Macro Skills Workbook

A Generalist Approach

Second Edition

Karen K. Kirst-Ashman
University of Wisconsin at Whitewater

Grafton H. Hull
University of Utah

BROOKS/COLE

™

THOMSON LEARNING

Australia • Canada • Mexico • Singapore • Spain • United Kingdom • United States

For permission to use material from this text,
contact us by **Web**: http://www.thomsonrights.com
Fax: 1-800-730-2215 **Phone:** 1-800-730-2214

For more information, contact
Wadsworth/Thomson Learning
10 Davis Drive
Belmont, CA 94002-3098
USA

For more information about our products, contact us:
Thomson Learning Academic Resource Center
1-800-423-0563
http://www.wadsworth.com

International Headquarters
Thomson Learning
International Division
290 Harbor Drive, 2nd Floor
Stamford, CT 06902-7477
USA

UK/Europe/Middle East/South Africa
Thomson Learning
Berkshire House
168-173 High Holborn
London WC1V 7AA
United Kingdom

Asia
Thomson Learning
60 Albert Complex, #15-01
Singapore 189969

Canada
Nelson Thomson Learning
1120 Birchmount Road
Toronto, Ontario M1K 5G4
Canada

ISBN 0-534-51302-6

Contents in Brief

✠ Table of Contents

Preface

Acknowledgments

✥ DEDICATION

To Vicki Vogel, our good friend and colleague

Students must practice skills in order to learn them. It is difficult, however, for instructors in classroom settings to provide students with opportunities to practice macro skills with organizations, communities, and political entities. This workbook is intended to solve that problem by offering a wide range of exercises, role plays, activities, and case scenarios that allow students to learn and employ specific macro skills based on a sound theoretical foundation.

This workbook can be used in the following four ways:

1. As the primary text in a practice course focusing on practice with organizations and communities
2. As a workbook accompanying other macro theory and practice texts
3. As a complement to the macro text *Generalist Practice with Organizations and Communities*, 2nd ed., (Kirst-Ashman & Hull, 2001), since the contents of the two books directly correspond
4. As a tool for integrating macro skill development for field internships

The content here aims to be relevant, practical, and coherent. Generalist practice is clearly defined, and macro practice skills are addressed from a generalist perspective. Specific macro practice skills are presented in a straightforward and interesting manner, and both applications to actual macro practice situations and the importance of client system strengths are emphasized throughout. Content is appropriate for both undergraduate and graduate generalist practice courses.

In addition to being a readable and practical guide to working in and with organizations and communities, the workbook also addresses a major concern in social work education today: the strong tendency for students to veer away from considering jobs in which they could help communities and organizations seek and achieve social change. Instead, students are frequently drawn to the perceived psychological drama and intensity of more clinically oriented practice with individuals, families, and small groups. Here, we emphasize the importance of macro practice for practitioners working in direct service or lower level supervisory job positions. The fact is that practitioners cannot simply assume that administrators will do the effective, efficient, or even *right* thing. In such cases, the practitioner may have to accept the responsibility for bringing about necessary changes. With that in mind, this book examines organizational and community theories and links these theories to practice applications.

This workbook aims to fulfill four major goals:

- First, it proposes a *generalist* perspective that emphasizes how micro, mezzo, and macro skills are interlinked. Our generalist approach assumes that group (i.e., mezzo) skills are built upon a firm foundation of individual (that is, micro) skills. Likewise, the skills involved in working with organizations and communities (that is, macro skills) rest upon a solid base of both micro and mezzo skills. We link the three levels of practice (micro, mezzo, and macro) to show students how all three levels of skills are utilized in everyday practice situations. Whole chapters and numerous examples throughout illustrate the application of micro and mezzo skills to macro practice situations. Other explanations and exercises demonstrate for students the importance of thinking about clients and their problems in ways that take into account the client's larger environment. Students are encouraged to explore automatically alternatives beyond the individual and small group levels.

- Second, the workbook includes clearly defined, step-by-step frameworks for thinking about and initiating macro change in organizations and communities. It proposes a model for decision making concerning whether or not to pursue macro intervention in a given situation. If such an intervention is judged necessary, a procedure is suggested for effective management of the macro change process.

- Third, the workbook identifies, explains, and examines specific skills useful in macro practice, including: working with the media, using new technological advances, fundraising, grant writing, working in court settings, evaluating macro practice effectiveness, resolving ethical dilemmas in macro contexts, advocating for populations-at-risk, and managing time and stress within macro environments. The book is flexible, easily adaptable to the instructor's needs. Specific exercises can be emphasized or omitted, depending on how workbook content corresponds to other course content.

- Fourth, this workbook presents students with material that is not only relevant and interesting, but also consistent with accreditation standards. This material targets social work values and ethics, human diversity, the promotion of social and economic justice, and the empowerment of populations-at-risk. In addition, this book aims to comply with accreditation standards by adopting a generalist perspective, emphasizing evaluation of practice, focusing on the differential use of communication skills with colleagues and community members, demonstrating the appropriate use of supervision, and examining practitioner functioning in organizational structures.

Many generalist curricula are structured so that practice courses oriented toward macro practice with organizations and communities follow practice courses concerned with micro systems and mezzo systems. We, therefore, assume that students will use this workbook close to the time when they will be completing their course work and seeking employment. For that reason we include chapters on constructing resumés and finding jobs, along with chapters on stress and time management. This material is vital to students and may not be addressed elsewhere in the curriculum.

✠ *Acknowledgments*

We wish to express sincere thanks to Vicki Vogel for her exceptional consultation, technical assistance, and support. Our heartfelt appreciation to Lisa Gebo of Wadsworth, who continually encouraged and supported our efforts. We extend our earnest thanks to Nick Ashman who provided support, encouragement, and patience in addition to many hours of cooking and other domestic sustenance while Karen Kirst-Ashman wrote. Finally, Stonehearth's Majestic Prince provided companionship interspersed with demands for long walks. His antics gave Grafton Hull his only exercise except for those brief moments when his mind wanders.

Chapter 1
Introduction to Generalist Practice with Organizations and Communities

Why Do You Need This Workbook?

Most social workers first entering professional practice view their jobs as dealing primarily with individuals and families. However, they actually practice in an agency environment, and the agency functions within a community. Through their workers, agencies provide resources and services to communities, and both your agency and its community will profoundly affect your ability to practice social work.

It is almost always easier to focus on the individual client(s) in front of you than on the larger picture of the agency and the community. It is tempting to believe that administrators and politicians will assume responsibility for all administrative and political matters. Indeed, in an ideal world, those functionaries *would* initiate and implement any and all changes necessary for the provision of the most effective and efficient service. In the real world, however, people in power are beset by multiple pressures and distractions, and they may choose not to make—or may fail even to see a valid need for—such macro changes.

Therefore, social workers must often take a much broader approach to their practice. As a generalist practitioner you will likely have to face community problems and gaps in services. Likewise, there will probably be times when your agency is ineffective in the performance of its task, is not doing something it should do, or is simply doing the wrong thing. Holloway (1987) describes some problems facing human service organizations as "profound" and others as very "subtle": "the agency does not reach out to potential clients, the agency is insensitive to clients' definitions of problems, it serves those for whom public sympathy is high and refuses to serve others, it makes referrals for its own rather than the client's convenience, or it offers one kind of service to meet all needs" (p. 731). In the face of such community or organizational problems, it is the practitioner's professional and ethical responsibility to consider helping the agency improve its service provision to clients.

Working in an agency or organization context requires an understanding of how such organizations function in their communities as well as in the larger political environment. Agency rules and policies will monumentally affect what you can and cannot do for your clients. For instance:

- Suppose your agency requires you to complete extensive and tedious paperwork for client intakes. You might suggest shortening this procedure for the sake of both clients and workers.

- Or suppose you want to add a new program to better serve your clients: You work in a domestic violence shelter traditionally oriented to helping survivors, and you want to start a new program for the treatment of abusers.

- Or suppose you want to implement a new project. This entails writing a grant proposal requesting funds to support an extensive in-service training program to teach workers new assessment techniques

These are three examples of internal agency issues that affect clients. Just as you function as a professional in an agency, you, your clients, and your agency must work in a community context. Community issues, therefore, can have major impacts on your own and your agency's ability to perform:

- You might need to address prejudice and racial discrimination in a community torn by racial tension and hatred.

- You might want to help clients and other community residents start a crime prevention program to increase neighborhood solidarity and make residents safer in their homes and on their streets.
- Community residents might seek your help in organizing themselves to exert political pressure in order to improve garbage cleanup and increase the frequency of police patrols.

Political forces, of course, also affect communities: Suppose the state legislature (or Congress) decides to discontinue subsidies for public transportation in your state's major urban areas. Without such subsidies, public transportation can no longer operate, and most of your clients depend on this transportation to get to work, shopping areas, and school. Your agency job description probably won't include mobilizing voters and taking political action. Nevertheless, the specific social service you provide (for example, counseling or financial assistance) can depend entirely on the availability of transportation, and that need can suddenly supersede all other problems. What if you can't do your job because your clients can't get to you? Can you ethically ignore the political debate over public transportation? What macro practice skills could you use in this situation?

One of this workbook's major assumptions is that generalist practitioners require a wide range of skills because they must be prepared to help individuals, groups, families, organizations, and communities in a multiplicity of situations—no matter what specific area they work in: children and families, health, justice, education, economic status, etc. To help you function more effectively as a generalist practitioner, we provide a series of exercises and activities to improve your skills for working in and with organizations and communities.

This chapter will:
- Define generalist practice and provide a generalist perspective for macro practice
- Formulate a systems perspective for macro practice, emphasizing macro client, target, change agent, and action systems
- Explore a variety of professional roles assumed in macro practice. Examine the concept of critical thinking

What Is Generalist Practice?

Generalist practice is the application of an *eclectic knowledge base, professional values,* and *a wide range of skills* to *target any size system* for change within the context of three primary processes (Kirst-Ashman & Hull, 1997).
- First, generalist practice involves working effectively within an *organizational structure* and doing so *under supervision.*
- Second, it requires the assumption of *a wide range of professional roles.*
- Third, generalist practice involves the application of *critical thinking skills* to the *planned change process.*[1]

---

[1] Note that another term often used to describe what generalist practitioners do is *problem-solving*. This term essentially refers to the same thing as planned change, although many debate the nuances of difference. Social work's more recent emphasis on client strengths may be at odds with the more negative connotations of the word "problem." The term "change" may have more positive connotations despite the fact that most social work intervention deals with problem situations. As there is some evidence that the term planned change is more frequently used in generalist practice, we will arbitrarily use it here (Hoffman & Sallee, 1993; Landon, 1995).

Eclectic Knowledge Base

Some of the terms inherent in that definition may need further clarification. An eclectic knowledge base is a foundation of information and skills that includes a wide range of methods and styles taken "from various sources" (Mish, 1995, p. 365). Generalist social workers must know about many things and must involve themselves in a wide variety of helping processes—helping a homeless family, a sexually abused child, a pregnant teenager, an elderly person no longer able to care for herself, an alcoholic parent, a community ravaged by a drug abuse problem, or a public assistance agency struggling to amend its policies in conformity with new federal regulations.

Professional Values

Values are principles, qualities, and practices that a designated group, individual, or culture deems inherently desirable (Mish, 1991, pp. 1302-1303). Professional values determine right and wrong behavior.

Wide Range of Practice Skills Targeting Any Size System

These dimensions of generalist practice are so intertwined that we address them together. Different specific skills are used with micro, mezzo, or macro systems, respectively, and the generalist perspective assumes a multi-level approach to intervention. That is, in a given situation, a generalist practitioner might have to intervene with individuals, families, groups, organizations, and/or communities. Therefore, social workers must master the skills needed to work with any of these entities.

Micro practice focuses on planned change with and for individuals. The context is usually "intervention on a case-by-case basis or in a clinical setting" (Barker, 1999, p. 302). The focus of attention is the individual, and the social worker must know how to communicate and work on a one-to-one basis.

Mezzo practice is generalist social work practice with small groups. In macro settings, this primarily involves task groups. Here, it is important to understand group dynamics and communication patterns. Working with families combines micro and mezzo practice. Because of the intimacy and intensity of family relationships and the importance of the family context to individuals, families deserve special status and attention.

Finally, *macro practice* is designed to affect change in large systems, including organizations and communities (Barker, 1999). Macro skills enable social workers to change agency or social policies, plan and implement programs, and initiate and direct projects in agency or community contexts. These are the skills this workbook stresses.

A generalist practitioner, however, is always open to the possibility of acting—either simultaneously or sequentially—on other levels of intervention. Generalist social workers, then, must be prepared to approach a problem from a wide variety of perspectives.

The figure below illustrates how you can focus your assessment on micro, mezzo, or macro levels of intervention.

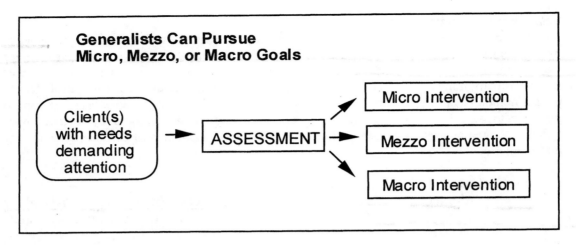

Generalists Can Pursue
Micro, Mezzo, or Macro Goals

Client(s) with needs demanding attention → ASSESSMENT → Micro Intervention / Mezzo Intervention / Macro Intervention

A Case Example: The Generalist Perspective

You are a generalist practitioner for a rural midwestern county. You receive referrals from your supervisor, who, in turn, receives them from an intake worker. It is your job to establish initial connections with clients (and with other persons referred to you) by engaging them in the planned change process, familiarizing them with the agency, and supplying them with information. You are also expected to solicit all necessary data to assist in service provision, provide short-term counseling when needed, and make appropriate referrals to agency units and other community resources.

You receive a referral involving an elderly individual, Murray Strewynskowski. The person who called, Duke Earl, is one of Mr. Strewynskowski's neighbors. Mr. Earl is concerned because Mr. Strewynskowski has twice fallen on his own icy sidewalk and been unable to get up without assistance. Fortunately, on both occasions, Mr. Earl observed the fall and was able to help Mr. Strewynskowski back into the house. Inside, Mr. Earl found chaotic conditions. Rotting garbage was strewn around the kitchen, and a dozen or more cats wandered through the house. Mr. Earl noticed one pitch-black cat with a white patch over her left eye eating what looked like canned creamed corn mixed with ketchup from a plate on the table; he wondered if the food had been intended for Mr. Strewynskowski's lunch. Mr. Earl was also worried about Mr. Strewynskowski's diet in general. The elderly man looked gaunt, and his neighbor was afraid that he was unable to shop or cook adequately.

You begin by calling Mr. Earl to clarify his report, ask a few additional questions, and thank him for his interest and help, thus *engaging Mr. Earl in the problem-defining process.* Engagement, then, is the process of orienting oneself to the problem at hand and of establishing communication and initiating a relationship with the individual or individuals involved.

Now you must figure out what to do about Mr. Strewynskowski, which means engaging *him*—the client—in the planned change process and determining what he needs and wants.

During the assessment phase of the planned change process, you may decide to intervene at the micro, mezzo, or macro level. Or you might decide that intervention at more than one level would be appropriate.

A Micro Approach

Employing a micro-level plan focused upon the individual might mean referring Mr. Strewynskowski to the appropriate services and overseeing the service provision. At this same level, you could then continue Mr. Strewynskowski's assessment and arrange for such services as a traveling homemaker and daily hot meal delivery. Does Mr. Strewynskowski need supportive services—assistance with paying his bills, obtaining medical attention, or purchasing groceries and other needed items?

Assuming a Wide Range of Roles

The seventh major element of generalist practice is the *wide range of professional roles* that generalist practitioners assume. A role is "a socially expected behavior pattern usually determined by an individual's status in a particular society" or unit of society (Mish, 1995, p. 1014). For example, people have certain expectations of how social workers will act and of the activities they will pursue. It is helpful to conceptualize the workers' roles in terms of the target, client, change agent, and action systems.

Note that professional roles are not necessarily mutually exclusive. A worker may perform the functions of more than one role at a time. The roles include enabler, mediator, integrator/coordinator, general manager, educator, analyst/evaluator, broker, facilitator, initiator, negotiator, and mobilizer.

The *enabler* provides support, encouragement, and suggestions to members of a macro client system, thus allowing the system to operate more easily and more successfully in completing tasks and/or solving problems. In the enabler role, a worker helps a client system become capable of coping with situational or transitional stress. Specific skills used in achieving this objective include conveying hope, reducing resistance and ambivalence, recognizing and managing feelings, identifying and supporting personal strengths and social assets, breaking down problems into parts that can more readily be solved [partialization], and maintaining a focus on goals and the means of achieving them (Barker, 1999, p. 154). For example, an enabler might help a community develop a program for identifying and shutting down crack houses. Community citizens do the work, but the enabler provides enthusiastic encouragement and helps participants identify their strengths and weaknesses and work out their interpersonal conflicts while keeping on task. Enablers, then, are helpers. Practitioners can function in the role of enabler for micro, mezzo, or macro systems.[2]

The *mediator* resolves arguments or disagreements among micro, mezzo, and/or macro systems in conflict (Yessian & Broskowski, 1983, pp. 183-84). At the macro level mediators help various factions (subsystems) in a community or community systems themselves work out their differences. For example, a community (or neighborhood) and a social services organization may require mediation over the placement of a substance abuse treatment center. Perhaps the social services organization has selected a prime spot, but the community or neighborhood is balking at the establishment of such a center within its boundaries.

The social worker may have to improve communication among dissident individuals or groups, or help those involved arrive at a compromise. A mediator remains neutral, does not side with either party in the dispute, and understands the positions of both parties. This allows her to clarify positions, recognize miscommunications, and help all parties present their cases clearly.

Integration is "the process of bringing together components into a unified whole" (Barker, 1999, p. 245), and coordination is the organizing of elements. The *integrator/coordinator*, therefore, brings the people involved in various systems together and organizes their activities (Yessian & Broskowski, 1983, pp. 183-84). A generalist social worker can function as an integrator/coordinator "in many ways, ranging from. . .advocacy and identification of coordination opportunities, to provision of technical assistance, to direct involvement in the development and implementation of service linkages" (Yessian & Broskowski, 1983, p.184). Integrator/coordinators function in macro systems in somewhat the same way that case managers function on behalf of individual clients or families.

The *general manager* assumes a particular level of administrative responsibility for a social services agency or some other organizational system (Yessian & Broskowski, 1983, pp.

---

2 Note that this definition of "enabler" is very different from that of the "enabler" as applied to cases of substance abuse. There the term refers to a family member or friend who facilitates the substance abuser in continuing to use and abuse the drug of his or her choice.

183-84). Administrators "determine organizational goals for a social agency or other unit; acquire resources and allocate them to carry out programs; coordinate activities toward the achievement of selected goals; and monitor, assess, and make necessary changes in processes and structure to improve effectiveness and efficiency" (Barker, 1999, p. 8). Managers perform a number of tasks including planning programs, getting and distributing resources, developing and establishing organizational structures and processes, evaluating programs, and implementing program changes when needed (Patti, 1983).

The *educator* gives information and teaches skills to other systems (Yessian & Broskowski, 1983, pp. 183-84). An effective educator must be knowledgeable, a good communicator who can convey information clearly and be readily understood by the receivers.

Analyst/evaluators analyze or evaluate effectiveness (Yessian & Broskowski, 1983, pp. 183-84). An analyst can determine the effectiveness of a program or even of an entire agency, and he can do this in an organizational or community context. Generalist social workers with a broad knowledge base can analyze or evaluate how well programs and systems work. Likewise, they can evaluate the effectiveness of their own interventions.

The *broker* links any size system (an individual, group, organization, or community) with community resources and services. A broker also helps put "various segments of the community in touch with one another to enhance their mutual interests" (Barker, 1999, p. 55). Getting resources for client systems is the broker's mission.

A *facilitator* "serves as a leader or catalyst for some group experience" (Barker, 1999, p. 165). Although the facilitator role is very useful in mezzo practice, workers also frequently assume it in macro practice. In the macro context a facilitator "brings participants together to promote the change process by improving communication, helping direct their efforts and resources, and linking them with needed information and expert help."

Kettner, Daley, & Nichols (1985) explain that the *initiator* calls attention to an issue. (From a systems perspective, this person is the change agent). The issue may be a community problem or need, or simply a situation that can be improved. *There need not be a problem.* In fact, preventing future problems or enhancing existing services are satisfactory reasons for initiating a change effort. Thus, a social worker may recognize that a certain policy creates problems for particular clients and bring this to the attention of her supervisor. Likewise, a client may identify ways that service could be improved and bring that to the attention of his social worker. In each case, the worker is playing the role of initiator. Usually, this role requires that other roles be undertaken, because pointing out problems does not guarantee they will be solved.

A *negotiator* acts to settle disputes and/or resolve disagreements. However, unlike mediators, negotiators clearly take the side of one of the parties involved.

The *mobilizer* identifies and gathers people from the community, and makes them responsive to unmet community need (Halley, Kopp, & Austin, 1998). The mobilizer's purpose is to match resources to needs in the community context. Sometimes, a mobilizer's goal is simply to make services more accessible to those in the community who need them. Other times, the goal is to initiate and develop services that will meet hitherto unmet needs. By our definition, the mobilizer operates in communities, not in organizations.

An *advocate* works "with and/or on behalf of clients (1) to obtain services or resources for clients that would not otherwise be provided; (2) to modify extant [currently operating] policies, procedures, or practices that adversely affect clients; or (3) to promote new legislation or policies that will result in the provision of needed resources or services" (Hepworth, Rooney, & Larsen, 1997, p. 468). In other words, the advocate speaks out on behalf of the client system in order to promote fair and equitable treatment or gain needed resources. In macro practice, of course, she would speak on behalf of some macro client system. This may be especially appropriate when a macro client system has little power to get what it needs.

www.afj.org

By the time you use this workbook, you will have acquired an assortment of skills for working with clients in micro and mezzo practice. It is on this foundation that you will build your macro skills and apply them in macro practice contexts. Agencies, mammoth bureaucracies, state governments, and even national arenas are made up of individuals with unique personalities, qualities, and quirks, all operating within their own unique contexts. Each powerful decision-maker—whether the director of a large agency or a prestigious politician—is simply another human being. Macro practice requires you to "live" and cooperate with colleagues and supervisors in agency settings.

Any individual can be part of a macro intervention, and macro practice *always* involves human interaction. Personal interaction, in turn, *always* involves communication. Many of the same communication and problem-solving skills you use in working with clients can be applied to interactions with colleagues and others in macro situations. Suppose you work in a protective services agency and want to initiate an in-service training program to teach new child-abuse assessment techniques. You will probably need the help of your immediate supervisor and/or other agency administrators to get the project off the ground. How likely are you to receive assistance from people you've antagonized or even alienated? Obviously, you'll have better luck if you've established open, positive relationships with the people whose help you need. In addition, you'll have to be appropriately assertive in proposing your idea to those who are in positions to help you. If an interpersonal conflict *does* arise, you'll need to know how to handle and resolve it.

This chapter will:

- Explore ways to establish rapport and build relationships with colleagues, supervisors, other staff, administrators, community leaders, politicians, and others in the macro environment
- Review a range of communication techniques and apply them to scenarios in macro practice
- Explore appropriate assertiveness in macro contexts and propose techniques for assertive interaction
- Suggest procedures for conflict resolution in macro settings
- Formulate suggestions for maximizing the benefits of supervisory relationships and enhancing the communication process

Warmth, Empathy, and Genuineness

You can learn a variety of relationship-enhancing behaviors and characteristics that will be useful in generalist social work practice. These include many aspects of verbal and nonverbal behavior that are most often learned in a micro practice context.

Three specific relationship-enhancing characteristics—*warmth*, *empathy*, and *genuineness*—are discussed in the social work literature as among the most basic and important in developing relationships (Halley, Kopp, & Austin, 1998; Hepworth et al., 1997; Kadushin & Kadushin, 1997). Demonstrating these traits requires the worker to employ certain verbal and nonverbal behaviors.

Warmth can be communicated to another person both nonverbally and verbally, using behaviors that can be defined, practiced, and learned. In general, it involves showing interest in other people and their ideas, demonstrating concern for their feelings, and simply making them feel accepted and liked. You can display this warmth nonverbally by maintaining eye contact, listening attentively, and presenting a pleasant facial expression.

Likewise, warmth can be communicated verbally:

"Hello. It's good to meet you."
"I'm glad we have the chance to talk about this."
"Please sit down. Can I get you a cup of coffee?"
"You are really a good listener."
"I do appreciate your efforts and your help."

Genuineness is the "sharing of self by relating in a natural, sincere, spontaneous, open and genuine manner" (Hepworth et al., 1997, p. 120). That is, you continue to be yourself while you are working to accomplish your professional goals.

Personality is that unique configuration of qualities and attributes that makes you an individual. Some personalities are effervescent, "bubbly," and outgoing. Others are subdued and quiet. Some people typically relate to others through their sense of humor; others prefer to relate more seriously. The point is that no one type of personality is "best," so there's no reason to pretend to be something or someone that you're not. Genuineness conveys a sense of honesty to others and generally makes them feel that you're someone they can trust.

Empathy is the quality of *being in tune* with other people's feelings and the ability to *communicate that understanding* both verbally and nonverbally. As a nonverbal example, you might furrow your brow to show that you are concentrating seriously on what someone is telling you and are concerned about the issue he or she is discussing. However, be careful. Sometimes, a frown can suggest displeasure or disapproval instead. It's important, therefore, to attend to your own nonverbal communication and be sensitive to others' reactions.

Verbally, there are a number of leading phrases that will indicate empathy:

- *I get the impression that . . .*
- *It seems to me that . . .*
- *Are you saying that . . .?*
- *Do I understand you correctly that . . .?*
- *I'm hearing you say that . . .*
- *Do you mean that . . .?*
- *Do you feel that . . .?*
- *I sense that you . . . .*
- *I'm getting the message that . . .*
- *You seem to be . . .*
- *When you say that, I think you . . .*
- *You look as if you . . .*
- *You sound so ___. Can we talk more about it?*
- *You look _____. What's been happening?*

You can convey empathy whether you think another individual's feelings are positive or negative. Having empathy does not mean having the same feelings yourself, only acknowledging that you understand the other person's situation.

When you work in a macro setting, you can use empathy to establish an initial rapport and to elicit feelings and talk about issues that might never be broached had feelings not been mentioned. Thus, empathy can help you draw out other people's feelings—even feelings that are not expressed verbally.

Exercise 2.1: Practicing Empathic Responses In Macro Practice Contexts

Below are several vignettes illustrating macro situations. Formulate and write down two empathic responses for each situation. (Responses for the first vignette are provided as an example.)

Vignette #1: You are a school social worker in an urban neighborhood. Residents inform you that a vacant lot in the neighborhood—two houses away from the school—was used as a dump for dangerous chemicals between ten and twenty years ago. In the past fifteen years, a dozen children attending the school have gotten cancer.

Addressing this type of issue is not part of your job description, but you see it as your professional and ethical responsibility to help the neighborhood residents explore their options for coping with this problem. For instance, a class-action lawsuit could be brought against the companies that dumped the chemicals. If it could be proved that the companies are at fault (that is, that they acted knowingly or negligently), they could be held financially liable for their actions.

The mother of one child (Eric, 14) who has leukemia makes an appointment to see you. When she enters your office, she bursts into tears: "I am so angry! How could people do this to little children? They must have known that dumping those wastes so close to children was dangerous."

How do you respond empathically?
- "You sound really angry. I don't blame you. What are your thoughts about what to do?"
- "I'm hearing you say that you are furious about this situation. What can I do to help you?"
- "This whole situation has been a horror story for you. Where do you think we can go from here?"

Vignette #2: You are a social worker in a health care facility for the elderly. You want to start a program that will bring middle-school children to visit your elderly clients. You believe that such interactions will be mutually beneficial for both your clients and the children. You have approached Kimberly, the other social worker in the facility, with this idea, but her response was hesitant and—in your opinion—negative. You think she is worried that this proposal will create a lot more work for her, work that she is neither ready nor willing to undertake.

In fact, you have pretty much paved the way for implementing the plan: You have contacted school administrators and teachers to obtain their permission and support. You've come up with a transportation plan and a proposed form for parental permissions. Before you have the chance to approach Kimberly again, she initiates a conversation with you: She states, "I know you're trying to do the right thing with this student visitation project [this is an empathic response on Kimberly's part], *but* you're pushing me into it. I don't have enough time to do my own work, let alone get involved in some petty little program you propose."

How do you respond empathically? (Remember that you *do not have to solve the problem* right now. You simply need to let Kimberly know that you understand how she feels.)

Alternative Response #1:

Alternative Response #2:

Vignette #3:   You are a social worker at a diagnostic and treatment center for children with multiple physical disabilities. Your primary function is helping parents cope with the pressures they are under and connecting them with needed resources. The Center's staff includes a wide range of disciplines such as occupational therapy,[1] physical therapy,[2] speech therapy, psychology, and nursing. Sometimes the professionals from these other disciplines ask you to talk parents out of asking them questions, especially when a child's condition is getting worse. One day a physical therapist approaches you and asks, "Do you think you could talk to Mrs. Harris? She keeps asking me these uncomfortable questions about Sally [Mrs. Harris's daughter]. Sally's condition is deteriorating. I don't know what to say."

How do you respond empathically?

Alternative Response #1:

Alternative Response #2:

Vignette #4:   You are an intake worker at a social services agency in a rural area. Your job is to take telephone calls, assess problems, and refer clients to the most appropriate services. You identify a gap in the services available to people with developmental disabilities. You think that a social activities center would help to fill this gap by meeting some hitherto unmet needs. You talk with administrators in your agency, and they generally support the idea—but they don't know where the funding would come from. They suggest that you talk with some local politicians. You make an appointment with the President of the County Board to explain your idea and ask about possible funding. She responds, "It certainly sounds good, but who's going to pay for it and run it?"

How do you respond empathetically?

Alternative Response #1:

---

[1] Occupational therapy is "a profession for helping people with physical disabilities use their bodies more effectively and people with mental impairment overcome emotional problems through specially designed work activity" (Barker, 1999, p. 334).

[2] Physical therapy is "the treatment of disease by physical and mechanical means (as massage, regulated exercise, water, light, heat, and electricity" (Mish, 1995, p. 877).

Alternative Response #2:

Using Verbal Responses in Macro Contexts

Communication to exchange information is the core of interpersonal interactions in macro settings. The vast array of possible communication techniques for use within agency, community, or political settings is much the same as those used in your micro and mezzo interventions with clients. There are various ways to initiate a communication, solicit information, encourage responses, and respond appropriately to another individual. Using appropriate communication techniques increases the chances that your *intent* (that is, what you want to convey) will match your *impact* (that is, what the receiver actually understands). A number of verbal responses are defined and discussed below.

Simple encouragement: Any verbal or nonverbal behavior intended to assure, comfort, or support the communication. Many times a simple one word response or nonverbal head nod combined with eye contact is enough to encourage the other person to continue. Verbal clues such as "mm-mm," "I see," "uh-huh" help convey that the communication's receiver really is listening and following what the sender is saying.

Please note that you should be cautious about the indiscriminate use of any verbal or nonverbal techniques. Sensitivity to cultural differences must be ongoing. For example, Ivey and Ivey (1999) describe a situation where a North American discusses an issue with a Chinese person. He utters "uh-huh" several times when the Chinese woman pauses briefly between sentences during her description of an event. However, "while 'uh-huh' is a good minimal encouragement in North America, it happens to convey a kind of arrogance in China. A self-respecting Chinese would say *er* (oh), or *shi* (yes) to show he or she is listening. How could the woman feel comfortable when she thought she was being slighted?" (p. 36).

Rephrasing: Repeating what the other person is saying by putting it into your own words. Rephrasing accomplishes several things: It communicates to the other person that you are listening to what she's saying. It notifies her that you did not understand, thus allowing her to clarify her meaning. It gives the other person time out to reflect on what she just said. Rephrasing does not involve *interpreting* what the other person has said, only repeating her statement in different words.

Reflective responding: Translating into words what you think the other person is feeling. Such empathic responding conveys your understanding of the other person's position and of how he feels about it. It is common for a person to *talk* about his problems without really articulating how he *feels*. You can help him identify and express his feelings so that he can do something about them. Both verbal and nonverbal behavior can be used as cues for reflective responding.

Clarification: Choosing and using words to make certain that what another person has said is clearly understood. The intent of clarification is to make a communication more understandable in one of two ways (Benjamin, 1974). First, you can help another person articulate—say more clearly—what she really means by providing the words for it. This is clarification for the other person's benefit. Second, you can explain what the other person is saying for your own benefit. Many times clarification will benefit both sender and receiver. In summary, use clarification when you are uncertain about what another person means; use restatement to paraphrase exactly what the other person said, thus showing that you already understand the communication; and use reflective responding to get at the feelings and emotions behind another person's statements.

Interpretation: Seeking meaning in an effort to help bring a matter to a conclusion, to enlighten, or to seek a greater depth of meaning in what someone has said. Interpretation helps the other person look deeper into the meaning of her own words and enhances her perception of that meaning.

For instance, a colleague might say, "I like Samson, but he always seems to get the most interesting cases. It's just not fair, that's all there is to it."

You could respond by interpreting this statement: "You seem to have some conflicting feelings about Samson. On the one hand, you like him. On the other, you apparently resent the fact that he gets more challenging cases than you do."

You have gone beyond your colleague's feelings of anger and resentment and focused on the reasons for those feelings.

Providing information: Communicating knowledge. Examples are infinite. A person may ask you a specific question, or you may determine that someone needs some particular input.

Emphasizing people's strengths: Articulating and emphasizing other people's positive characteristics and behaviors. Your instructors have probably drilled into you the importance of emphasizing client strengths, but it is also important to emphasize the strengths of colleagues, administrators, and others you deal with. Each individual in the macro environment has personal strengths, weaknesses, concerns, and defenses. When you feel you must offer a constructive suggestion or criticism, a strengths perspective allows you to do so while still supporting the other person's ego. You want to convey to that person that you are on her side, and by emphasizing her strengths, you show that you are not the enemy.

Summarization: Briefly and concisely covering the main points of a discussion or series of communications. Summarization can be difficult because you must carefully select only the most important facts, issues, and themes. Exclude less essential detail. Condense so that you emphasize only the most salient points.

You can use summarization to bring a discussion to a close while focusing the main issues in others' minds. At the end of a staff meeting, you can summarize recommendations about who is to do what before the next meeting, thereby crystallizing in all participants' minds whatever plans were made. Summarizing information periodically throughout a discussion also serves to keep the discussion on track and/or "as a transition to new topics" (Whittaker & Tracy, 1989, p.135).

Eliciting information: Requesting knowledge you need. One way to elicit information is simply to ask questions—either closed-ended or open-ended. *Closed-ended questions* seek simple, definite answers from a predetermined range of possibilities, such as "yes" or "no," or "male" or "female." Such questions do not encourage or even allow for explanation or elaboration. Open-ended questions seek more extensive presentations of thoughts, ideas, and explanations.

Overlap of Techniques

Sometimes it is difficult to label a technique specifically as "clarification" or "interpretation," but some techniques fulfill only one purpose and thus fit obviously into one category. Others combine two or more techniques because they fulfill two or more functions. The important thing is to master a variety of techniques and thereby become more flexible and more effective in communicating with others.

Exercise 2.2: Responding to Others in the Macro Environment

Look at the statements below. They might come from colleagues, supervisors, administrators, and others in the macro working environment. For each statement, give examples of the different types of possible responses. (Types of responses are listed under each statement.) The first statement is an example.

Statement #1: **(From a worker at another agency)** "I've been meaning to talk to you about your agency's policy regarding the treatment of poor clients."

Possible Responses:

> **Simple encouragement:** "I see. Please go on."
>
> **Rephrasing:** "You have some concerns about my agency's procedures for working with impoverished clients."
>
> **Reflective responding:** "You're upset about the way my agency treats poor clients."
>
> **Clarification:** "You're concerned about the effect of our sliding fee scale on clients who can't afford it."
>
> **Interpretation:** "You have some ethical concerns about our policy on treatment of poor clients."
>
> **Providing information:** "Let me give you a copy of our new policy and some data on how it affects clients."
>
> **Emphasizing people's strengths:** "You always have been an exceptional advocate for the poor."
>
> **Summarization:** (Since it is almost impossible to summarize one line, assume that there has been an ongoing discussion of this matter.) "Over the past few weeks, we've talked about a number of your concerns about agency policy, including treatment of staff, of people of color, and of the poor."
>
> **Eliciting information:** "Can you tell me exactly which policy you are referring to?"

Statement #2: **(From a colleague at your agency)** "I'm furious with my supervisor. He never gives me credit for anything!"

Simple encouragement:

Rephrasing:

Reflective responding:

Clarification:

Interpretation:

27

Providing information:

Emphasizing people's strengths:

Summarization: (Since it is almost impossible to summarize one line, assume that you have had an ongoing discussion on this matter.)

Eliciting information:

**Statement #3:** **(From another agency's director)** "I think your agency ought to get more involved in our program."[3]

Simple encouragement:

Rephrasing:

Reflective responding:

Clarification:

---

[3] Vocational rehabilitation involves training people who have physical or mental disabilities "so they can do useful work, become more self-sufficient, and be less reliant on public financial assistance" (Barker, 1999, p. 512).

Interpretation:

Providing information:

Emphasizing people's strengths:

Summarization: (Since it is almost impossible to summarize one line, assume that you have had an ongoing discussion on this matter.)

Eliciting information:

Statement #4: **(From a local politician who has significant influence over your agency's funding)** "I'd like to know why your agency's staff hasn't submitted any grants for external funding."

Simple encouragement:

Rephrasing:

Reflective responding:

Clarification:

Interpretation:

Providing information:

Emphasizing people's strengths:

Summarization: (Since it is almost impossible to summarize one line, assume that you have had an ongoing discussion on this matter.)

Eliciting information:

The Use of "Why?"

It is easy to use the word *why* when asking questions, but be aware that "why" can sound threatening. It can "put people on the spot," and it can imply that the person to whom it's directed is at fault. Consider the question, "Why are you late?" You can rephrase it: "You're late. Is everything all right?" or "We're so glad you got here. Was traffic terrible?"

Exercise 2.3: Avoiding the Use of "Why?"

Rephrase the following "why" questions.

Question #1: *"We agreed at the last meeting that you'd talk to Fred—why didn't you?"*

Alternative Phrasing:

Question #2: *"Why are you always complaining about that policy?"*

Alternative Phrasing:

Alternative Phrasing:

Question #4: _"Why are public assistance and social security so complicated?"_

Alternative Phrasing:

Appropriate Assertiveness in the Macro Environment

Most people wish they'd been more assertive on certain occasions. Yet in the midst of an interaction, they may feel uncomfortable about such behavior or find themselves caught off guard. For example, Verne and Shirley are social work practitioners in the same agency. One day Verne catches Shirley in the hall as she's rushing off to an important meeting. He asks her to finish up a report of his that is due immediately. He assures her that it won't take very long and that he will be eternally grateful. Shirley, having no time to think, agrees and hurries to the meeting. On second thought, she is disgusted with herself. She decides that Verne purposely approached her in a moment of distraction and asked a very inappropriate favor. His reports are _his_ responsibility, and she curses herself for not being more assertive.

Other people actually maintain a _pattern_ of nonassertiveness. Suppose a supervisor asks a worker to put in regular overtime because the supervisor knows that worker _will never say no._ The worker doesn't _want_ to work overtime, and other employees are not asked to do so. Sometimes chronically nonassertive people allow their frustration to build until they can't stand being taken advantage of and simply "lose it." All their emotions explode in a burst of anger.

Nonassertive, Assertive, and Aggressive Communication

On an assertiveness continuum, communication can be rated nonassertive, assertive, or aggressive. _Assertive_ communication is verbal and nonverbal behavior through which you can get your points across clearly and straightforwardly, taking into consideration both your own value and the value of whomever is receiving your message.

In _nonassertive_ communication, you devalue yourself, placing the other person and his or her priorities ahead of yourself and your agenda.

Aggressiveness is at the other end of the assertiveness continuum. It is characterized by bold and dominating verbal and nonverbal behavior through which you claim precedence for your point of view over all others.

In micro, mezzo, and macro practice, appropriate assertiveness gives you a substantial advantage (Lewinsohn et al., 1978; Sundel & Sundel, 1980): more control over your work and in other interpersonal environments, the ability to avoid uncomfortable or hostile interactions with others, the sense that other people understand you better than they did before, and the enhancement of your self-concept and your interpersonal effectiveness. Appropriate assertiveness helps to reduce tension and stress.

There's no assertiveness "script" to cover every situation. You must simply consider both your own rights and the rights of the person with whom you are interacting. The following are a few examples of possible nonassertive, aggressive, and assertive responses to work situations:

Situation #1: Amorette is a social worker at a residential treatment center for adolescents with severe emotional and behavioral problems. She completes the draft of a grant application for funds to start a sex education program in the center. The proposal stipulates that experts will provide both educational programming and contraceptives. Agency policy requires that all grant proposal drafts be reviewed by the Grants Committee before they are submitted. Prunella, one of the center's teachers, is a member of the Grants Committee.

When Prunella sees the proposal, she flies through the roof. She contends that—for this population—explicit discussion of sex will only encourage experimentation. She is also appalled that the proposal includes providing contraceptives directly to the girls. "Why not show them pornographic movies too?" she mutters.

Prunella approaches Amorette and declares, "That grant proposal you wrote is totally inappropriate. Under no circumstances will I condone it!" How should Amorette reply?

> **Nonassertive Response:** "You're probably right. I'll just forget about it."
>
> **Aggressive Response:** "What's wrong with you? Are you still living in the Dark Ages or something? Maybe what you need is a little action yourself."
>
> **Assertive Response:** "I understand your concerns. However, I still think this is an important issue to address. Let's talk further about it."

Situation #2: Gigette is a social worker for a public agency that provides supportive home-based services for the elderly. The agency's intent is to help people maintain their independence and reside in their own homes as long as possible. A county policy states that clients may receive a maximum of eight service hours per month from Gigette's agency or others like it. Many of Gigette's clients require more help than this. She understands that the policy was instituted to keep costs down, but she is convinced that increasing the maximum hours of service from eight to sixteen would allow many clients to remain in their own homes much longer. In the long run, this would save money, because providing or subsidizing nursing home care is monstrously expensive.

Gigette gains the support of her agency's administration and is authorized to approach Biff Bunslinger, the County Board President and explain her proposal and its rationale. His support will be crucial in changing the county's policy.

Biff listens, then says, "It's a good idea, but where will you get the money for it? What else do you want to cut? Do you have any idea what repercussions such a major policy change would have?" How can Gigette respond?

> **Nonassertive Response:** "I don't know. I'm sorry. Let's forget it."
>
> **Aggressive Response:** "You haven't heard a word I've said. Get off your butt, Biff, and start thinking about those people out there who really need help!"
>
> **Assertive Response:** "I know funding is tight and that you have to balance all sorts of competing financial needs. Let me show you how in the long run this plan can help your elderly constituents *and* save the county money."

Situation #3: Bo, an outreach worker for urban homeless people, is on the Board of Directors of another agency, the AIDS Support Network.[4] Eleni, another board member who is also a local lawyer, bluntly tells him, "I wish you would be more specific in your comments during meetings. I can never understand what you're talking about." What can Bo reply?

---

[4] A Board of Directors is "a group of people empowered to establish an organization's objectives and policies and to oversee the activities of the personnel responsible for day-to-day implementation of those policies" (Barker, 1991, p. 25).

Nonassertive Response: "You're right. I'll try to speak more clearly in the future."

Aggressive Response: "I'm not nearly as unclear as you are—nor, by the way, as arrogant. If you don't understand me, maybe what I'm saying is just over your head."

Assertive Response: "I'm sorry you feel that way. Maybe you could let me know right there at the meeting when I've said something you don't understand. Also, I want you to know that I appreciate this feedback, but you might have given it with greater sensitivity to my feelings."

Exercise 2.4: Nonassertive, Aggressive, and Assertive Responses

For each of the following case vignettes, propose nonassertive, aggressive, and assertive responses that the worker involved in each case might make.

Case Vignette #1: Mohammed, a school social worker, applies for a state grant to start a summer activity program for adolescents in an urban neighborhood. Although he has already solicited support from his direct supervisor and from the school board, a principal from another school in the district objects to Mohammed's proposal: "Trying to get money for that project is inappropriate. It will result in significant differences in services between one school district and another, which is completely unfair. I think we should forget the idea."

Nonassertive Response:

Aggressive Response:

Assertive Response:

Case Vignette #2: Audrey directs a group home for adults with physical disabilities. The home is run by a conservative religious organization which has publicly declared its anti-abortion stance. Her direct supervisor, the organization's director, is also strongly anti-abortion. Audrey, however, maintains a pro-choice position.

A pro-choice rally is being held this weekend, and Audrey plans to attend and participate. She even expects to carry a pro-choice banner and march in a planned procession through the main area of town. Audrey's supervisor finds out about her plans, calls her aside, and says, "I forbid you to participate in that rally. Our agency has a reputation to maintain, and I won't allow you to jeopardize it."

Nonassertive Response:

Aggressive Response:

Assertive Response:

Case Vignette #3: Hiroko is a public assistance worker for a large county bureaucracy. She is very dedicated to her job and often spends extra time with clients to make certain that they receive all possible benefits. Her colleague Bill, who has the same job title, tells Hiroko, "Either you're a fool and a drudge to work overtime like that, or you're trying to be a 'star' to feed your ego."

Nonassertive Response:

Aggressive Response:

Assertive Response:

Case Vignette #4: Manuella is a social worker for Heterogeneous County Department of Social Services. Paperwork recording her activities with clients is due promptly the Monday following the last day of each month. For whatever reason, Manuela simply forgets to get it in by 5:00 p.m. Monday the day it's due. Her supervisor Kong calls her at noon the next day. He raises his voice and reprimands, "you know that reports are due promptly so that funding is not jeopardized. How many times do I have to tell you that?"

Nonassertive Response:

Aggressive Response:

Assertive Response:

Case Vignette #5: Fred works with a colleague, Ethel, who consistently comes late to their social work unit's biweekly meetings. Ethel typically saunters leisurely into the meeting room with a cup of decaf in hand, noisily situates herself in a chair at the rectangular meeting table, and casually interrupts whomever is speaking, asking for a brief review of what she missed. Fred is sick and tired of such rude, time-wasting behavior. Finally, after the last meeting, Fred pulls Ethel aside.

Nonassertive Response:

Aggressive Response:

Assertive Response:

Case Vignette #6: Julia represents her social services agency at a community meeting where twelve community residents and five workers from other agencies are discussing what additional social services the community needs. Some possible grant funding has become available to develop services. The person chairing the meeting, Chandra, asks for input from each person present except Julia. Apparently, Chandra simply overlooked that Julia had not gotten an opportunity to speak.

Nonassertive Response:

Aggressive Response:

Assertive Response:

Assertiveness training helps people analyze their own behavior and become more assertive. Alberti & Emmons (1976) developed a number of steps that will lead to the habit of assertive behavior. They form the basis for the following exercise.

1. Recall a situation in which you could have acted more assertively. Perhaps you were too nonassertive or too aggressive. Describe the situation below.

2. Analyze the way you reacted in this situation. Critically examine both your verbal and nonverbal behavior. Describe and explain that behavior.

3. Choose a role model for assertive behavior in a situation similar to the one you have described. Identify the person you've chosen, then describe what happened and how she reacted assertively.

4.   Identify two or three other assertive verbal and nonverbal responses that you could have employed in the situation you described.

5.   Imagine yourself acting assertively in the situation you described. Explain what you would say and do.

6.   After you have completed these five steps, try behaving assertively in real life. Continue practicing until assertiveness becomes part of your personal interactive style. Give yourself a pat on the back when you succeed in becoming more assertive. Be patient with yourself—it's not easy to change long-standing patterns of behavior.

Conflict and Its Resolution

An *interpersonal conflict* occurs "when the actions of one person attempting to reach his or her goals prevent, block, or interfere with the actions of another person attempting to reach his or her goals" (Johnson, 1997, p. 226). Conflict can occur in an infinite number of ways in an unending array of contexts—micro, mezzo, and macro. This chapter focuses on conflicts between individuals in macro contexts. Chapter 3 will address specific types of conflict and conflict management guidelines for mezzo situations in macro environments.

Conflict is not always (or completely) negative (Johnson, 1997). On the positive side, it forces adversaries to examine their perspectives more thoroughly, enhances self-awareness, generates new energy for problem-solving, releases pent-up emotional steam, improves the quality of problem resolution and decision making through the infusion of new ideas, and increases excitement in otherwise humdrum daily routines. On the negative side, it requires the expenditure of considerable energy, carries with it the risk of loss (of face, position, influence, etc.), and diminishes the quality of collaboration and teamwork if hard feelings arise (Daft, 1998).

Personal Styles for Addressing Conflict

Just as each of us has a unique personality, so also does each have an individual style of conflict. Johnson (1997, pp. 240-41) describes five conflict-management styles. The categories are somewhat oversimplified, but they do illustrate broad types of behaviors people display in a conflict.

1. *Turtles* "withdraw into their shells to avoid conflicts" (p. 208). For them, this is easier than mustering up the initiative and energy needed to address a conflict. Turtles typically have relatively poor self-concepts and are nonassertive.

2. *Sharks,* unlike turtles, are aggressors. They move into conflict boldly, pushing aside any opponents. Sharks like power and want to win. They have very little interest in nurturing a relationship with an opponent.

3. *Teddy bears* are essentially the opposite of sharks. They value their relationships with their opponent more than the achievement of their own goals. Teddy bears are more assertive than turtles because they do value their own ideas, but they will put those ideas aside in deference to an opponent's beliefs if they believe their relationship is threatened.

4. *Foxes* are compromisers. Slyly, they work toward an agreement acceptable to them and to their opponent. Foxes are willing to relinquish some of their demands in order to come to a reasonable compromise. They are pretty slick at finding ways to satisfy everyone.

5. *Owls,* like foxes, believe in compromise, but they are much more assertive in conflict. Their style can be called confrontational. Owls walk willingly, even eagerly, into conflict situations because they value *the conflict itself* as a means of brainstorming solutions, attacking problems, and enhancing relationships.

Exercise 2.6: What's Your Style of Conflict ?

We cannot overstress the importance of getting to know yourself and your own reactions better in order to control your behavior and increase your interpersonal effectiveness. To this end, answer the following questions.

1. What style of conflict—or combination of styles—described above comes closest to the way you usually handle a conflict? Explain why.

2. To what extent is your approach to handling conflict effective? Explain.

3. In what ways would you like to change your approach to conflict management? (If you are satisfied with your behavior in conflictual situations, say so.)

Steps in Conflict Resolution

Johnson (1986) proposes seven steps for conflict resolution. Although it is not always possible to go through each one, it is important to keep them in mind.

Step 1: Initiate a confrontation ("the act of bringing together opposing ideas, impulses, or groups for the purpose of systematic examination or comparison" [Barker, 1999, p. 98]). First, clearly identify your goals and recognize their importance to you.

Then keep in mind the importance of nurturing your interpersonal relationship with the other person (Hooyman, 1973; Johnson, 1997; Weissman, Epstein, & Savage, 1983). You will need the support of others to achieve any macro goals you may establish. Therefore, the stronger your various relationships in the macro environment, the more likely you are to perform your job well and achieve your intervention goals.

Step 2: Agree on a definition of the problem. This definition should make neither you nor your opponent defensive or resistant to compromise. Emphasize how important the issue is to both of you.

Step 3: Recognize the importance of maintaining communication with your opponent(s) in the conflict. Many of the communication techniques already discussed can be put to excellent use in this process. Additionally, Sheafor, Horejsi, & Horejsi (1991, pp. 337-38) propose the following general communication guidelines:
- Do not begin a confrontation when you are angry. Anger makes you lose your objectivity.
- Do not enter into a conflict unless you are willing to work toward resolution. Otherwise, you are wasting your time.
- If you absolutely despise your opponent or have immense difficulty finding any positive, empathic feelings about him, do not confront him. Explore other ways of addressing the conflict (for example, through finding support from others who can deal more calmly with your opponent) or drop the matter completely.
- Include positive statements and feedback along with your negative input.
- Explain your concerns in a "descriptive and nonjudgmental" manner (Sheafor et al., 1991, p. 338). Prepare details beforehand in your head so that you can explain and clarify the issues and behaviors involved.
- Supply relevant data in support of your position. Be able to articulate your position clearly and have both your ideal solution and some potential compromises clearly established in your mind.
- Use "I-messages" frequently. Rephrasing your thoughts in this manner emphasizes your personal caring and empathy.

Step 4: Indicate your own willingness to work with your opponent to find a mutually satisfactory solution. To minimize disagreement (or at least to develop a viable plan of action) stress whatever you and your opponent have in common.

Step 5: Empathize with your opponent. Think carefully about why she thinks, feels, or acts as she does.

Step 6: Evaluate both your own and your opponent's motivation to address the conflict. Is it worthwhile to expend the energy necessary to resolve this conflict?

Step 7: Come to some mutual agreement by following these five suggestions (Johnson, 1997). (1) Articulate exactly what your agreement entails. (2) Indicate how you will behave toward the other person in the future as compared to in the past. (3) Indicate how the other person has agreed to behave toward you. (4) Outline ways of addressing any future difficulties (such as might arise if you or the other person violates the agreement). (5) Decide how and when you and the other person will meet to continue your cooperative behavior and to minimize future conflict.

Exercise 2.7: Conflict Resolution

Recall a conflict in which you have been involved. For the purposes of this exercise, it may be work-related, school-related, or personal.

1. Describe the conflict in detail. Who was involved? What was the issue? Explain the positions taken by the opposing sides. What were the circumstances of the actual confrontation?

2. Did you follow the suggestions in Step 1 for beginning a confrontation—that is, did you identify your goals and nurture your relationship with your opponent? What, if anything, could you have done differently to improve your handling of this conflict?

3.   Did you follow Step 2 by finding some common ground with your opponent? What, if anything, could you have done differently to discover some common ground?

4.   Did you follow Step 3 by maintaining communication with your opponent? What, if anything, could you have done differently to improve communication?

5.   Did you follow Step 4 by indicating your willingness to cooperate with your opponent? What, if anything, could you have done differently to demonstrate this willingness?

6.   Did you follow Step 5 by empathizing with your opponent and trying to understand his or her perspective? What, if anything, could you have done differently to achieve this empathy and understanding?

7.   Did you follow Step 6 by evaluating both your own and your opponent's motivations in this conflict? What, if anything, could you could have done differently to discern and evaluate those motives?

8.   Did you follow Step 7 by arriving at some mutually satisfactory agreement? What, if anything, could you have done differently to make such an agreement possible?

Working Under Supervisors

Your interpersonal relationships with agency supervisors are especially significant in the macro environment. Social work, in general, embraces the use of supervision as a professional value. Barker (1999) defines it as "an administrative and educational process used extensively in social agencies to help social workers further develop and refine their skills and provide quality assurance for the clients" (p. 473), and Shulman, (1999) reinforces that the purpose of supervision is improvement of service to clients.

If you can empathize with supervisors and understand their position, you will be able to maximize the benefits of your relationships with them. On one hand, they are responsible for you and your work performance. On the other, supervisors must answer to upper levels of administration in fulfilling their other agency responsibilities.

Workers generally expect supervisors (Halley et al., 1998; Sheafor, Horejsi, & Horejsi, 1999; Shulman, 1993):

- To be readily available for consultation—i.e., to provide help based on professional or expert opinion
- To ascertain that workers are knowledgeable about relevant agency policies and are aware of what they should and should not do
- To inform higher levels of administration about line workers' needs
- To facilitate cooperation among staff and resolve disputes
- To nurture workers, provide support, and give positive feedback whenever possible
- To evaluate workers' job performance
- To facilitate workers' development of new and needed skills

---

Exercise 2.8: Evaluating Supervisors

Think of a supervisor you have or one you had in the past. You may choose someone you consider very good or downright terrible. In this exercise, you will evaluate that supervisor in terms of the expectations listed above, so choose someone you remember well. If you've never had a supervisor, imagine one of your instructors in that role. In this evaluation concerning this person's supervisory behavior, cite pros, cons, and suggestions for improvement. It may help to mention specific interactions you had or issues you confronted with this supervisor.

1.   How readily available was this supervisor to provide help based on professional or expert opinion?

Pros:

Cons:

Suggestions for Improvement:

2. Did this supervisor fulfill your expectations in ascertaining that you were knowledgeable about relevant agency policies so that you could do your jobs as well as possible?

   Pros:

   Cons:

   Suggestions for Improvement:

3. Did this supervisor fulfill your expectations in informing higher levels of administration about line workers' needs?

   Pros:

Cons:

Suggestions for Improvement:

4.   Did this supervisor fulfill your expectations in facilitating cooperation among staff and helping to resolve disputes?

Pros:

Cons:

Suggestions for Improvement:

5.   Did this supervisor fulfill your expectations in nurturing you, providing support, and giving positive feedback?

Pros:

Cons:

Suggestions for Improvement:

6.   Did this supervisor fulfill your expectations in accurately and effectively evaluating your job performance?

Pros:

Cons:

Suggestions for Improvement:

7.   Did this supervisor fulfill your expectations in facilitating your development of new and needed skills?

      Pros:

      Cons:

      Suggestions for Improvement:

Using Supervision Effectively

Effective use of supervision hinges partly on your own behaviors and characteristics. Communicating clearly and regularly with your supervisor can get you the help you need in working with exceptionally difficult clients and finding resources you would not otherwise know about. The following are some helpful suggestions for maximizing your use of supervision (Halley et al., 1998; Sheafor et al., 1997):

1.   Use your micro communication skills with your supervisor. Check to be certain that you clearly understand the messages you hear. Ask questions. Rephrase a question if you don't think your supervisor understands what you mean. Paraphrase your supervisor's answer to ensure that you understand what was said.

47

2.   Keep your records up-to-date. Record-keeping is essential for accountability and your supervisor is ultimately responsible for your work. If you fail to keep up with required record-keeping, it will reflect badly on your supervisor. I promise you she will not like that.

3.   Plan ahead in terms of the items you include on your supervisory agenda. This gives the supervisor time to provide the information and help you need.

4.   Put yourself in your supervisor's shoes. Use empathy. He is an individual with his own feelings, interests, biases, and opinions. Think about both what he needs to know and what he needs to communicate to you. It is helpful to get to know your supervisor as well as possible.

5.   Display an openness to learning and improving yourself. Demonstrate a willingness to accept criticism and use it to improve your work.

6.   Display a liking for your work. You can emphasize the positive aspects of your work, emphasizing those facets you especially like. Whiners get old pretty fast.

7.   Work cooperatively with other staff and use teamwork. Be sensitive to the effect of your behavior on others. Show respect for the competence and talents of your peers and coworkers. Be tolerant of what you see as their shortcomings. Try to see the world from their perspective and understand why they feel and act the way they do.

8.   Give your supervisor feedback. *Tactfully* let her know what you like and dislike. If you have specific needs that your supervisor can appropriately meet, express them.

9.   Forewarn your supervisor about potential problems. When you don't know all the possible implications of a particular course of action or how it might affect the agency, ask your supervisor. *Don't* wait until the situation has reached crisis proportions.

10.   Learn your supervisor's evaluation system so that you can adequately respond to his expectations.

Exercise 2.9: Addressing Problems in Supervision

Sometimes, for whatever reason, problems develop. They may be your own, your supervisor's, or no one's fault, but when they occur, you must address them, adjust to them, or leave for another job.

The following scenarios are taken from actual supervisory experiences. Each involves real problems that you too could confront. In each case, think about how you would use the recommendations we have just discussed to resolve the difficulties. Then answer the questions that follow.

Scenario A: Taking Your Credit

You are a school social worker in a large urban high school. Your primary role is "to help students, families, teachers, and educational administrators deal with a range of problems that affect students" including "truancy, depression, withdrawal, aggressive or violent behavior, rebelliousness, and the effects of physical or emotional problems" (Gibelman, 1995, p. 175). In essence, you work with students to combat truancy, enhance academic performance, encourage responsible decision-making, and prevent disasters such as the 1999 teen shootings in Columbine High School, Littleton, Colorado. This allows numerous possibilities for development and implementation of creative projects.

You come up with what you consider a brilliant idea. What about starting a program where interested high school teens would provide tutoring, craft project supervision, and recreational activities for children living at a local homeless shelter?[5] This would not only furnish a needed community service, but also provide opportunities for youth to learn empathy, feel useful, and responsibly help others.

You briefly mention the idea to your supervisor Harmony for her approval. Without hesitation she gives you the go-ahead. You meet with personnel from the shelter, parents of some of the homeless children who may be involved, potential student participants, members of the Parent/Teacher Association at your school, and school administrators. You contact people from other communities that have similar programs and put in a significant amount of work writing up the proposal. Finally, you submit it to Harmony for her endorsement. She states, "I'll take it from here. Higher administration supports this."

You don't quite believe your ears. Does she really mean she's taking it over after all the work you put into it? That can't be. You reply, "Just say okay, and I'll start implementation. One of the first things will be to solicit student volunteers."

She responds, "No, you've got lots of other things to do. I'll take over now." You emphasize how the whole thing was your idea, how hard you've worked, and how you are *really* committed to carry out the plan. You hear yourself pleading with her. You suggest working on the project together.

"No," she confirms, "I'll do it. Don't worry about it anymore." You are devastated. Worse yet, three days later, you see a big write up about the project in the local newspaper giving Harmony all the credit. Your name isn't even mentioned.

1.   Try to empathize with this supervisor by discerning what her reasons might be for reacting like this.

2.   In this situation, how could you use the suggestions for assertiveness and confrontation described earlier in this chapter?

---

[5] The idea for the program described in this vignette was adapted from one proposed by J. P. Kretzmann and J. L. McKnight in *Building Communities from the Inside Out* (Chicago: ACTA Publications, 1993, p. 41).

3.   Consider the suggestions for using supervision effectively. Which of them could help you in this case?

4.   If you were the supervisee portrayed here, how important would it be to you to receive credit for your accomplishment? Would you feel that it was the goal that mattered rather than *who* achieved it?

5.   If you are the supervisee portrayed here and you *do* care about receiving credit for your work, what will you do if all the suggestions you have proposed thus far fail? (For example, will you go to an administrator above your supervisor for help and risk your supervisor's wrath? Will you learn a lesson from the experience and keep your successes to yourself in the future? Will you try to put it out of your mind and go on with your daily business? Will you start looking for another job?) There is no "correct" answer. You must identify various options, weigh the pros and cons of each, and decide what to do.

Scenario B: The Communication Gap

You are a newly hired social worker for a unit of boys, ages 11 to 13, at a residential treatment center for youths with serious behavioral and emotional problems. Your responsibilities include counseling, group work, case management, some family counseling, and consultation with child-care staff on matters of behavioral programming. Two of the twelve boys in the unit have been causing you particular trouble. They are late for their weekly counseling sessions and sometimes skip them altogether. When you do talk to them, they don't respond to your questions. Instead, they walk around the room, tell you you don't know what you're doing, poke holes in the furniture with their pencils, and call you vulgar names.

You are at a loss regarding what to do with these two clients. In your weekly one-hour session with your supervisor, you explain the situation. He makes several vague suggestions about videotaping some of your sessions, making home visits, and talking about the boys' behavior with them. At the end of the session, you feel you've gotten nowhere, and you still don't understand what you should do. You have difficulty following what your supervisor is saying. You can't "read" him. Sometimes you think he's joking, but you can't be sure.

1. Try to empathize with this supervisor by discerning what his reasons might be for reacting like this.

2. In this situation, how could you use the suggestions for assertiveness and confrontation described earlier in this chapter?

3.   Consider the suggestions for using supervision effectively. Which of them could help you in this case?

4.   Consider the possibility that you tried a range of approaches and none worked. If you decided that your supervisor was incompetent and really unable to help you, what would you do? Might you consider turning to other people in the agency for help? If so, how would you do so?

Scenario C: The Angry Response

You are a social worker at a health care center (nursing home) who has a variety of clients diagnosed as having a mental illness. Every six months, a staffing is held at which social workers, nurses, therapists (speech, occupational, physical), physicians, psychologists, and psychiatrists summarize clients' progress and make recommendations. It is your job to run the staffing and write a summary of what is said.

You are new at your job and unfamiliar with this agency. During the staffing, the psychiatrist is very verbal—in fact, you would describe him as "pushy." You feel intimidated and are uncomfortable asserting your own opinions when they are different from, or even opposed to, his. Because of his advanced education, his professional status, and his self-confident demeanor, you feel that his views are probably more important and valid than yours. After the staffing, your supervisor calls you aside. His face is red and his voice has a deadly, steel-like calm. He reams you out for letting the psychiatrist take over the staffing. This surprises and upsets you so much that you do not hear many of the specific things he says. You just know that he is furious with you and has implied—or even stated—that you are an incompetent wimp. He walks off in a huff.

1.   Try to empathize with this supervisor by discerning what his reasons might be for reacting like this.

2.   In this situation, how could you use the suggestions for assertiveness and confrontation described earlier in this chapter?

3.   Consider the suggestions for using supervision effectively. Which of them could help you in this case?

Scenario D: Gender Discrimination

You have the strong feeling that you supervisor, who is of the same gender as you, gives opposite gender supervisees preferential treatment. For instance, he acts friendlier and more casual with them, directs more comments and questions to them during meetings, and seems to give them preference for their vacation choices. You also have heard they're getting higher raises when you feel your own work performance is at least as good or better than theirs.

1. Try to empathize with this supervisor by discerning what his reasons might be for reacting like this.

2. In this situation, how could you use the suggestions for assertiveness and confrontation described earlier in this chapter?

3. Consider the suggestions for using supervision effectively. Which of them could help you in this case?

4.   In the event that your efforts to improve the situation fail, what would you do?

Scenario E: Problems with Delegation[6]

You are a caseworker for a social services agency in a rural county. Your job includes a wide range of social work practice, from investigating child abuse cases to working with families of truants to providing supplementary services to the elderly who want to remain in their own homes. You have a heavy caseload, but feel very useful. In general, you really like your job.

The problem is that your supervisor insists on reading every letter and report you write before it goes out. You think this is a terribly time-consuming waste of effort. In many instances, it also delays your provision of service, and you feel that it's condescending and implies a lack of confidence in your professional abilities.

1.   Try to empathize with this supervisor by discerning what her reasons might be for reacting like this.

---

[6] A primary administrative task for supervisors is mastering the art of delegation. Delegation is "assigning responsibility or authority to others" (Mish, 1991, p. 336).

2.   In this situation, how could you use the suggestions for assertiveness and confrontation described earlier in this chapter?

3.   Consider the suggestions for using supervision effectively. Which of them could help you in this case?

4.   In the event that your efforts to improve this situation fail, what would you do?

Scenario F: No Action

You are a social worker in a large urban community center serving multiple community needs. Services include counseling for emotional and behavior problems, provision of contraception, recreational activities for adults and youth, day care for working parents, meals for elderly citizens, some health care, and a variety of other services. Your job focuses primarily on counseling the center's clients referred for this purpose. You enjoy your job and are proud of being a professional social worker.

The problem is another social worker whose office is next to yours. He has a similar job but is assigned a different caseload and a slightly different range of responsibilities. The bottom line is that you seriously question his professional competence. You've observed him using what you'd describe as "comic book therapy" with the children and adolescents on his caseload. In other words, his clients come in and select comic books from his vast collection instead of receiving any real counseling. He has boasted on several occasions that he only went into social work because he was eligible for a scholarship.

One day you approach one of your clients, a fairly bright and articulate boy of 13. You are surprised to see him reading something in the center's waiting room, and you are disturbed when he obtrusively places his hand over a portion of a picture in the book. It strikes you as odd that his hand is placed over the rear half of a horse. He looks surprised to see you and he comments on the horse's long white mane. The mane is indeed remarkable: it reaches to the ground and extends another foot. When you ask your client what the book is about, he sheepishly shows you the picture, which depicts a castrated horse (hence, the mane and tail elongated due to hormonal changes). The book's title is *Washington Death Trips*. Among other items pictured in the book are dead babies in caskets, people who have butchered over 500 chickens by hand for no reason, and various infamous murderers. The boy tells you that your colleague lent him this book.

You are furious. Not only does this colleague offend your professionalism and your professional ethics, he even has the gall to interfere with your clients. You immediately go to your supervisor, who is also his supervisor, and complain about the incident.

Your supervisor—a well-liked, easy-going, but knowledgeable and helpful person—hems and haws. He implies that methods of counseling are each professional's own business, but you believe that your supervisor is afraid to confront your colleague.

1.   Try to empathize with this supervisor by discerning what his reasons might be for reacting like this.

2.   In this situation, how could you use the suggestions for assertiveness and confrontation described earlier in this chapter?

3.   Consider the suggestions for using supervision effectively. Which of them could help you in this case?

4.   If your efforts to improve this situation fail, what will you do? Can you ignore this issue?

Postscript

In summary, life with supervisors will not always be ideal. When a problem occurs, all you can do is use your communication skills to your best advantage, identify your alternatives, weigh the pros and cons of each, and choose your course of action.

Fortunately, you will probably also have supervisors who will serve as primary mentors. A mentor is someone who encourages you to do your best, exposes you to new knowledge and ideas, and provides you with opportunities to develop your skills and competence.

For this exercise students pair off, with one person playing a supervisee and the other a supervisor. You and your partner choose who will play which role. The supervisee should use the suggestions provided in this chapter to confront the supervisor assertively and use supervision effectively. Allow five to ten minutes for the role play, then answer the questions.

Supervisee: *You are a generalist practitioner in a foster care placement unit in a large county social services agency. You received your annual performance review report from your supervisor. The format requires a summary statement by the supervisor. Yours reads, "This worker does a pretty good job of completing her work on time." You feel this is a very negative statement, substantially detracting from a positive evaluation. You believe that you work exceptionally hard, often volunteer to accept difficult cases, and take pride in your performance.*

Supervisor: *You have two dozen supervisees. You don't like to give radically different performance reviews to your workers because these can make for hard feelings and jealousy among staff. You don't think the review is really relevant anyway since salaries are based solely on seniority, not on merit. In your view, your significant communication with workers is carried on during your biweekly individual supervisory conferences, and you think this particular supervisee is doing a good job.*

1.   What communication, confrontation, assertiveness, and supervisory techniques did the supervisee use during the role play?

2. How effective were these techniques in resolving the issue?

3. What other techniques, if any, might the supervisee have used to improve her effectiveness?

As the previous chapter emphasizes, generalist social workers use a variety of skills in macro practice. These include micro and mezzo skills such as networking, working with groups, planning and conducting meetings, and dealing with conflict. In fact, we begin with the perspective that it is nearly impossible to engage in effective macro practice without a solid grounding in micro and mezzo skills. While a single person can sometimes achieve great ends much that gets accomplished within organizations and communities is the result of several people working together. That is the focus of this chapter.

Specifically, this chapter will:

- Examine networking skills useful for working with organizations and communities
- Discuss the importance of teamwork in social work macro practice
- Provide suggestions for organizing and conducting meetings
- Introduce basic skills for dealing with conflict

What Is Networking?

Networks are groups or individuals, organizations or agencies that are linked together either formally or informally. Networks allow sharing of resources (e.g., money, emotional or social support, knowledge or skills) among the participants. Social workers often refer to our efforts to connect or reconnect individuals and families as networking. It is a skill used routinely on the micro and mezzo levels of practice.

Networking also refers to the development of connections at the macro level among professionals and between social workers and organizations or agencies. This networking is designed to facilitate dealing with a variety of systems. For example, it allows social workers to function more effectively in their own agencies and with other organizations because they know the important people, procedures, and policies needed to get things accomplished. At the macro level, social workers also use networking to link people and groups interested in large-scale change efforts—for example, by creating a community coalition focused on stopping drive-by shootings. Such a coalition was formed when several community organizations decided they had to combine resources to have any real chance of stopping the violence in their city. Using the relationships and connections built up among the leadership and members of the various organizations, they were able to maximize their influence. The coalition included leaders from law enforcement, social services, the school system, a ministerial association, and neighborhood associations affected directly by the violence. Getting these disparate groups together would have been much harder without the networking that had gone on before.

Why Is Networking Important?

Networking is important for a number of reasons. First, many people benefit directly from a variety of informal networks. The interdependence of individuals and our need to lean on others from time to time is a strong argument for networking. Clients experiencing serious mental illness in a community can often benefit significantly by strengthening their networks of family and friends. In addition, informal networks can often respond faster than larger, more formalized organizations.

Networks can also help those who would not normally seek help—for instance, people confronting language or cultural barriers, or those who are afraid of being stigmatized if they go to traditional agencies—can often get help from informal networks. Again, the aid provided can range from financial assistance to help with legal, social, or interpersonal problems. Informal networks can be drawn from one's work environment, social organizations, or church, among many others. Even when an informal network itself cannot provide help, it may support the use of formal community resources.

Networking is also important in rural areas where more formal resources are lacking. Here one's informal network might include everyone from the grocer to the county sheriff. The absence of formal agencies and services makes it essential that social workers know about and use these resources.

Informal networks are also important for the help they can offer to formal networks. No formal agency can meet all the needs of clients or groups of clients. Informal networks provide personal advice, concrete resources, and feedback not available from formal networks.

Networking can also assist people in using formal resources which are cumbersome, confusing, or otherwise difficult to utilize. Sometimes formal organizations need a kick in the pants to get things moving. A social worker who has developed contacts in a troublesome agency may be able to help clients deal with roadblocks, red tape, or other barriers.

Networking can improve the services rendered by formal organizations. Agency directors and others in leadership roles have a responsibility to improve services in their own agencies. By networking, they can learn from their contacts in other agencies what innovations are proving successful, when they can avoid unnecessary duplication of services, and how to identify gaps in service.

Finally, networks can help workers manage their own difficult times. Social workers regularly experience stress, frustrations, and challenges. It is often helpful to have a personal/professional network to turn to for advice, suggestions, emotional support, and a certain degree of reality testing.

Exercise 3.1: Networking

List at least four reasons why networking is important in social work.

Recommendations for Developing Networks

Developing effective networks is an important skill for social workers working in the community. The suggestions below can help you achieve this.

Identify Significant Informal Networks

Learn the names of the service clubs, fraternal organizations, and neighborhood associations in your community. Find out what special interests or focuses these groups may have. Identify all the major churches in your community and learn the names of their pastors. Find out whether these churches offer support groups or other services targeted at specific problems. In rural communities, try to learn the names of most community leaders, professionals in the health care and human services fields, and elected officials. If you are new to a community, ask established friends and colleagues to introduce you to those on your "need to know" list.

In addition, learn the names, functions, and services offered by all formal social service providers in your community. Keep a file, Rolodex, or database of these organizations, with the names of your contact people. Make a point of visiting each agency or organization and participating in any activities—such as Christmas open houses, anniversary celebrations, and similar activities—that further your learning.

Strengthen your ties to other networks by learning names, responding promptly to requests for information or assistance, and thanking people for their help. When the time comes that you need assistance for your clients, it will be much easier if you have laid the groundwork first. Recognize that networks change over time and that there is a mutuality at work: those who give help reasonably expect to be able to ask for it themselves later.

Exercise 3.2: Your Personal Network

You have learned about the importance of personal networks in helping social workers cope with their own stresses and frustrations. List at least five individuals you would include in your support network.

Recognize Different Types of Networks

Networks differ in a variety of ways. For example, some networks provide help with very complex problems. Others offer only minor or modest assistance. Formal networks tend to have greater resources available for dealing with major problems. Informal networks generally lack either the resources or the scope of formal networks. Some networks, such as church groups, are characterized by a high degree of intimacy between members. Again, more formal networks often lack this degree of intimacy since relationships are based upon professional contact. From time to time, a network may come into existence and then disappear. Sometimes a community is confronted with a particular problem. Those with mutual interests come together, respond to the problem, and then go their separate ways. This tends to happen when tragedy—a flood, a major fire, an outbreak of illness—strikes a community or organization or when another transient stressor appears.

Exercise 3.3: Tapping Your Own Network

Consider each of the following situations. Then identify a resource from your network that you could rely on to help you. These resources may or may not be on the list you made in exercise 3.2.

1.   Your car breaks down on the way to your first day at your field placement. You need a ride to work for the next two days. Who would help and why?

2.   Payday is still a week away and you need another $50 to get a wart removed from your nose. Who would lend you $50 and why?

3. Your computer and printer just quit, you have a paper due tomorrow morning at 8:00 A.M., and the campus computer labs are closed. Whose computer and printer could you use and why?

4. You have decided to come out of the closet and acknowledge that you are gay (or lesbian). Who is the first person you could depend on for support and why?

Exercise 3.4: Professional Networking

As you can see, networks come in handy in personal situations. They are equally important in your professional roles. Respond to the situation below:

Your new client is a woman with chronic mental illness who can function as long as she takes her medication. However, because of her illness she often forgets and decompensates. To whom would you go to help her develop (or redevelop) a network that she could rely on? List at least three possible individuals or groups that might be of assistance.

Team Work in Macro Practice

Social workers often work in teams composed of other social workers, various professionals, or citizens. Teams composed of members from several disciplines are often called interdisciplinary or multidisciplinary teams. Their membership might include social workers, psychologists, psychiatrists, nurses, and others with needed expertise. Other opportunities to work on teams arise when you participate as a member of an agency board of directors, an advisory committee, or a task force.

The most effective teams have a number of things in common (Larson & LaFasto, 1989; Fatout & Rose, 1995). Those commonalities are enumerated below:

1. Clear Goals: As might be expected, lack of clarity about a team's purpose can be devastating. Ideally, the goals should be clear to all members and represent ends that members believe in.

2. Team Structure and Membership Tied to Goals: Both the people on a team and the way the team organizes its work are important variables. Problem-solving teams require different skills than do teams trying to create a new agency or program. Similarly, those who are skilled at planning are helpful in the latter

situations but they may not function as well when the task is to carry out day-to-day operations.

3. Membership Commitment: The best teams show an *esprit de corps* (team spirit). They enjoy working together and look forward to achieving the team's goals.

4. A Climate of Collaboration: Collaboration is more likely to exist when members know and trust each other. The more team members can come to rely on each other, the greater the potential for collaboration. In a true collaborative environment, members value one another's contributions and trust one another.

5. Commitment to Excellence: A team committed to excellence measures its individual and corporate actions and achievements against some benchmark. All members of the team—or at least most of them—commit themselves to meet this standard and may pressure other members to do the same. Poor quality work is not acceptable.

6. Information-Based Decision Making: Effective teams make rational decisions based upon analysis of available data. Ideally, information available would be complete, accurate, and timely but this is not always the case. Incomplete information is often all we have to use. Effective groups recognize and identify information gaps. Occasionally, teams have more information than they can use and must make decisions about the most important data to consider.

    Accurate information requires that teams use multiple sources of information and cross-check data. Facts and figures should be double-checked with official statistics and an effort made to obtain current information (Fatout & Rose, 1995).

7. External Recognition and Support: Teams benefit from the recognition and support of outside individuals or groups. This recognition helps insure a "we" feeling and cements the members' connections to the team.

8. Principled Leadership: The best team leaders are clear and consistent in what they say to and about the team. Members need to know that the leader trusts and respects their abilities. Principled leadership shows itself through praise for the contributions of individual members and the ability to shed or control one's own tendency to "showboat."

Whether you're a member or a team leader, be aware of what makes a team effective. That awareness will help ensure both the achievement of team goals and the satisfaction of team members. You must be sensitive to the presence or absence of these characteristics, work to strengthen the team, and contribute your talents to achieving your team's goals.

Exercise 3.5: Practicing Team Work

Social workers participate as members of teams on a fairly routine basis. Respond to each of the situations below.

A. It is your first week of work at a residential treatment center for adolescents with emotional problems. At 10:00 AM you have your first meeting with the "M" team, which consists of you (the social worker), a Ph.D. psychologist, a psychiatrist, a nurse, and the cottage parents from cottage B (your cottage). Just prior to the meeting your supervisor asks you to list the professional knowledge and skills each of these people will bring to the meeting. This isn't "busy work." She wants you to appreciate the value of all the professionals on this team. List the professional contributions each might bring to this meeting based upon their professions and positions.

Psychiatrist

Psychologist

Nurse

Cottage Parents

B. You have been assigned to work with a team of community citizens seeking to "improve the quality of life in Tanktown." The team has been floundering for several months. Read the information provided about the team and review the characteristics of effective teams. Then identify what you see as the possible problems that may be causing this group's inability to get things done.

> The Quality of Life Team (or Q-Team as they like to call themselves) has been meeting for the past four months. They were appointed by the mayor to "improve the quality of life in Tanktown." Members include residents of the community, business owners, students, and several ministers. The mayor chose people who worked in his last election campaign. Meetings have been spent arguing about what the team should focus on. Discussions center around members' very different opinions about what Tanktown's most important problems are. Several members have missed at least five meetings, and the others tend to push ideas that are not supported by a majority of the team. The mayor told the group he'd check back in a year to see how they were doing. List the characteristics of effective teams that this group appears to lack. Explain each item.

How to Plan and Conduct Meetings

"Meetings, meetings, meetings! I don't have time for all these meetings." This is a lament that you are likely to hear from time to time in your practice. Meetings can be an important means of getting work done, but often they seem to waste precious time. Social workers spend time in all kinds of meetings—staff meetings, team meetings, community meetings—so it is important that this time be used efficiently. When meetings waste people's time, they typically react negatively. So how do you increase the likelihood that a meeting will be productive? Several recommendations are in order.

1. *Establish Purpose and Objective of Meeting*

    Everyone invited to a meeting should know why it's being held. Without clarity about the basic agenda, the meeting is likely to evolve into a confused mess.

2. *Choose Meeting Participants*

    Whenever possible, select those who will come to the meeting. Depending upon the meeting's purpose, you may need people who are critical thinkers, who possess certain expertise, and who work well together. You also want people who are committed to the meeting's purpose and who will actually show up, so take into account any possible barriers to participation.

3. *Choose a Time and Place*

    Where will you meet? When will you meet? These are not insignificant decisions. The time of day may encourage or discourage attendance. The location must be accessible to all participants and conducive to doing business. Take into account such things as room size in relation to size of group, ventilation, and availability of aids such as blackboards. Give clear directions to the meeting site and to parking areas. Don't expect people who use public transportation to make a meeting at the county seat fifteen miles away. Ideally, schedule your meeting far enough in advance so that people can put it on their calendars. Be sure to remind them as the day of the meeting approaches. Don't assume that everyone will come to a meeting that was scheduled two months ago.
    Consider possible seating arrangements. Do you need a table and chairs? Should the room be set up theater-style? The purpose of the meeting helps determine room layout.

4. *Send Out an Agenda*

The agenda is simply a list of the things you expect to cover at the meeting. It includes the date, time, and place of the meeting, and alerts participants to what they will be doing and when. The list of items to be addressed should be brief and requires no details. Bring extra copies of the agenda to the meeting. Someone will forget his agenda—count on it.

Background material should accompany the agenda. It's a waste of time to have people read documents at the meeting itself. Be aware that the difficulty level of the decisions to be made at the meeting will probably dictate how much you can get done in the time allotted. Usually the agenda is arranged so that housekeeping items such as approval of minutes, brief reports, and announcements are covered at the very beginning. The most important and difficult items should appear in the middle of the agenda after people warm up. Save the end of the agenda (and meeting) for routine items or those which can be put off until later. Remember, you have only so much time to work with.

5. *Manage the Time*

Start the meeting on time. Ignore the stragglers, and reward those who come on time. Introduce people if they don't already know one another. Announce the purpose of the meeting, and begin to move through the agenda. Remind people when the meeting will end and end it sooner if you get your business done ahead of time. If time expires and you have not covered everything, bring the last item to closure and adjourn. When you promise people the meeting will end at 5:00 p.m., stick to it. This encourages participants to stay on the topic and get the work done in a timely fashion. If the meeting is mired in muck and a decision can't be reached, don't be afraid to end the meeting. Sometimes a decision *can't* be reached because additional facts are required, important participants are absent, more time is needed for discussion, or the matter should be dealt with by another group (such as a subcommittee) (Jay, 1984).

Plan for any follow-up meetings, scheduling these as soon as possible. Make sure that decisions made at the meeting are carried out and identify the person(s) responsible for this. Ensure that minutes are prepared and distributed to participants prior to the next meeting.

6. *Manage the Discussion*

Whether you are a leader or a member in a meeting, you have a role to play in keeping the group on target. Test whether items under discussion are related to the agenda. If not, you've gotten off the subject. Contribute your ideas, but make sure they're always on target. Encourage everyone to speak, allowing and encouraging dissent and differences of opinion. Critical thinking demands that opposing ideas be considered. Test for real acceptance of compromises rather than accepting a false sense of harmony.

Don't let the discussion become personal. Some meetings get a bit hot, and so do the participants. Poke fun at yourself, but not at others. Reframe comments that seem to attack people rather than challenge ideas. Model fairness, impartiality, and concern for all participants.

Encourage or arrange for *brief* reports. There is nothing more boring than listening to long reports that should have been reduced to writing and distributed before the meeting.

Doing a meeting right takes careful planning and attention to detail. The exercise below is designed to help you identify and plan for some of the most important considerations in setting and conducting a meeting.

The agency director has asked you to handle the details for a forthcoming meeting. The participants are community representatives interested in services for people with disabilities. Your director wants to impress upon her guests the agency's commitment to serving this population, and she tells you to set the meeting for either August 1st or September 1st at your option. All of the other details are also up to you.

A.   Identify below all the major decisions you will have to make (for example, setting the meeting date and time).

B.   Now identify specifically what you decided about each item above (for example, set meeting for September 1st).

C.   What further information, if any, do you need from the Director?

You are invited to observe a meeting of a community coalition created to reduce street violence. Below is a summary of the minutes of the meeting.. Read it, and identify any improvements you think are warranted in the conducting of this group's meetings.

> The meeting began at 1:20 p.m. after a short delay to locate the light switches for the meeting room and to accommodate late-comers who were confused about the meeting location. Since agendas were not mailed ahead of time, Chairperson Reno opened the meeting by reading the agenda aloud. The agenda included (1) action on the curfew ordinance, (2) planning for next week's community forum, and (3) discussion of adding to the coalition a representative from the Parents-Teachers Association at the high school. There being no objections, the agenda was adopted as read.
>
> The secretary reminded the group that we had decided at the last meeting to talk about proposing changes to the curfew ordinance. The group discussed this matter and voted to talk to the City Council about changing the curfew. It was agreed that the coalition would meet again later this month to review progress on this matter. The meeting adjourned at 3:00 p.m.

List the actual or potential problems you noted in this brief record. Discuss briefly what should have been done.

Actual or Potential Problems   What Should Have Been Done

Understanding Parliamentary Procedure

It's almost impossible for a group to accomplish anything without first agreeing on a set of rules and procedures. Imagine, for instance, a group of 10 social workers all shouting out ideas and expecting that anyone who could yell loud enough would get his way. Suppose one person said, "I propose the rest of you give all your money to me for my vacation. You have to because I said it first." Without a method for handling routine business, dispatching harebrained ideas without too much fuss, and ensuring that everyone gets a chance to participate in decision making, anarchy would reign.

Robert's Rules of Order (Robert, 1989) provides a systematic and fair way of transacting business. Because they were originally used in British legislative sessions during the nineteenth century, these rules are generally referred to as "parliamentary procedure." Many groups—legislative bodies, committees, task forces, etc.—use parliamentary procedure to conduct their business. Often the group's official documents such as their constitution or bylaws state that business is to be conducted in accordance with *Robert's Rules of Order*.

Like any set of rules, parliamentary procedure has strengths and limitations. It is an effective means of dealing with proposals from group members, making formal decisions, and ensuring that all members have the right to be heard. It is also a much quicker way of reaching a decision. Imagine having to talk everyone into agreeing to something rather than relying on a decision by the majority. Unfortunately, parliamentary procedure can be misused by group members—for example, there are tactics they can use to stall. Even under normal circumstances, debate and voting on a proposal usually produce clear winners and losers, which can lead to hard feelings and impede the ability of members to compromise on other issues. Finally, anyone who doesn't understand parliamentary procedure will feel left out of the discussion or afraid to share her ideas for fear of making some mistake.

What Must I Know?

A variety of terms are routinely used in parliamentary procedure. They include:

Motions: Motions are the primary means of conducting business under parliamentary procedure. They fall into four primary categories: privileged, incidental, subsidiary, and main motions. Motions are usually stated in this form: "I move approval of the budget for 1998," or "I move we refer this matter to the finance committee." Some categories of motions, however, are stated differently.

- *Privileged motions* influence or impact on the formal agenda. For example, a motion to adjourn and a motion to recess—both of which mean the group will cease deliberation for a period of time—are privileged. As their name implies, these are motions of the greatest importance.

- *Incidental motions* concern procedures. A body's failure to follow proper procedure might be met with a motion expressed in the words, "Point of order!" This motion and its sibling "Point of information" must be addressed immediately. When a member raises one of these motions, the presider (group leader) is required to let that person speak. This is known as "recognizing" the person who has raised the motion. A point of information might be raised when something in the discussion is unclear, which is why it takes precedence over other motions. After all, you don't want to vote on something you don't understand (unless you're practicing for a future job in the U.S. Congress).

- *Subsidiary motions* include moving to table, postpone, or amend a motion already being discussed. We refer to motions being discussed as "on the floor." Thus, you might say "I move to amend the proposed budget to add 5% salary increases for the staff for next year."

  A motion to table a motion already on the floor is an attempt to postpone any discussion or decision on the proposal indefinitely. Tabling motions are raised when it becomes clear that no decision is going to be reached or that debate is going in circles. A motion to "refer to committee" is used when a matter is best left in the hands of a smaller group for study and recommendation.

- The last category is *main motions*, which accomplish most of a group's business. Although these are of the lowest priority among motions, they are nevertheless important. Without a main motion on the floor, group discussion can wander all over the place because it has no clear focal point. Moving to approve the purchase of new furniture or the proposed budget is a typical example of a main motion. Essentially, main motions bring matters to the floor for

71

discussion and decision. When you make such a motion you are usually accorded the right to speak first. Others may follow until all have had an opportunity to present their ideas.

Seconds: Most motions require a second before discussion is permitted. A second is simply a statement ("I second the motion") indicating support for a motion. Usually, without a second, a motion dies. Exceptions include point of order and point of information, neither of which requires a second.

Debate: Debate is almost always required on a motion, but there are exceptions. Point of order and point of information motions are not debatable. Debate is not allowed on motions to table, to "call the question" (that is, to end debate and vote on the motion), or to remove an item previously tabled.

Amendments: An amendment is a proposal to modify a motion on the floor. Each proposed amendment must be voted on before the original motion. Amendments are a way of modifying a motion to gain support from other members. Each proposed amendment is voted on until no further amendments are suggested. At that point a vote is taken on the motion as amended.

Voting: Generally speaking, most motions must be voted on by the group. Voting is usually done by voice vote or a show of hands. The presider will say, "All those in favor of the motion, say aye." Following the ayes there will be a similar call for no votes and sometimes for abstentions (those who choose not to vote). Paper ballots are used in some groups for elections of officers and similar votes. In some groups the presiding officer may also vote. This is specified in the bylaws of the organization under most circumstances. A simple majority (over 50 percent) of those present supporting a motion is needed for passage. Amendments to the group's constitution or bylaws usually require a two-thirds vote to pass. The presider is responsible for announcing the results of the vote. The secretary (official recorder of actions of the group) will enter this decision in the minutes of the body. The minutes are the official record of actions taken by the group.

Other Important Concepts: Almost every group has subgroups (usually called committees) responsible for handling certain types of business. Committees do some of the business of the group between meetings and prepare materials for consideration by the larger group. For example, the board of directors of a group I serve on has committees dealing with personnel, finance, the annual dinner, buildings and grounds, and membership. Each committee has a specific area of responsibility. Any time a matter that falls into one of those areas comes before the board of directors, it is referred to the appropriate committee for a recommendation or decision. Often, after discussing a matter, the committee makes a report and a recommendation to the entire board.

Committees fall into three general categories. *Standing committees* (such as personnel and finance) exist all of the time. Their existence is spelled out in the organization's constitution or bylaws. The constitution is the primary set of rules for an organization, establishing its purpose and outlining its operational system—such as membership, elections, and officers. Bylaws are the guiding rules for the organization's conduct and rank just below the constitution in importance.

From time to time the board I mentioned above finds it necessary to establish other committees to handle specific, one-time issues. For example, an *ad hoc committee* was established to plan a retirement party for the executive director. Since we do not anticipate having such parties on a regular basis, it makes sense to create a temporary committee.

An *executive committee* is responsible for making decisions for the board between meetings. The executive committee is usually empowered to expend funds for emergencies and to handle any other decisions needing immediate action. Most executive committees are composed of the officers of the board (president, vice president, secretary, treasurer) and a few other members chosen at large. The president of the organization usually presides over both the executive committee and the organization as a whole. The treasurer handles financial affairs, and the secretary is the official record-keeper of the organization. Duties of the vice-president vary from organization to organization.

Other rules that govern most organizations and groups include:

- A quorum—a minimum number of members, usually specified in the bylaws—is needed to transact business.
- Rules may specify the categories of members eligible to vote on certain issues.

Skill in using parliamentary procedure is very helpful for a social worker working with groups, committees, and other decision-making bodies. A knowledgeable worker can assist the group to conduct its business efficiently and effectively.

Exercise 3.8: Parliamentary Quick Quiz

Without peeking back at the chapter, quickly match the terms on the left with the definitions on the right.

_____	1.	Robert's Rules of Order
_____	2.	Secretary
_____	3.	Point of Order
_____	4.	Minutes
_____	5.	Second
_____	6.	Amendment
_____	7.	Debate
_____	8.	Executive Committee
_____	9.	Standing Committee
_____	10.	Constitution and by-laws
_____	11.	Main Motions
_____	12.	Quorum

A. Official recorder of group decisions
B. Accomplish primary business of group
C. Guidelines used in parliamentary procedure
D. Minimum number of members needed to transact business
E. Motion indicating proper procedure is not being followed
F. Committee that exists continuously
G. Proposed modification to a motion
H. Discussion about a motion
I. Governing rules of an organization
J. Composed of organization officers and charged with acting for the body between meetings
K. An indication of support for a motion which has just been proposed
L. Official record of actions taken by a group

Conflict Management

You may wonder why we talk about managing conflict instead of preventing or stopping it. The fact is that conflict is a normal characteristic of society. Conflict occurs over ideas, philosophies, resources, personalities, goals, and objectives. Ideally, conflict should be kept on a substantive level rather than on a personal or emotional level. Conflict on substantive matters can generate new ideas, open up alternatives, and allow for a clear airing of positions. Conflict on affective or emotional matters can be personally hurtful, is usually unproductive, and may preclude reaching a mutually satisfactory conclusion.

Few of us look forward to dealing with conflict. In fact, some people will do anything to avoid it, but it is nearly impossible to be effective in a group if you are unwilling or unable to handle conflictual situations. This is certainly true at the macro level. If you are trying to get approval of a law prohibiting discrimination against people on the basis of their sexual orientation, you will most certainly engender conflict. Similarly, if you attempt to get a landlord to fix up his rundown slum buildings, you can expect resistance and conflict because your goal and his are on a collision course. Conflict is also a normal developmental phase in most groups.

Thus, as a group leader you must anticipate this and be prepared to manage it. To do so requires that you be able to identify different types of conflict. Each type is described briefly below in figure 3.1.

Figure 3.1: Types of Conflict		
Type of Conflict	**Characteristics**	**Example**
Interpersonal Conflict	Involves at least 2 individuals and strong disagreements over whose argument is right	Two neighborhood social workers arguing over whether to support an anti-drug program
Resource Conflict	Differences arise when resources are insufficient to satisfy all parties	Residents demand that the city council provide a police sub-station in their neighborhood
Representational Conflict	Occurs when one attempts to represent one's group	Worker representing local group creates conflict by advocating for better drug law enforcement
Intercessional Conflict	Occurs when one attempts to intercede between or among warring factions	Worker intervening between groups with drastically different goals is embroiled in conflict

We can help groups and individuals by enabling them to recognize when they are in conflict and to carefully identify their differing perspectives. We must do this in a way that validates people's rights to have different opinions and needs while at the same time making it clear that differences can be discussed, negotiated, and resolved. Helping differing parties present their perspectives, using good listening skills, and searching for common ground between them is a service for which each social worker should be prepared. This is an appropriate place to use one's critical thinking skills—especially those that challenge assumptions—and to recognize emotional as opposed to rational arguments.

Exercise 3.9: Recognizing Types of Conflict

It is important to be able to recognize the type of conflict existing in a group or organization. Identify the type of conflict displayed in each of the following vignettes, and explain your reasons for that choice.

A.   "As chair of the homeless coalition, I can't sit here and let this city council tear down the old courthouse without a fight. We have 50 homeless families in this city and the city owns a building that would make a wonderful shelter. Mayor Jones, why can't you see the benefits that using this structure for a shelter would bring to the community?"

"The city council has to be concerned about more than just homeless people, Ed. We need the space occupied by the old courthouse for downtown parking. We're losing business to the mall outside of town because we have no place for people to park downtown. The city council asked me to work with you to find some other solution for this homeless problem."

Type of Conflict:

Explain:

B.   "If we add money to the budget so we can hire another building inspector, we won't be able to put another police officer on the force. What with the increase in gang activity here, I believe we need more cops, not more building inspectors."

        "Figuring out what makes the most sense within the budget is important, Mary. We have only $75,000 left in the personnel budget. I think the money will produce better benefits for the community if we add the inspector. There are too many substandard homes and apartments in the community, some of which are being used as drug houses. An inspector could help us cope with this at least as well as another police officer."

Type of Conflict:

Explain:

C.   "Constanza, I am tired of hearing of the so-called benefits of the DARE program. Show me an ounce of research that proves this program actually keeps school kids from using drugs. The whole thing is just a big public relations program. I think we should concentrate our efforts on something we *know* works—like the Police Dog Sniffer program. We know the dogs can sniff out drugs in school lockers."

        "José, police dogs are fine after the fact, but they do nothing to prevent drug use. We should spend our money on prevention, not intervention."

Type of Conflict:

Explain:

D.   "You're on their side! Why don't you ever see our perspective? All you ever do is agree with the Razers."

        "Oh, right. Man, if he's on our side we're in big trouble. He can't understand anything cause he's not a home boy."

        "Washington, Alonzo, I'm not on anyone's side. I'm supposed to find a way to keep you from stomping each other and keep you out of jail besides. My point is that I think the Guns proposal to keep the downtown area off limits to gang activity makes sense. It lets both your groups use the downtown as individuals, *and* it keeps the police off your butts. The minute you start something downtown, you've got the mayor, the council, and business owners turning up the heat. Both of your gangs get fried whenever that happens. Just because Alonzo suggested it, doesn't make it automatically a bad idea. Now get out of my face unless you have a better idea."

Type of Conflict:

Explain:

Conflict Management Strategies

Strategies for managing conflict fall into two general categories: There are some we use when we try to mediate a conflict in order to reduce its impact. Mediational conflict resolution aims at getting the opposing sides to work out a compromise. This approach is discussed by Johnson (1998) and outlined below:

Figure 3.2: Mediational Conflict Resolution Strategies

1. Anticipate conflict and be alert to its signs.
2. Reframe individual conflict as a matter for the entire group.
3. Seek and listen to all viewpoints, identifying similar and dissimilar positions.
4. Avoid situations and solutions that produce clear winners and losers.
5. Ask groups to cooperate and compromise rather than compete with one another.

Sometimes we do not wish to reduce conflict, but to use it to achieve goals for our clients. Maybe we are trying to force a change in some situation. Unfortunately, one side is not budging, so mediational strategies are inappropriate. Figure 3.3 describes the use of conflict as a specific strategy.

Figure 3.3: Using Conflict Strategy

Conflict Strategy	Rationale for Use
Assess your power and your adversary's power	Knowing whether you have the power (money, time, votes, etc.) to overcome your opponent is critical
Never disclose all your power	This keeps your opponents off balance and leaves them wondering if you have more influence than they can observe
Use power sparingly	This keeps your real strength a secret and keeps you from wasting a precious resource
Avoid unnecessary conflict	Conflict should not be the chosen approach when other less polarizing methods will achieve the same end
Generate conflict when other nonconflictual approaches have failed	Conflict can force others to see how something will affect them, challenge weak agreements, and encourage differences of opinion
Use covert methods to avoid direct conflict	Useful when the risk of direct conflict is too high—get others to fight for you, or employ passive resistance

---

Of course conflict can also be managed by other methods. One side can change its mind when confronted with evidence. The two sides may negotiate their differences. Both might agree to abide by the decision of an outside party (perhaps an arbitrator). In other situations the use of authority by either side or by an outside party may end the conflict. For example, the federal government has periodically ordered railroad workers and their employers back to work, thus forcing an agreement because the nation would be badly hurt by a railroad strike.

Exercise 3.10: Managing Conflict

In the following case example, a conflict is brewing within the staff of a hospital social work department. Assume you are a new worker in this unit and that you are concerned about the apparent split developing over the best way to handle a hospital-proposed reduction in patient services.

Miguel, the most senior social worker in the unit is speaking angrily about the situation: "We have always been a department that offered help to anyone we felt was at high risk. That risk could be financial, emotional, social, or medical. We've never set some group aside and said, 'We won't help you.' That's not what social work is all about."

"Micky, I know you're upset. But we don't own the hospital—we just work here. If the hospital director says we have to focus our services rather than take all comers, I don't see what we can do", says Betty, the acting department director.

"You can't fight city hall", says Mel, another worker.

"Baloney," Todd chimes in. "This hospital has built a fine reputation and we're not going to let it get destroyed without a fight."

Discuss what you might say to the group members to build cooperation, encourage compromise, hear their various viewpoints, find a common ground among members, and produce an environment of respect for everyone's ideas. In short, how would you keep the conflict from escalating?

Refer back to the case scenario described in Exercise 3.10. Assume that you are successful in getting your colleagues to form a united front against the proposed changes in hospital rules. Identify and list some strategies or guidelines mentioned in the book that you might find useful for getting the hospital administrator to change her mind.

We have established that an organization is a type of macro system. When you begin working in an organization, you become part of that larger system so it is important that you understand how such large systems work. There may be times when "the system" does not work as well as it should, and you may decide you need to try to change it.

Early in their professional careers, most social workers find the direct interaction and work with clients fascinating and exciting. Larger systems such as organizations and communities seem far less interesting, yet they frequently determine how good a job the worker can do for his clients.

This chapter will:

- Define organizations, social service, and social agencies
- Identify some major organizational theories, including systems theories, classical scientific management theories, human relations theories, the cultural perspective, the economics perspective, and the contingency perspective
- Explain organizational operations from a systems perspective
- Explore predominantly social work and host agency settings, organizational goals, organizational structure, and organizational culture
- Investigate sources of power held by individuals in organizations
- Discuss working within a bureaucracy
- Describe total quality management as one example of a management style that differs significantly from traditional bureaucracy

Organizations, Social Services, and Social Agencies

Social work is usually practiced in the context of an agency—a type of organization. *Organizations* are defined as "(1) social entities that (2) are goal directed, (3) are designed as deliberately structured and coordinated activity systems, and (4) are linked to the external environment" (Daft, 1998, p. 11). An organization is a *social entity* because it is made up of people with both strengths and failings who develop their own patterns of behavior. It is *goal-directed* because it exists for a specified purpose. It involves *deliberately structured and coordinated activity systems*, clusters of work activities performed by designated units or departments within an organization. Organizations coordinate the functioning of various activity systems to enhance efficiency in attaining desired goals. Organizations have structures that include policies for how the organization should be run, hierarchies of how personnel are supervised and by whom, and different units working in various ways to help the organization function. An intake unit for a large county department of social services is an example of an activity system. Workers under supervision process new cases by following established procedures, obtaining required information, and making referrals to the appropriate service providers within other agency units.

Linkage to the external environment concerns how any organization is in constant interaction with other systems in the social environment including individuals, groups, other organizations, and communities. Agencies providing social services interact dynamically with clients, funding sources, legislative and regulatory agencies, politicians, community leaders, and other social service agencies.

This chapter focuses on organizations that provide social services to clients. *Social services* are the functions that social work practitioners and other helping professionals perform for: improving people's health; enhancing their quality of life; "helping people to become more self-sufficient; preventing dependency; strengthening family relationships; and restoring individuals, families, groups, or communities to successful social functioning" (Barker, 1999, p.

453). In essence, the term "social services" covers the wide range of activities that social workers perform to help people solve problems and improve their personal well-being. *Institutional* social services include such services as financial assistance, housing programs, or education provided by public organizations (Barker, 1999). *Personal* social services are those "with a basic purpose to enhance the relationships between people and between people and their environments and to provide opportunities for social fulfillment" (Barker, 1999, p. 359). Such services usually target specific groups or particular problems such as family planning, counseling, or services directed at groups such as children or the elderly (Barker, 1995). The term *human services* is often used interchangeably with *social services*.

A *social agency* "is usually staffed by human services personnel (including professional social workers, members of other professions, paraprofessionals); clerical personnel"; and sometimes volunteers (Barker, 1999, p.447). Social agencies generally serve a defined client population which experiences a defined need. Services are provided in accordance with a prescribed set of policies that stipulate how the agency staff will accomplish its purpose. *Public* social agencies are run by designated units of government and are usually regulated by laws that affect their policies. For example, a county board committee oversees a public welfare department and is responsible for establishing its major policies. (Of course, such a committee must function under the regulations set by state or federal governments that at least partially fund the agency.)

Private social agencies, on the other hand, are privately owned and run by people not employed by government. The services they provide include personal social services. Note that sometimes services resemble those furnished by public social agencies such as corrections, protective services for children, and job preparation and training for public assistance recipients.

Private social agencies may be either nonprofit or proprietary. *Nonprofit* social agencies are run to accomplish some service provision goal, not to make financial profit for private owners. *Proprietary* or *for-profit* social agencies provide some designated social services, often quite similar to those provided by private social agencies, but with the additional aim of making a profit for their owners.

Exercise 4.1: Defining Types of Agencies

Match the following terms with their respective definitions:

a. Social services
b. Institutional services
c. Personal social services
d. Social agency

e. Public social agency
f. Private social agency
g. Nonprofit social agency
h. Proprietary agency

_____: A social agency that provides some designated social services, often quite similar to those provided by private social agencies, but with the additional aim of making a profit for its owners.

_____: An agency "usually staffed by human services personnel (including professional social workers, members of other professions, paraprofessionals); clerical personnel"; and sometimes volunteers (Barker, 1999, p. 447.)

_____: An agency run by designated units of government and usually regulated by laws that affect its policies.

_____: A social agency not run by the government, the purpose of which is to accomplish some service provision goal, not to make financial profit for its owners.

_____: Services "with a basic purpose to enhance the relationships between people, and between people and their environments, and to provide opportunities for social fulfillment" (Barker, 1999).

_____: Services including financial assistance, housing programs, or education provided by public organizations (Barker, 1999).

_____: An agency that is privately owned and run by people not employed by government.

_____: The functions that social work practitioners and other helping professionals perform for: improving people's health; enhancing their quality of life; "helping people become more self-sufficient; preventing dependency; strengthening family relationships; and restoring individuals, families, groups, or communities to successful social functioning" (Barker, 1999, p. 453).

Address the following questions:

a. What are the key components involved in defining each of these agency types?
b. In what ways are some of the eight agency types different?
c. In what ways are some of the eight agency types similar?
d. In what ways are the key components involved in each agency type important for understanding how the agency functions?

Organizational Theories

There are several major theoretical perspectives on how organizations are or should be run. Some theories emphasize similar dimensions such as expectations for staff treatment, the importance placed on profits, or the degree to which new ideas are encouraged. However, each theory stresses various concepts somewhat differently.

A range of theories are reviewed here. First, a number of traditional theories are explained including systems, classical scientific management, and human relations. Subsequently, new perspectives including the cultural, economic, and contingency perspectives are introduced.

Systems Theories

Systems theories emphasize how all parts of the organization (subsystems) are interrelated and function together to produce output (Holland & Petchers, 1987; Hodge, Anthony, & Gales, 1996). An organization is more than the sum of its individual parts. It is an intricate mechanism where parts work together to take resources (input) and process them into some kind of product or service (output) (Holland, 1995).

Systems theories emphasize the interactions of the various subsystems involved. Additionally, the importance of the environment and the impacts of other systems upon the organization are stressed. In some ways, systems theories are more flexible than many other theories. Irrational, spontaneous interactions are expected rather than ignored. Systems theories emphasize constant assessment and adjustment.

Classical scientific management theories emphasize a specifically designed, formal structure and a consistent, rigid organizational network of employees (Hodge, Anthony, & Gales, 1996; Holland & Petchers, 1987; Sarri, 1987). Each employee has a clearly defined task calling for minimal independent functioning. Supervisors closely scrutinize the workers' activities. Efficiency is paramount and performance is quantified (that is, made very explicit regarding what is expected), regulated, and measured. Worker morale is relatively insignificant. Administration discourages employee input regarding how organizational goals can best be reached. Employees are required to do their jobs as instructed and as quietly and efficiently as possible. Traditional bureaucracies operate according to classical scientific management theories.

Human relations theories emphasize "the role of the informal, psychosocial components of organizational functioning" (Holland & Petchers, 1987, p. 206), on the grounds that satisfied, happy employees will be most productive. These theories are concerned with "employee morale and productivity; . . . satisfaction, motivation, and leadership; and . . . the dynamics of small-group behavior" (Sarri, 1987, p. 31). Administrators are responsible for enhancing workers' morale, so effective, capable administrators are vital. The immediate work group (a mezzo system) is also crucial in human relations theories. Employees are encouraged to work cooperatively together and to participate in group decision making. Employers encourage employee input concerning organizational policies and practices.

Cultural Perspective

Organizational culture is "the constellation of values, beliefs, assumptions, and expectations that underlie and organize the organization's behavior as a group" (Holland, 1995, p. 1789). The cultural perspective on organizations assumes that each organization develops a unique mixture of values, standards, presumptions, and practices about how things should be done that eventually becomes habit (Hodge et al., 1996; Holland, 1995).

Management and other personnel may not be consciously aware that such patterns and expectations have developed. They become ingrained in established means of accomplishing tasks and goals. If it worked before, it'll work again. "If it ain't broke, don't fix it." The result is the establishment of an ideological structure that frames how organizational members think about the organization and how it should work. Employees tend to view new ideas by shaping them to conform to old, tried and true practices.

It should be noted that the organization's culture might support "innovation" and "risk-taking" instead of the status quo (Johns, 1996, p. 289). Here organizational culture would encourage personnel to shy away from old techniques and search for new ones.

Economics Perspective

The economics perspective emphasizes how organizations should proceed in whatever way necessary to maximize profits or output (Hodge et al., 1996; Holland, 1995). Serious attention is paid to the relationships between inputs or investments and the resulting outputs or production. Efficiency is paramount. Emphasis is placed on evaluating processes and programs to determine which is the most cost effective, that is, which produces the most results for the least money.

The economics perspective also frames the transactions between management and employees (Hodge et al., 1996). Just as the organization is viewed as being out to get as much as it can, so are the employees. Thus, management must assume that employees will act in their own best interests rather than the organization's. Management, thus, must ensure that procedural structure is sufficient so that employees have difficulty acting selfishly.

In some ways the economics perspective resembles classical scientific management approaches. Efficiency is emphasized and the employees are closely supervised. However, the economics perspective stresses the examination of numerous alternatives to achieve the same end. Flexibility and creativity may provide potential means to higher productivity for less cost. In contrast, the classical scientific management approaches focus on structured, established ways to accomplish tasks, such as has often been demonstrated in traditional bureaucracies. Change is often the enemy because it tends to interfere with following established procedures.

Contingency Perspective

The contingency perspective maintains that each element involved in an organization depends on other elements; therefore, there is no one generally best way to accomplish tasks or goals (Daft, 1998; Hodge et al., 1996). Each organization with its units or subsystems is unique. Thus, the best way to accomplish goals is to make individual determinations in view of the goal's context. Different means are required to solve various problems depending on all of the variables involved. The best approaches for organizations to take are ones reflecting a good fit with those in the external environment (Daft, 1998).

A strength of this perspective is its flexibility. It can be applied to any situation in any organization. However, a potential weakness is its lack of direction. The core idea suggests that all variables should be evaluated and any may be significant. Where does one start when evaluating a problem or planning a procedure? Staff? Input? Process? It's difficult to determine.

Exercise 4.2: Relating Concepts to Theory

Each concept listed below characterizes one or more of the organizational theories. Identify which organizational theory or theories it reflects and explain the concept's significance to the relevant theories.

1. *Concept:* **Importance of the environment**

    Organizational theory(ies) it characterizes:

    Explain the concept's significance:

2. *Concept:* **A unique mixture of values, standards, presumptions and practices formulating an established pattern for accomplishing tasks**

    Organizational theory(ies) it characterizes:

    Explain the concept's significance:

3. *Concept:* **Emphasis on control of employees**

    Organizational theory(ies) it characterizes:

    Explain the concept's significance:

4. *Concept:* **Flexibility in achieving goals**

    Organizational theory(ies) it characterizes:

    Explain the concept's significance:

5. *Concept:* **Evaluation of all variables and development of a unique plan to achieve goals**

    Organizational theory(ies) it characterizes:

    Explain the concept's significance:

6.   *Concept:* **Work group cooperation**

       Organizational theory(ies) it characterizes:

       Explain the concept's significance:

7.   *Concept:* **Efficiency and flexibility to achieve maximum production**

       Organizational theory(ies) it characterizes:

       Explain the concept's significance:

8.   *Concept:* **Constant assessment and adjustment**

       Organizational theory(ies) it characterizes:

       Explain the concept's significance:

9.   *Concept:* **Evaluation of all variables and the development of a unique plan to achieve goals**

       Organizational theory(ies) it characterizes:

       Explain the concept's significance:

10.   *Concept:* **Employee satisfaction**

       Organizational theory(ies) it characterizes:

       Explain the concept's significance:

Social Agencies as Systems

Systems theories provide one theoretical or conceptual perspective on the world of organizations. They stress the relationships among various systems including "individuals, groups, organizations, or communities" (Barker, 1999, p. 477), so they furnish an exceptionally useful way for social work practitioners to conceptualize service provision to clients. The following concepts are especially significant in understanding the macro environment.

A *system* is a set of orderly and interrelated elements that form a functional whole. A nation, a public social services department, and a newly married couple are all *social systems*—that is, they are composed of people and affect people.

Agency A

1a.   What sources comprise Agency A's financial input?

1b.   What are the characteristics of Agency A's clientele input (for example, problem type, age range, needs, strengths)?

2.   Describe the treatment or service provision process that Agency A employs.

3.   How does Agency A determine or measure its service effectiveness or output?

Agency B

1a.   What sources comprise Agency B's financial input?

1b.   What are the characteristics of Agency B's clientele input (for example, problem type, age range, needs, strengths)?

2.   Describe the treatment or service provision process that Agency B employs.

3.   How does Agency B determine or measure its service effectiveness or output?

Use the information above to answer the following questions:

1.   How are Agencies A and B similar or different in terms of their financial input?

2.   How are Agencies A and B similar or different concerning their clientele input?

3.   How are Agencies A and B similar or different concerning their process of service provision?

4.   How are Agencies A and B similar or different concerning their determination and measurement of service effectiveness?

The Nature of Organizations

Organizations are particularly important to you for three basic reasons. First, you will most likely be employed by one. Second, the organization itself can create problems for you. Third, Hasenfeld (1984) stresses that you need to understand organizations in order to plan the implementation of macro changes. The ensuing discussion stresses the following concepts: agency settings; organizational goals; the macro context of organizations; and organizational structure.

Agency Settings—Predominantly Social Work or Host

Social workers usually work in either predominantly social work or host organizational settings. Each setting has particular implications for effective practice.

Predominantly social work settings are agencies where social work is the main or primary profession employed. Most public social service agencies are predominantly social work settings. Administrators, supervisors, and most employees are social workers with social work titles, though the agency may also employ homemakers, psychologists, or other professionals.

Social workers tend to share similar professional values and perspectives because they've had similar education and training. In such an agency, therefore, social workers understand their role. Note that sometimes, particularly in public settings, decision-makers may not be professional social workers. Rather, they may be elected officials, lawyers, or political appointees to boards and commissions that interpret legislative policy and tell agency staff how to operate and what to do. In these cases, social workers may be at the mercy of decision-makers with other agendas than practice effectiveness and client satisfaction such as power, cost efficiency, and personal values.

Host settings usually employ a variety of professional staff and social services are not their main business. Consider hospitals and schools. Medical care of patients is the primary service of the hospital. Medical personnel (including nurses and physicians) comprise the largest segment of the professional staff. Most administrative staff and supervisors have medical backgrounds. Social work is just one of several ancillary professions—including dietitians, pharmacists, and chaplains—contributing to the overall goal of providing medical care.

Such an environment can prove challenging for social workers. Typically social workers must learn the language (for instance, medical terminology or relevant abbreviations) used by the other professions. Unlike many predominantly social work settings, the hospital is likely to operate on the basis of a definite pecking order with physicians at the top. Sometimes social work values and perspectives will clash with those of the physicians and other medical personnel.

Exercise 4.5: Predominantly Social Work and Host Social Agency Settings

1.   Name two predominantly social work social agency settings. Describe the professional role of social workers in each setting.

2.   Name two host social agency settings other than hospitals and schools. Describe the professional role of social workers in each setting.

Organizational Structure

Organizational structure is "the manner in which an organization divides its labor into specific tasks and achieves coordination among these tasks" (Johns, 1996, p. 490). All large agencies (and most smaller ones as well) have a *formal* structure. Sometimes it is explicated in an organizational chart showing who reports to whom (Daft, 1998; Hodge et al., 1996). Such charts depict lines of authority and communication, and many agencies operate according to this chart at least with respect to some functions such as how information is disseminated.

Equally often, however, agencies also develop *informal* structures and lines of communication. Many structure their units so that all workers in the unit report to one supervisor. Consider the Rocky County Foster Care Unit, comprising five workers and a supervisor. When workers have questions or problems, they often discuss their cases with other workers in the unit or with Natasha, the senior worker in another unit, instead of taking the problem to Boris, the Foster Care Unit Supervisor. As a result, Boris lacks information that might be important in doing his job.

While confiding in Natasha may seem like a bad arrangement, it has some beneficial aspects. Workers are sometimes uncomfortable talking with their supervisors, but they are willing to seek help from other more experienced workers. Sharing of ideas and problems fosters camaraderie among the workers, which decreases their stress levels and can lead to better job performance. Human relations theories stress the importance of such interpersonal communication and support in organizations.

We neither praise nor criticize the existence of informal structures and communication channels. We simply acknowledge that they do exist and must be dealt with. Being aware of both formal and informal avenues within your agency can strengthen your ability to do your job. Once you know all your options and alternatives, you can make more informed choices.

Keep three concepts in mind when you appraise an agency's formal and informal structures. These are *lines of authority, channels of communication,* and *dimensions of power.*

Lines of Authority

An agency's formal structure depends on *lines of authority* (Daft, 1998; Johns, 1996). For our purposes, authority is the specific administrative and supervisory responsibilities of supervisors for their supervisees. Agency policy usually specifies these lines of authority in writing.

Often, an agency's formal structure is outlined in an organizational chart (Lauffer, Nybell, & Overberger, 1977). Individual staff positions are indicated by labeled squares or circles. The hierarchy of authority in an organizational chart is depicted by vertical lines leading from supervisors down to supervisees (Daft, 1998). Generally, positions higher on the chart have greater authority than those placed lower. In essence, these lines represent "who is responsible for whom" (Lauffer et al., 1977, p. 31).

The chart in figure 4.1 reflects the hierarchy of authority for Multihelp, an agency providing assessment and therapeutic treatment to children with multiple developmental and physical disabilities.

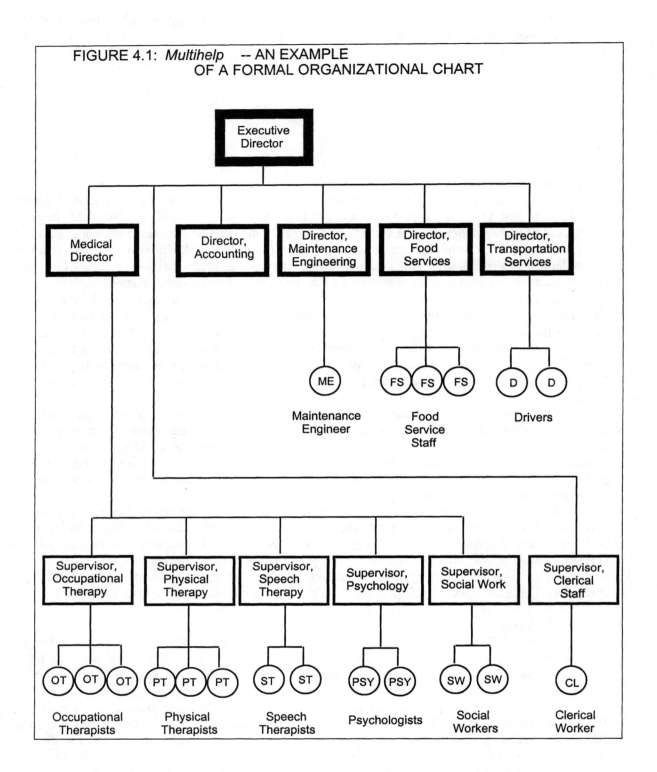

FIGURE 4.1: *Multihelp* -- AN EXAMPLE OF A FORMAL ORGANIZATIONAL CHART

Rectangles in figure 4.1 designate positions with some degree of administrative responsibility. The bolder the rectangle, the more authority and responsibility the position entails.

The Executive Director has the most authority and is responsible for the overall performance of Multihelp. Below him are five agency directors—the Medical Director (a physician), and the directors of accounting, maintenance engineering, food services for clients and staff, and transportation services for clients. Each director (except the Director of Accounting) is, in turn, responsible for the supervision of other staff further down the hierarchy of authority. The Medical Director oversees the entire clinical program—occupational therapy, physical therapy, speech therapy, psychology, and social work—including the work of the various departmental supervisors. Circles at the bottom of the chart represent line staff who work directly with clients.

Does the chart make clear how this agency is run? Look at the Social Work Department: two direct service workers report directly to their Social Work Supervisor. They serve their clients, look to their own supervisor for direction, and live happily ever after—right?

The "catch" is that formal organizational charts depict lines of *formal* authority within agencies. An agency's actual chain of command may follow the formal chart fairly closely, but an agency is equally likely to develop *informal* channels of communication and power.

Channels of Communication

All agencies have "multiple networks of communication by which members relay and receive information" (Resnick & Patti, 1980, p.51). Communication, of course, is "a process by which information is exchanged between individuals through a common system of symbols, signs, or behavior" (Mish, 1995, p. 233).

Formal lines of authority suggest that such communication flows harmoniously and synchronously along these designated channels. Supervisees are *supposed* to communicate primarily with their identified supervisors for direction and feedback. Supervisors are *supposed* to communicate directly with their supervisees and the managers who supervise them. But Multihelp does not work this way.

Dimensions of Power

Power is the potential ability to move people on a chosen course to produce an effect or achieve some goal (Homan, 1995; Martinez-Brawley, 1995). Like channels of communication, dimensions of power are supposed to follow the lines of authority. That is, those in supervisory positions are supposed to have actual power (that is, clear-cut influence and control) over their employees. In a real-life agency, this may or may not be the case.

Informal Structure: The Multihelp Example

Look at Multihelp's Social Work and Psychology Departments, illustrated in figure 4.2. This subsection of the organizational chart contrasts the formal and informal structures for these two agency departments. The *real* channels of communication and dimensions of power among supervisors and direct service staff are very different from those depicted in the formal organizational chart. The real relationships reflect the personalities and interactions among people with unique perspectives and identities, strengths and weaknesses, and problems and needs.

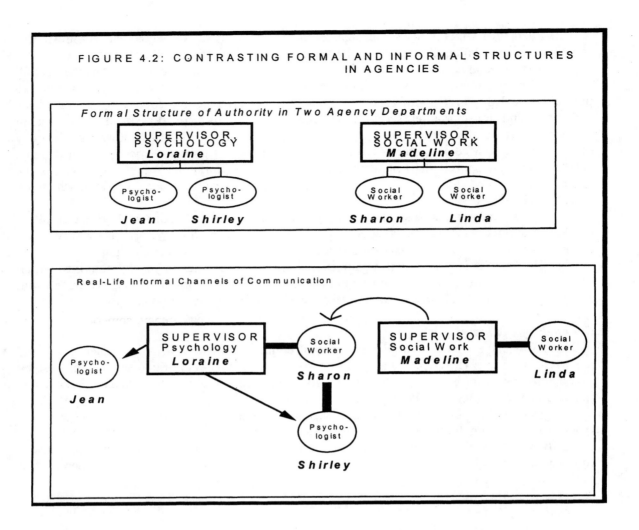

FIGURE 4.2: CONTRASTING FORMAL AND INFORMAL STRUCTURES IN AGENCIES

Formal Structure of Authority in Two Agency Departments

Real-Life Informal Channels of Communication

The formal structure shows that Loraine, the Psychology Department's Supervisor, is responsible for the administration and supervision of both Jean's and Shirley's job performances. Both these workers have master's degrees in psychology. Likewise, the formal structure reveals that Madeline, the Social Work Department's Supervisor, has direct supervisory authority over both Sharon and Linda, each of whom has a master's degree in social work.

The lower box portrays the real-life informal structure of these departments. Sharon, one of the social workers, is a good friend of Loraine's. They are both single, so they frequently socialize and even vacation together. (See the bold line connecting them in figure 4.2.)

Sharon, on the other hand, does not get along with Madeline, her Supervisor. It is fair to say that they have a personality conflict—though the term is difficult to define. For whatever reason, they do not like each other. Sharon considers Madeline incompetent, lazy, and interested in doing as little work as possible. Madeline perceives Sharon as an overly energetic, impulsive "go-getter"—"a bull in a china shop." They interact as little as possible, and most of their communication is in the form of memos—usually direct commands from Madeline to Sharon. (Note the arrow that swoops up from Madeline and down again to Sharon. Communication and power consistently flow downward from Madeline to Sharon in a dictatorial, hierarchical fashion.)

Madeline, however, has much in common with Linda, the other social worker. They meet socially and frequently eat lunch together. Madeline views Linda as a calm, competent worker who communicates well and as an enjoyable social companion. She treats Linda as a friend and an equal. (The thick bold bond linking Madeline and Linda horizontally illustrates this relationship.)

Psychology Department Supervisor Loraine sees Jean as a competent professional colleague. (Note that Jean appears slightly below Loraine in figure 4.2. The connecting arrow flows from Loraine down to Jean because Loraine maintains her supervisory and administrative status.) They like each other on a professional basis, but they do not have a personal friendship.

Loraine perceives Shirley in a much different light. She regrets hiring her and has begun to document Shirley's difficulties in performance in preparation for "letting her go"—dismissing her from the agency. (Thus, Shirley is positioned significantly below Loraine, the arrow connecting them running from Loraine down to Shirley. The chain of communication and power clearly positions Loraine in the more powerful, communication-controlling position, and Shirley in an inferior, less powerful, communication-receiving status.

However, the plot is even more complicated. Sharon is substantially younger than Loraine and about the same age as Shirley, who is also single. Sharon and Shirley have much in common and are close friends. (See the bold vertical line connecting them. This indicates that they consider each other equals, friends, and colleagues.)

Sharon is in an uncomfortable and tenuous position. On the one hand, she values her friendship with Loraine and sees Loraine as a professional ally in the agency, someone who can provide her with some leverage against Madeline. On the other hand, Sharon also likes Shirley, and understands that Loraine is not perfect. Sharon can listen to Shirley's complaints against Loraine and provide some sympathy, but she must be extremely careful not to speak against either Loraine or Shirley to the other person. It is not easy to maintain such a balancing act.

We neither praise nor criticize informal structures of communication and authority. We simply acknowledge that they do exist in almost every agency—including yours. In practice, being aware of both formal and informal agency structures may strengthen your ability to do your job.

What eventually happened at Multihelp? Shirley left to take a position in another state, and she and Sharon soon lost contact. Six months later, Sharon also left the agency for another social work position better suited to her energetic, enthusiastic style. She became a counselor for teens with serious behavioral and family problems. Sharon and Loraine maintained their personal friendship for many years after Sharon left the agency. No one knows what happened to Madeline, Linda, or Jean.

Exercise 4.6: Analyzing Formal and Informal Organizational Structure

Choose an organization, preferably some type of social services agency. For the purposes of this assignment, however, any agency—including your university or some segment of the university—will do. Contact an employee, a supervisor, or an administrator in the agency you selected, and ask for a copy of the organizational chart. Explain to your contact person that you want to study the formal *lines of authority,* the *channels of communication,* and the *dimensions of power* illustrated in the chart. Define the terms for your contact, then ask the following questions and record his or her answers:

1.   A.   To what extent do the channels of communication in the agency follow the formal lines of authority depicted in the organizational chart?

B.   If there are specific differences between the chart and the reality describe them.

C.   What are the positive and negative effects of these differences?

2.   A.   How closely do the dimensions of power in the agency match the formal lines of authority depicted in the organizational chart?

B.   If there are specific differences between the chart and the reality, describe them.

C.   What are the positive and negative effects of these differences?

should be accomplished. This school of thought calls for minimal independent functioning on the part of employees. Supervisors closely scrutinize the latter's work. Efficiency is of utmost importance. How people feel about their jobs is insignificant. Administration avoids allowing employees to have any input regarding how organizational goals can best be reached. Rather, employees are expected to do their jobs as instructed—and as quietly and efficiently as possible.

Its polar opposite is *Total Quality Management (TQM)*, a style currently employed by many social service organizations.[1] This management perspective emphasizes organizational process, attainment of excellent quality service, and empowerment of employees. Barker (1999) defines TQM as "an orientation to management of organizations, including social services agencies, in which quality, as defined by clients and consumers, is the overriding goal, and client satisfaction, employee empowerment, and long-term relationships determine procedures" (p. 488).

Bedwell (1993) provides a more straightforward description of TQM: "The essence of total quality is simple: Ask your customers what they want; then give it to them!" (p. 29).

Essentially, TQM considers clients, other agencies that purchase services from the TQM-oriented agency, and the agency's staff very important. Agency staff most directly involved with clients are significant because their interactions with clients directly affect client (customer) satisfaction. TQM maintains that quality of service provision is also critical. Each social services agency must specify its own definition of quality in the context of its own purpose. Dimensions may include accuracy, consistency, responsiveness, availability, perceived value (by clients), and service experience—the entirety of the service event as perceived by clients (Lutheran Social Services of Wisconsin and Upper Michigan, 1993, p. 8). In contrast to traditional bureaucracies, TQM empowers employees to perform their jobs as effectively and efficiently as possible. It emphasizes participative management that places the major responsibility for effective service provision on direct service workers. Teamwork and shared responsibility among workers are top priorities. TQM encourages teams to stress the importance of open communication, identify problems and issues, discuss potential alternatives, make decisions about how to proceed, set goals, and evaluate progress. Employees are consistently encouraged to assess processes and procedures and make improvements. Essentially, supervisors and administrators should "serve as integrators and facilitators, not as watchdogs and interventionists" (Kanter, 1989, p. 89). Agencies adapting TQM eagerly solicit feedback from clients about service effectiveness.

Exercise 4.8: Organizational Culture Investigation

The two questionnaires below contain questions you can ask to evaluate organizational culture. They compare two organizational cultures—a traditional bureaucracy and a client/employee centered agency employing TQM. This exercise will sensitize you to differences in organizational culture and to how those differences may affect you professionally.

Select a social services agency—large or small, public or private—in your area. You may interview a worker, a supervisor or agency administrator, or both a worker *and* an administrator. (If you choose this last option, you can compare their impressions of the organizational culture. Frequently, workers—who are in direct contact with clients and their views—perceive an organization very differently than do administrators—who are exposed to political, funding, and regulatory pressures from the external macro environment.) This questionnaire will not yield a specific score to precisely define organizational culture, but it will provide you with some thought-provoking information about agency life.

---

[1]The concepts involved in Total Quality Management were developed by W. Edward Deming (1982, 1986) and others (Crosby, 1980; Feigenbaum, 1983; Juran, 1989).

Instruct the interviewee(s) to answer both questionnaires to the best of her ability, using this scale: (1) never; (2) infrequently; (3) sometimes; (4) frequently; and (5) always. Record her responses below.

Add up the scores for each questionnaire separately and divide each by ten. The two average scores will range from 1—low organizational commitment to that management style—to 5—very high commitment to that management style. You may find an inverse relationship between scores on the Bureaucratic and Customer/Employee Orientation questionnaires, reflecting the extreme differences between the two.

Bureaucratic Orientation Questionnaire[2]

1. Most professional employees in this organization hold a clearly defined job with clearly designated responsibilities.

Never	Infrequently	Sometimes	Frequently	Always
1	2	3	4	5

2. Most professional employees in this organization are told straightforwardly and specifically how their jobs should be accomplished.

Never	Infrequently	Sometimes	Frequently	Always
1	2	3	4	5

3. Supervisors closely scrutinize employees' work.

Never	Infrequently	Sometimes	Frequently	Always
1	2	3	4	5

4. The administration considers efficiency to be of the utmost importance.

Never	Infrequently	Sometimes	Frequently	Always
1	2	3	4	5

5. Decisions about agency policy and practice tend to be made by higher administration and flow from the top down.

Never	Infrequently	Sometimes	Frequently	Always
1	2	3	4	5

6. Power in the agency is held primarily by top executives.

Never	Infrequently	Sometimes	Frequently	Always
1	2	3	4	5

7. Communication in the organization flows from the top down.

Never	Infrequently	Sometimes	Frequently	Always
1	2	3	4	5

---

[2]Many of the questions listed below are derived from the conflicts posed by Knopf (1979) that occur between the orientations of helping professionals and bureaucratic systems.

8. There is little communication among horizontal units—that is, units of approximately equal status that perform different functions.

Never	Infrequently	Sometimes	Frequently	Always
1	2	3	4	5

9. The organization emphasizes a rigid structure of power and authority that works to maintain stability and the status quo.

Never	Infrequently	Sometimes	Frequently	Always
1	2	3	4	5

10. The organization and its administration place great importance on specified rules and policies and expect employees to adhere to them.

Never	Infrequently	Sometimes	Frequently	Always
1	2	3	4	5

TOTAL: = _____ ÷ 10 = _____ (AVERAGE SCORE)

Customer/Employee Orientation Questionnaire

1. The organization places primary importance on the client (customer) and on effective service to clients.

Never	Infrequently	Sometimes	Frequently	Always
1	2	3	4	5

2. The organization holds in high regard practitioners who provide services directly to clients.

Never	Infrequently	Sometimes	Frequently	Always
1	2	3	4	5

3. The organization's administrative structure is viewed primarily as a support system for clients and direct service workers.

Never	Infrequently	Sometimes	Frequently	Always
1	2	3	4	5

4. The organization's administration considers quality of service—consistency of service provision, responsiveness to clients' needs, and service availability—its major goal.

Never	Infrequently	Sometimes	Frequently	Always
1	2	3	4	5

5. Organizational leadership seeks to empower agency practitioners so that they can do their jobs as effectively as possible.

Never	Infrequently	Sometimes	Frequently	Always
1	2	3	4	5

6. Professional employees are encouraged to provide input into how the organization is run.

Never	Infrequently	Sometimes	Frequently	Always
1	2	3	4	5

7. The organization values client feedback and incorporates it into improving service provision.

Never	Infrequently	Sometimes	Frequently	Always
1	2	3	4	5

8. Professional employees are encouraged to work together to improve service provision.

Never	Infrequently	Sometimes	Frequently	Always
1	2	3	4	5

9. Communication flow is open and frequent among most agency units.

Never	Infrequently	Sometimes	Frequently	Always
1	2	3	4	5

10. Professional employees feel that their input to upper levels of administration is valued and put to use.

Never	Infrequently	Sometimes	Frequently	Always
1	2	3	4	5

TOTAL = _____ ÷ 10 = _____ (AVERAGE SCORE)

After calculating scores, explain to the interviewee(s) which organizational culture his agency reflects. Give brief examples of traditional bureaucracy and of TQM. Then ask the following questions about the organization's culture and effectiveness.

1.   How would you describe the organization's culture?

2.   To what extent do you feel the organization's culture enhances or detracts from practitioners' ability to do their work effectively?

3.   What are the strengths of the organization's culture?

4. What are the weaknesses of the organization's culture?

5. Ideally, what changes, if any, would you make in the organizational culture?

This chapter takes you through the decision-making process behind undertaking a macro practice change. You might assume that administrators and politicians will implement the changes in policies and programs necessary for optimum service to clients, but often that is not the case.   In the real world, administrators must adhere to complicated regulations, operate with tight monetary restrictions, and act on insufficient information about what's going on below them. In addition, some make personal gain their top priority.

We assume, therefore, that organizational change will be instigated by practitioners with little or no administrative power (that is, those with lower-level supervisory status who work directly with clients)—even though such action is not part of their job descriptions.

This chapter will:

- Discuss macro practice changes involving projects, program development, and agency policy
- Explain the seven-step PREPARE process, a guideline for assessing an organization's potential for change
- Use case examples to demonstrate the PREPARE process

Change in Organizations: Projects, Programs, and Policy

Most of the macro changes you will consider pursuing will involve either improvement of client services or enhancement of the work environment (with the intent of improving service provision) (Netting, Kettner, & McMurtry, 1993). These changes may take the form of new projects, new programs, and/or changes in formal agency policies (Kettner et al., 1985).

A *project* is a "specific set of short-term, result-oriented activities providing support or direct services in response to unique conditions, problems, needs, or issues, in a community or organizational context" (Kettner et al., 1985, p. 39).[1] Projects are generally time-limited, usually lasting no more than one year. Unlike program development or policy changes, projects are temporary.   They are also usually very specific in terms of the client population they serve and the final objectives they pursue. Partly for this reason, they generally cost less than new programs and have fewer repercussions than major agency policy changes. All this makes them more appealing to administrators.

Projects can be undertaken in response to an issue that requires a new, innovative, or untried approach. You might want to implement a new technique or evaluate the effectiveness of some agency procedure. Projects may be very short-term endeavors aimed at supporting other agency activities—for example, fundraising projects and staff-training seminars.

You might need to bring about a macro change in the form of a new *program*, usually because you've discovered a gap in service. Programs are "relatively permanent structures designed to meet ongoing client needs"; they "carry out policies that are intended to meet community or organizational goals" (Kettner et al., 1985, p. 33)—for example, a sexual harassment awareness program in a large agency, a contraception counseling program in a school system, or a recreational program for the elderly in a neighborhood community center.

Finally, you may need to change, add, or remove an *agency policy*. Such policies are guidelines that govern how an agency operates, what should and should not be done within the agency setting.   Policies cover both internal operations (process) and provision of services to clients (output). You might target a policy that interferes with service provision—such as a

---

[1] Other definitions and uses of the term "project" are applied to ongoing, permanent, or semi-permanent organized, goal-oriented activities. Consider, for example, the Milwaukee AIDS Project which has served persons living with AIDS and their families for many years and will most likely continue to do so.

requirement for excessive paperwork—or a policy prescribing when and where an intervention must take place. You might seek to alter regulations dealing with worker caseloads or overtime.

Considering Organizational Change: PREPARE

Macro interventions are often complex. Practitioners must begin by considering the problem and the potential solutions in a general way. Maybe you will decide that a macro change is not the option you should pursue and turn your attention to the mezzo or micro levels. Maybe you will decide that no macro change is feasible and drop the whole idea.

If you decide to go ahead, you must determine what type of macro change is desirable— A change in your agency? A change in your community? A change in local, state, or federal social policy? For now, we will discuss organizational change.

Suppose you have determined that a problem exists. Do you have the potential resources to bring about a change that will solve the problem? Figure 5.1 ("PREPARE: An Assessment of Organizational Change Potential") summarizes this process.[2]

Figure 5.1:		PREPARE: An Assessment of Organizational or Community Change Potential
Step		
1.	P	Identify **PROBLEMS** to address.
2.	R	Review your macro and personal **REALITY**.
3.	E	**ESTABLISH** your macro reality.
4.	P	Identify relevant **PEOPLE** of influence.
5.	A	**ASSESS** potential financial costs and potential benefits to clients and agency
6.	R	Review professional and personal **RISK**.
7.	E	**EVALUATE** the potential success of the macro change process.

Step 1: *PREPARE—Identify* Problems *to Address*

There are problems in every work environment. Organizational change requires that you begin by identifying the problems you feel are most severe.

Substep 1: Decide to seriously evaluate the potential for macro level intervention. Address the following questions:

a.   How severely does the problem impact clients' well-being?
b.   Is the problem serious enough to merit macro change?
c.   Are you willing to expend the effort necessary to analyze and appraise the possibilities of effecting a change?
d.   Will your clients support such a macro change? Will it be in their best interest?

If you feel in your gut and determine rationally that a macro change is necessary, proceed to Substep 2.

---

[2] You need not necessarily follow PREPARE's steps in the exact order in which they are presented. What is important is that you do remember all the variables involved when you consider undertaking a macro level change.

Substep 2: Define and prioritize the problems you've identified. Choose those that you will start with. Consider the client population that will be affected by your proposed change, define the components of the problem, and determine its primary cause.

Substep 3: Translate problems into needs. Problems are sources of perplexity or distress. Needs are "physical, psychological, economic, cultural, and social requirements for survival, well-being, and fulfillment" (Barker, 1999, p. 323). Poverty is a problem. Food, shelter, education, and work are needs. To substantiate the needs connected with the problem you mean to address, compile background data and statistics (for example, from public records or census data), make certain other agencies aren't already meeting the needs, and seek related ideas and suggestions from other professionals and from clients (Hasenfeld, 1987).[3]

Substep 4: Determine which need or needs you will address.

Step 2: PREPARE—Review Your Macro and Personal Reality

You need to assess both your macro and personal realities to realistically evaluate your chances of making a successful macro change. Your *macro reality* is the macro environment in which you work—the systems, subsystems, and other elements of your agency's internal operation, as well as the agency's own macro environment. Your *personal reality* consists of your own strengths and weaknesses.

Substep 1: Evaluate the organizational and other macro variables: (1) availability of resources and funding; (2) constraining regulations or laws that might limit the potential for change; (3) degree to which the internal political climate of the agency is or is not supportive; (4) external political climate; and (5) other relevant factors (Holloway, 1987).

Substep 2: Assess your personal reality—that is, the strengths and weaknesses that may act for or against a successful change effort. Consider your own personal qualities, both positive and negative. For example, assets: your personal relationships with colleagues and administrators in the agency, well-developed persuasion and conflict-resolution skills; liabilities: lack of sufficient information about the problem you want to address, lack of self-confidence.

Exercise 5.1: Evaluating Personal Characteristics for Macro Practice

Evaluating your own characteristics, strengths, and weaknesses is as important in macro practice as in micro or mezzo practice. Indeed, macro practice skills are built upon micro and mezzo practice skills, and you will use the same interpersonal skills in macro practice as you do at the other levels. Picture yourself working with staff, administrators, and clients in an agency. Answer the questions and follow the instructions below:

1. Complete the following four "Who are you?" statements, using adjectives, nouns, or phrases. If you had to summarize who you are, what would you say?

    I am

    I am

    I am

---

[3] You can also undertake a more formal needs assessment. Needs assessments are "systematic appraisals made by social workers and other professionals in evaluating their clients for problems, existing resources, potential solutions, and obstacles to problem solving" (Barker, 1999, p. 323).

I am

2.   What adjectives would you use to describe yourself? Underline all that apply.

HAPPY SAD HONEST DISHONEST SENSITIVE INSENSITIVE
TRUSTWORTHY UNTRUSTWORTHY CARING UNCARING OUTGOING
SHY WITHDRAWN FRIENDLY UNFRIENDLY RELIGIOUS NOT-VERY-
RELIGIOUS NERVOUS CALM FORMAL INFORMAL AGGRESSIVE
ASSERTIVE TIMID CONFIDENT NOT-VERY-CONFIDENT CAREFUL
CARELESS CAPABLE INCAPABLE INDEPENDENT DEPENDENT
AFFECTIONATE COOL WARY BOLD CHEERFUL WITTY UNASSUMING
THOROUGH EASY-GOING DETERMINED CLEVER RESPONSIVE STRONG-
MINDED LEISURELY INDUSTRIOUS WEAK-WILLED (AT LEAST SOMETIMES)
CONTROLLED SPONTANEOUS SERIOUS FUNNY TOUGH PLEASANT
DARING EAGER EFFICIENT NOT-SO-EFFICIENT ARTISTIC TACTFUL
INTOLERANT VULNERABLE LIKABLE SMART UNDERSTANDING
IMPATIENT PATIENT IMAGINATIVE WORDY CONCISE OPEN-MINDED
FUNNY ORGANIZED SOMEWHAT-DISORGANIZED CONSCIENTIOUS LATE
EMOTIONAL UNEMOTIONAL CONTROLLED OPEN CREATIVE CURIOUS
SENSITIVE SINCERE PRECISE A-LITTLE-HAPHAZARD COOPERATIVE
PLEASANT ETHICAL BRAVE MATURE EAGER SPUNKY

3.   Cite your four greatest strengths—personal qualities, talents, or accomplishments.

        Strength A

        Strength B

        Strength C

        Strength D

4.   Several weakness are listed below. To what extent do you suffer from each? Rate
        yourself on each one by placing the appropriate number beside it.

        1. Very serious 2. Moderately serious 3. Mildly serious 4. Not at all serious

        Lack of understanding of community service system   _____
        Personal stress   _____
        Exhaustion and fatigue   _____
        Over-involvement with job   _____
        Insufficient time   _____
        Lack of self-confidence   _____

5.   Cite your four greatest weaknesses.

       Weakness A

       Weakness B

       Weakness C

       Weakness D

6.   How do you think your personal strengths will help you work with other staff, administrators, and clients in macro practice situations?

7.   What weaknesses, if any, do you think you need to address to improve your ability to work with staff, administrators, and clients in macro practice situations?

Step 3: PREPARE—Establish *Primary Goals*

What is required to fulfill your identified needs? What goals do you think you might be able to accomplish in your own macro environment? It is too early to establish detailed, specific objectives, but identifying a primary goal will give you a sense of direction.

> Examples of goals may range from the establishment of regular meeting times for physicians, social workers, and nurses in a hospital to discuss cases, to the shifting of the program focus of a social work unit from individual services to group or community service. A goal may be as minute as designing a new face sheet on a case record or as major as establishing a workshop to improve administration-staff relationships (Resnick, 1980c, p. 212).

Step 4: PREPARE—*Identify Relevant* People *of Influence*

Who might be available to help you make the changes you've identified? There might be specific individuals or groups in the organization or the community, people or groups with access to influence or power—such as agency supervisors, administrators, or community leaders. Subjectively consider to what extent you can anticipate support from each person or group identified.

Step 5: PREP_A_RE—Assess *Potential Financial Costs and Potential Benefits to Clients and Agency*

Any macro change requires some new input. Such input can take the form of actual money spent or of staff time—another expensive resource (Rubin & Rubin, 1992).

It may be difficult to estimate actual costs, but you do need to think about costs in a general way. Does your macro change require $500,000 for new staff and office space expansion when your agency is strapped for funds? Or does your macro proposal require a few hours per week of several staff members' time, plus the cost of supplies and funding for publicity to advertise a new service?

Rubin and Rubin (1992, p. 391) suggest asking three basic questions before pursuing a new project. First, "Will the results be worth the effort"? Second, "Might alternative solutions produce more benefits at less cost"? Third, "Who gets the benefits and who pays the costs"?

Step 6: PREP_A_RE—Review *Professional and Personal* Risk

There are three more questions to ask yourself before you undertake macro change in an organization (Resnick & Patti, 1980). Evaluate the potential risk of each.

- First, to what extent are you in danger of losing your job if you seek to make this change? Do you perceive no, some, moderate, or serious danger?
- Second, to what extent will such macro change efforts decrease your potential for upward mobility in the agency? Might you make enemies who could stand in the way of your future promotions?
- Third, to what extent would your efforts for macro change seriously strain your interpersonal relationships at work? Risk factors include the need to pressure administrators who do not want to be pressured and may seek to punish you; the chance that you will be viewed as a troublemaker or will annoy your colleagues by asking them to contribute their time and effort.

Of course, sometimes involvement in macro activity will *enhance* your standing in an agency. It can demonstrate initiative and a sense of responsibility that others might highly respect.

Step 7: PREP_A_RE—Evaluate *the Potential Success of a Macro Change Process*

The last step in the PREPARE process determines whether you should continue your change efforts or stop right here. It consists, essentially, of the following two substeps.

Substep 1: Review the prior PREPARE process, and weigh the pros and cons of proceeding with the change process. Specifically, appraise client need (as established in Step 1), positive organizational variables in your macro reality and your personal assets (Step 2), potential support from people of influence (Step 4), and potential financial benefits (Step 5). Then weigh these variables against negative organizational variables in your macro reality and your personal deficiencies (Step 2), potential resistance from people of influence (Step 4), potential financial costs (Step 5), and your own potential risk (Step 6). Figure 5.2 illustrates Step 7 in the PREPARE process.

At the end of this decision-making process, you will be left with one of three decisions: to make a definite commitment to the change process, to accept that the time is not right and postpone your plans, or to forget the idea altogether.

Substep 2: Assuming that you are committed to the macro change, identify possible approaches, roughly estimate their potential effectiveness, and select the most appropriate one. Approaches may be directed at changing agency policy, at developing a new program, or at undertaking some more limited project. Chapter 6 will continue where this chapter leaves off in the macro change process.

Figure 5.2: PREPARE-- **Evaluate** the Potential Success of a Macro Change Process

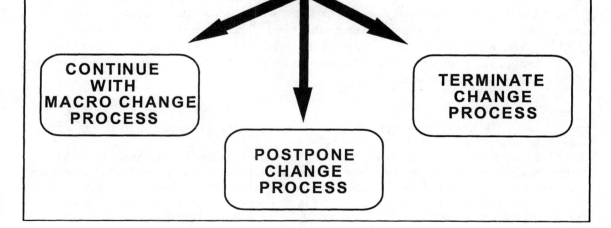

Evaluate the _PROS_ that include:

	Established in Step
Client Need	1
Positive Organizational and Other Macro Variables	2
Your Own Strengths	2
Potential Support	4
Financial Benefits	5

Weigh the pros against the_CONS_ that include:

	Established in Step
Negative Organizational and Other Macro Variables	2
Your Own Weaknesses	2
Potential Resistance	4
Financial costs	5
Your Risks	6

CONTINUE WITH MACRO CHANGE PROCESS

POSTPONE CHANGE PROCESS

TERMINATE CHANGE PROCESS

Read the following case vignette and answer the subsequent questions using each step of the PREPARE process. Feel free to add creative ideas and solutions to each phase of the decision-making process.

You are a social worker for Shatterproof County Department of Social Services in the Public Assistance Division.[4] Shatterproof is a huge urban county populated primarily by people of color. Following the demise of Aid to Families with Dependent Children (AFDC),[5] your agency is struggling to adapt to new policies, regulations, and requirements concerning the distribution of clients' needed resources. You and your colleagues are working to adjust and conform to new expectations. However, that is not the immediate focus of your concern.

In working for the county these past three years, you have become increasingly disturbed about the way many workers treat clients, most of whom are women of color. You feel that workers are pressured to process clients through the planned change process as quickly as possible and that too little emphasis is placed on client empowerment. Empowerment is the "process of increasing personal, interpersonal, or political power so that individuals can take action to improve their life situations" (Gutierrez, 1995, p. 205).[6] You feel strongly that if workers assumed an empowerment-oriented approach, more clients would be able to gain control of the solutions to their own problems. Such an approach might involve teaching workers how to focus on empowerment approaches and techniques, including "accepting the client's definition of the problem," "identifying and building upon existing strengths," engaging in a realistic assessment of the client's power in her personal situation, "teaching specific skills" (such as "skills for community or organizational change; life skills, such as parenting, job seeking, and self-defense; and interpersonal skills, such as assertiveness, social competency, and self-advocacy"), and "mobilizing resources and advocating for clients" (Gutierrez, 1995, pp. 208-10).

So you begin to wonder what you might be able to do about this situation. Clients ought to be allowed more input into the definition and solution of their problems, but workers are not as receptive to clients as they should be. Adopting an empowerment approach could greatly help in successfully implementing the new public assistance programs. Of course, this is not the agency's only problem. Workers are overly burdened with paperwork, and computers and programs are already outdated. Nevertheless, in your mind empowerment remains the dominant issue. You think social workers, supervisors, and administrators should be educated about empowerment issues and trained to implement empowerment approaches in practice. Emphasis should be placed on both empowerment values and skills. How can you increase awareness and implementation of a philosophy of empowerment in your huge agency? Upper-level administrators seem to inhabit some unreachable plane. There are only so many hours in your workday. What are your options? Can you start small by trying to reach workers in your own unit? (There are seven of you who report to one supervisor. Can you initiate training for yourself and the other six workers in your unit?

---

[4] Public assistance is "a government's provision of minimum financial aid to people who have no other means of supporting themselves" (Barker, 1999, p. 390).

[5] AFDC was "a public assistance program, originating in the Social Security Act as Aid to Dependent Children, funded by the federal and state governments to provide financial aid for needy children who are deprived of parental support because of death, incapacitation, or absence" (Barker, 1995, p. 14).

[6] Many of the concepts presented here are taken from L. M. Gutierrez (1995). "Working with women of color: An empowerment perspective." In J. Rothman, J. L. Erlich, & J.E. Tropman (eds.), *Strategies of Community Intervention* (pp. 204-220). Itasca, IL: F. E. Peacock.

Will the unit and the agency accept an empowerment approach? What factors will help you and what will hinder you? What will training the unit staff cost? The agency may have some funding available to provide in-service training for workers,[7] because it does require every worker to complete continuing education units (CEUs)[8] on a regular basis. As a matter of fact, you have a flyer announcing an empowerment training seminar led by an expert in the field. You also know of a social work professor in the local university who might be able to do some training or to refer you to someone who can. What would that cost? Is there any possibility of getting volunteers to do the training on a limited basis?

Are there other potential barriers to training besides cost? Certainly the agency's CEU requirements are in your favor. Although the agency is in some turmoil due to new programs and requirements, it seems there has always been some degree of hubbub. That's really nothing new. Training a single unit is a relatively small task. Ideally, you'd like to include the entire agency, but that's something to think about in the future. You can think of no one outside the agency who would actively oppose your plan.

Do you think you can "pull off" such a project, even though training programs aren't in your job description? What personal characteristics will work to your advantage in the process? For example, are you capable, responsible, and/or assertive? Do you have exceptionally strong communication or negotiation skills? On the other hand, what weaknesses do you have that might act against a successful change process? For example, is it difficult for you to ask for things? Do you consider yourself shy or lacking in confidence?

The bottom line is that you really want other workers to work with clients more effectively by adopting an empowerment approach. Your goal, then, is to figure out how to provide training to help them do just that. You've discussed the idea with colleagues who seemed mildly positive about it. You don't think they'd be willing to take on primary responsibilities for the project, but it would be worthwhile speaking with some of them further.

Your colleague and friend Ortrude has some difficulties organizing and following through on details, but she usually speaks up for anything she believes in. Maybe you can win her support. There is also Virgilia, a hard, responsible worker who usually keeps her opinions to herself. You don't feel you know her very well, but she might be in favor of your idea. On the downside, there's your colleague and non-friend Bentley who typically "pooh-poohs" any innovative idea.

The agency's voluntary In-service Training Committee suggests and plans training for various agency units, so you will have to approach its members, and they might be supportive—even though their funding is limited and fluctuating. Since you don't personally know any committee members, you have no natural "in."

As to people in the community, you've already established that at least one expert is available (though you don't know what her fee would be) and that the professor at the university is another possibility.

What about your own position and how initiating such a project might affect you both professionally and personally? Your supervisor Astral is a "laid-back" type who generally gets her work done in a leisurely fashion. (Actually, you think she's kind of "spacy.") She is not someone to depend upon for high-powered consultations or for strong support for this initiative. On the other hand, if you're willing to do the work yourself, she will probably approve the project and send it up for higher level authorization. All agency in-service training must be approved by

---

[7] In-service training is "an educational program provided by an employer and usually carried out by a supervisor or specialist to help an employee become more productive and effective in accomplishing a specific task or meeting the overall objectives of the organization" (Barker, 1999, p. 243).

[8] Acquiring CEUs often involves successful completion of "qualified academic or professional courses" (Barker, 1999, p. 103). One intent is to keep professionals in a range of professions updated with current knowledge relevant to their fields.

the agency's Assistant Director, Harvey. You think Harvey, a scrooge-like accountant at heart, is more likely to approve such a plan if it isn't extremely costly.

Step 1: Identify Problems to Address

Substep 1.1: Evaluate the potential for macro level intervention. Discuss the seriousness of the identified problem situation in the case example above. In your own words, describe what you see as the core issue(s).

Substep 1.2: Define and prioritize the problems you've identified in the case example.

Substep 1.3: Translate problems into needs.

116

Substep 1.4: Determine which need or needs you would address if you were in this worker's situation. Explain why.

Step 2: Review Your Macro and Personal Reality
        Substep 2.1: Evaluate the organizational and other macro variables potentially working for or against you in the macro change process as portrayed in the above case example. Fill out figure 5.3, then explain the reasons for your responses below.

Figure 5.3: PREPARE--Evaluate Your Professional and Personal **Risk**

To what extent are you in danger of:	No danger	Some danger	Moderate danger	Serious danger
1. losing your job?				
2. decreasing your potential for upward mobility?				
3. seriously straining work relationships?				

Explain the reasons for your responses.

Substep 2.2: Assess your personal reality—that is, the strengths and weaknesses that may act for or against a successful change effort. Exercise 5.1 may help you with this question.

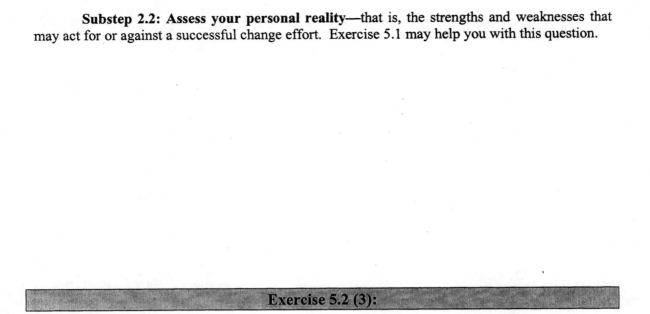

Exercise 5.2 (3):

Step 3: Establish Primary Goals
List the goals you would pursue if you were in the position described above.

Exercise 5.2 (4):

Step 4: Identify Relevant People of Influence
In figure 5.4, list individuals and groups both inside and outside of the agency.

Figure 5.4: PREPARE—Identify Relevant **People** of Influence

Potential Action Systems	*Name*	*Potential Support*			
		Very good	Mildly good	Mildly bad	Very bad
Individuals in the Organization					
Groups in the Organization					
Individuals in the Community					
Groups in the the Community					
Others					

Give a brief explanation of your choices.

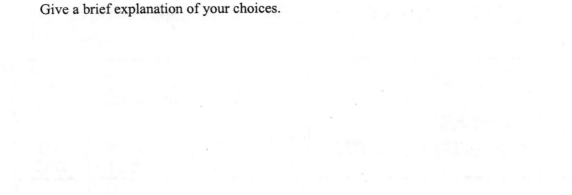

Exercise 5.2 (5):

Step 5: Assess Potential Financial Costs and Potential Benefits to Clients and Agency
Use the case example in your response.

Exercise 5.2 (6):

Step 6: Review Professional and Personal Risk
What are the possibilities that you might lose your job, decrease your potential for upward mobility, and/or seriously strain your work relationships?

Step 7: Evaluate the Potential Success of a Macro Change Process

Substep 7.1: Review (and summarize) the prior PREPARE process, and weigh the pros and cons of proceeding with the macro change process.

PROS

Client need (see Step 1):

Positive organizational and other macro variables (see Step 2):

Your own strengths (see Step 2):

Potential support from people of influence (see Step 4):

Potential financial benefits (see Step 5):

CONS

Negative organizational and other macro variables (see Step 2):

Your own weaknesses (see Step 2):

Potential resistance of people who have influence (see Step 4):

Financial costs (see Step 5):

Your risks (see Step 6):

Substep 7.2: Identify possible macro approaches to use in the case example and determine how you would proceed (that is, continue the macro change process, postpone it, or drop the whole idea).

Below are three case scenarios that might involve project implementation, program development, or policy change. For each, determine what type of change should be pursued, provide a rationale for your answer, and discuss potential benefits and problems of this change.

Case Scenario A: You are the social worker at an elementary school. You notice that an increasing number of children come from turbulent homes. With each passing year these children present more problems with truancy. Their grades deteriorate and their illicit drug use soars. They need help. But what kind? Your job is to intervene individually with children suffering the most severe crises. You do some individual counseling, make some family visits, run a few support and treatment groups, and attend numerous assessment and planning meetings.

In a social work journal, you read about a new type of alternative approach for children at risk for the very problems you're seeing. One idea in particular catches your eye: A school in Illinois developed a "Friendship System" for children-at-risk. Volunteers solicited from among social work students at a nearby university attended a dozen training sessions, learning how to deal with these children. Each volunteer was then paired with a child and became the child's "special friend." The required commitment period was one year. Volunteers' responsibilities included spending time with the child at least once a week, being available when the child needed to talk, and generally being a positive role model for the child.

The program seems similar to Big Brothers/Big Sisters in which volunteers "work under professional supervision, usually by social workers, providing individual guidance and companionship to boys and girls deprived of a parent" (Barker, 1999, p. 45). But children in the Friendship System might or might not be from single-parent homes. The Friendship System's only prerequisite for the children is that school staff designate them as at-risk of problems including truancy, deteriorating school performance, and drug use, and school staff have substantial latitude in determining a child's eligibility for the program. Typical criteria include a recent divorce in the family, extreme shyness and withdrawal, academic problems, or other social problems. You think, "Wouldn't it be great if my school system had something like that in operation?"

What type of change would you consider pursuing—implementing a project, developing a program, or changing a school policy? Provide a rationale for the proposed change and discuss its potential benefits and problems.

A.   What type of change should be pursued?

B.   Explain your reasons for choosing this change.

C.   What are the potential benefits and problems of this change?

Case Scenario B: Your agency requires clients to fill out a 27-page admissions form before they can receive services. A large percentage of the agency's clients are Hispanic, and they speak very little English so the admissions form effectively prohibits Hispanic clients from receiving service. Because of the language difference, the agency blocks clients from receiving service.

What type of change would you consider pursuing—implementing a project, developing a program, or changing an agency policy? Provide a rationale for the proposed change and discuss its potential benefits and problems.

A.   What type of change should be pursued?

B.   Explain your reasons for choosing this change.

C.   What are the potential benefits and problems of this change?

Case Scenario C: You are a social worker in a rural county social services agency. The towns in the county range in size from 1500 to 10,000 people, and the area has become increasingly impoverished as a number of small cheese and leather factories have left the area. Many people are struggling to survive in old shacks with little clothing and food. You know you can't overhaul the entire public assistance system, but you would like to initiate a food drive or collection to temporarily relieve people's suffering.

What type of change would you consider pursuing—implementing a project, developing a program, or changing an agency policy? Provide a rationale for the proposed change and discuss its potential benefits and problems.

A.   What type of change should be pursued?

B.   Explain your reasons for choosing this change.

C.   What are the potential benefits and problems of this change?

This chapter builds on Chapter 5's explanation of the decision-making process. PREPARE helps you decide whether or not to pursue some type of macro intervention. In this chapter, we assume that the decision is positive, and we discuss how you can go about implementing a macro change.

This chapter will:

- Explain the IMAGINE process for proceeding with a macro intervention
- Discuss concepts involved in conceptualizing the macro environment for change, including the client, change agent, target, and action systems
- Explain the importance of establishing clear goals and action steps to attain them
- Evaluate the use of persuasion and pressuring strategies when neutralizing opposition to the proposed plan
- Provide an opportunity to apply IMAGINE to a case example focusing on agency policy change
- Define the concept of cultural competence and raise questions with respect to organizations

The Planned Change Process and Organizational Change

We take the perspective of a direct-service generalist practitioner with little or no administrative power. Your job requires you to participate in certain types of work with clients. For example, if part of your job is to counsel jobless people and assist in their job search, that is exactly what you do. You do not have to ask permission or try to influence decision-makers to get the job done. In macro generalist practice, however, you must often go beyond your specified job role, and the change you initiate will affect more than just your own work. Therefore, macro generalist practice differs from micro and mezzo generalist practice in the way you go about effecting a change.

Macro generalist practice follows the basic planned change process of engagement, assessment, planning, implementation, evaluation, termination, and follow-up, but it differs from micro and mezzo practice in two distinct ways: First, the change process involves many more people and systems than work with individual clients or groups of clients. Second, it requires that you muster support from colleagues and influence decision-makers in order to bring about a change. Therefore, the macro planned change process is more complicated than the micro or mezzo process would be.

Chapter 5 introduced the three major types of macro change you are likely to target: changing a policy, implementing some kind of project, and developing a program. It also explained the first phase of the procedure for assessing organizational change potential. In the second phase, you actually pursue the organizational change process you are initiating. The remainder of the chapter will explore and discuss this process.

IMAGINE: A Process for Initiating Organizational Change

The paradigm (model) IMAGINE outlines a guide for initiating and pursuing macro change within organizations. Figure 6.1 illustrates the meanings of each letter in the acronym.

Figure 6.1: IMAGINE: A Process for Initiating and Implementing Macro Change
I   Start with an innovative **IDEA**.
M   **MUSTER** support and formulate an action system.
A   Identify **ASSETS**.
G   Specify **GOALS** and objectives.
I   **IMPLEMENT** the plan.
N   **NEUTRALIZE** opposition.
E   **EVALUATE** progress.

Step 1: IMAGINE—Start with an *Innovative* Idea

At this point in the process, we assume that you have already expended time and effort thinking about this potential macro change. Specifically, you have determined which to pursue—a limited project, the development of a more extensive program, or a change in agency policy.

Step 2: IMAGINE—*Muster* Support and Formulate an Action System.

We assume that your job role carries with it no agency-designated power to initiate macro change all by yourself. Therefore, regardless of the type of macro change you have chosen, you need help. You will already have identified some relevant people of influence in making your decision to commit to this change. Now you must determine specifically whom you want to influence and how to do it most effectively.

To better understand the macro change process, think of the various systems—the client, target, change agent, and action systems (Netting, Kettner, & McMurtry, 1998; Pincus & Minahan, 1973; Resnick, 1980b; Resnick 1980c)—that interact in the environment.

The *macro client system* is made up of everyone who will ultimately benefit from the change process. It usually includes individual client systems that have similar characteristics and receive similar agency services. For instance, the macro client system might include all the clients with developmental disabilities who work at a sheltered workshop[1], as well as these clients' families.

The *change agent* is the individual who initiates the macro change process. In this context you—at least initially—are the change agent. Later on as you gain support and join in coalitions with others who also believe in the proposed macro change, you become part of a larger action system dedicated to changing the status quo.

The *target system* is "the individual, group, or community to be changed or influenced to achieve the social work goals" (Barker, 1999, p. 480). We have already indicated that this is frequently your own agency or some subsystem within your agency.

The *action system* includes those people who agree and are committed to working together to attain the proposed macro change. As a change agent, you need to select supporters for your action system very carefully. It is best to muster support from staff who are well respected and competent because they probably have substantial credibility with decision-makers (Resnick, 1980c).

---

[1] A sheltered workshop or sheltered employment offers job training and vocational rehabilitation services for people with various disabilities (in this case, developmental disability) or needs for rehabilitation; such workshops also provide testing services and social skills training (Barker, 1999).

Read the following vignette and identify the systems involved.

You are a hospital social worker who works with patients in the geriatric unit. Their problems typically include broken bones, onset of diseases such as diabetes, increasing mental confusion, and many accompanying physical difficulties. Patients usually remain hospitalized two days to two weeks. Most patients come to the hospital from their homes, and your job often involves placing patients in more structured settings because injuries or diseases have restricted their ability to function independently. Many are placed in health care centers (nursing homes).

You have been assigned Olga, 82, who fell and broke her hip. She also has diabetes and is increasingly incontinent. Prior to her fall, she barely subsisted in a second story one-room apartment, dependent on her monthly Social Security check for survival, and she has consumed all of her meager savings. She is an extremely pleasant woman who continues to emphasize that she doesn't want to be a burden on anyone. All of her family are dead. You worry that placement in an inferior setting will be tortuous for her if she doesn't receive the relatively intensive care she needs.

You notice that nursing homes vary dramatically in their levels of care, their appearance, the attention they give to patients, their ratios of staff to patients, the activities they offer, and their overall cleanliness. Patients with private insurance can easily enter one of the better facilities, while impoverished patients on Medicaid must go to inferior settings. You consider this both unfair and unethical.

You see yourself as a possible change agent. At least three of your colleagues in the hospital's social work unit have similar concerns about their own clients and the hospital's elderly clients in general. Your immediate supervisor is not really an "eager beaver" when it comes to initiating change, but you think you might be able to solicit some support from her. You are not certain whether upper levels of hospital administration believe that nursing home conditions are any of their business. In your state all nursing homes must be licensed, but licensing regulations require the maintenance of only the most minimal standards.

a.   Identify the macro client system in this case.

b.   Who might make up the action system? Explain why.

c.   Who might be your target system? Explain why.

Step 3: IM**A**GINE—Identify *Assets*

Whatever the type of macro level change, a change agent must determine what *assets* are available to implement the change. Assets are any resources and any advantages you have that will help in your proposed change process. Assets can include readily available funding, personnel who are able and willing to devote their time to implementing the change, and office space from which the change activities can be managed.

Exercise 6.2: Identifying Assets

Read the following case scenario and identify the assets it reveals.

> Louise, a financial counselor at a private mental health agency, knows that the agency has access to special funding through personal donations made on behalf of persons "with special needs." She is not certain how the administration defines "special needs." But since the agency is privately owned, it is not subject to the same requirements and regulations that would limit a public agency. Louise learned about this special fund via the informal agency grapevine. It has never been publicly announced.
>
> Louise is working with several families whom she feels are in exceptional need. Their problems—including unemployment, depression, mental illness, poverty, unwanted pregnancy, and truancy—make them truly multiproblem families. Neither her agency nor any local public agency has been able to provide adequate resources for these families. Louise has established clear documentation of their extreme circumstances.
>
> Having worked at the agency for eight years, she feels she has gained substantial respect for her work and her ideas. She knows one member of the agency's board of directors fairly well, because she's worked with him on several projects in the past. (A board of directors is "a group of people empowered to establish an organization's objectives and policies and to oversee the activities of the personnel responsible for day-to-day implementation of those policies," and board members are often highly respected and influential volunteers from the community (Barker, 1999, p. 50). Louise might be able to contact this man to get information about the special-needs funding.
>
> She is aware, however, that her agency administration discourages workers from seeking access to this "secret" fund. Amounts available are limited, so the administration must dispense these funds extremely cautiously. In any case, Louise decides to approach the agency's Executive Director and request funding for the families in need.

Identify the assets available to Louise.

Step 4: IM**A**GINE—Specify *Goals* and Objectives

After formulating an innovative idea, mustering support from others, and identifying assets, it is time to specify your goals and objectives in the macro change process. You have already identified your primary goals during your assessment of macro change potential in Chapter 5. Goals give you direction, but goals are usually so broadly stated that it is virtually impossible to specify how they will be achieved. For example, you might want to improve conditions in the Family Planning Center where you work. In order to accomplish this, you must break down that primary goal into a series of objectives. Objectives are smaller, behaviorally specific subgoals that are stepping stones on the way to the accomplishment of the primary goal.

Presenting your plan to your target system is a critical point in the macro change process. Before you do this, determine who—in your ideal version of events—will assume what roles. *Role determination* means deciding in advance who will attend the meeting and who will contribute what. It is wise to choose action system members who you think will have the strongest positive impact on the target system (for example, decision-making administrators). You want to maximize your potential to influence decision-makers on your behalf. Next, you should determine who will introduce the idea, who should present the rationale, who should respond to what types of questions, and so on.

Second, before a formal meeting, you must decide how *you will describe and portray the issue, your concern, and your recommendations for change.* This should be crystal clear in your mind. Try to anticipate any arguments against the proposal, and formulate responses to those arguments. For example, suppose administrators say that the proposal will cost too much or that existing staff would not be able to complete the necessary tasks. How will you answer them? It is extremely important that you examine and understand the change from an administrative point of view, and that you be able to respond to administrative objections. After all, administrators may have constraints such as licensing regulations or funding requirements of which you are unaware.

In neutralizing opposition, you may pursue a range of strategies from persuading to pressuring (Halley et al., 1998.). Persuading means using logical and convincing arguments to bring decision-makers around to your point of view. It works best when decision-makers are not dead set against your proposal and are open to rational arguments and innovative ideas.

There are three basic ways to initiate persuasion.

- First, *establishing something in common*—that is, presenting some aspect of the problem or proposed solution with which you know both action and target systems will agree. For example, you might say, "I know that we all are seeking effective service delivery for our clients."

- Second, *sharing honest feelings*—which may entail getting right to the point, even if the target system receives the point negatively. For instance, you might say, "I understand that you are opposed to a major change. However, I feel it is necessary to share my serious concerns with you."

- Third, the *blunt assault* (p. 226)—a step beyond just sharing your feelings. (This approach should be used rarely, because it comes close to pressuring.) For example, you might say, "I have to be honest. I totally disagree with your position, and I will be forced to fight you on this one. Let me explain to you why I feel so strongly. . . ."

Austin et al. (1986) cite additional persuasive strategies.

- Educate the decision-makers by providing detailed, specific information.

- Help decision-makers understand the problem and see it more clearly from your point of view.

- Discuss options and potential solutions to your described problem. Review the advantages and disadvantages of each.

- Appeal to the decision-makers' sense of fairness, ethics, and right and wrong. What is the most ethical approach to service provision for clients? What goals are most important for the agency to pursue?

- Develop a rational argument to support your proposed plan. Choose information that strongly supports your macro proposal.

- Finally, specify to decision-makers what the negative consequences of the identified problem might be. What will ignoring the problem or maintaining the status quo cost them in money, morale, public opinion, etc.?

Pressuring is a much "pushier" approach than persuading because it means using force and even coercion to achieve your goals. As a result, it involves much higher potential risks than persuading. Decision-makers are far more likely to react with hostility and dogged resistance. Use pressuring only when three conditions are present (Halley et al., 1998).

- First, you have tried everything else, including persuasion, and nothing has worked.
- Second, you are determined to pursue this macro change for the sake of your clients.
- Third, you believe you have a reasonable chance of attaining your goals. Otherwise, why waste your energy and expose yourself to risk?

Pressuring strategies include circulating a petition to gain collective support, calling on sanctioning agencies in the external environment (such as regulatory agencies, referral agencies, or powerful political entities), going to the media, or initiating a strike or lawsuit. Please note, however, that an administration may feel betrayed by Benedict Arnolds who air the agency's "dirty laundry" for all the world to see.

Step 7: IMAGINE—*Evaluate* Progress

In the final step in the IMAGINE macro change process, you *evaluate* the intervention's progress and effectiveness. Evaluation can focus on either the *ongoing operation* and activities involved in achieving a macro level change or on the *results* of the effort. How effective is or was the change effort?

Application of IMAGINE to Macro Intervention: Changing Agency Policy

IMAGINE can also be applied to changing an agency policy. Policy is "the explicit or implicit standing plan that an organization or government uses as a guide for action" (Barker, 1999, p. 366). Policies thus provide rules or directions for the functions and activities of a macro system. Policy's purpose is to provide rational, predictable guidelines for a system's operation, especially with respect to how resources are distributed. Thus, policy dictates what should and should not be done in the agency setting, especially with respect to how resources are distributed (Kettner et al., 1985).

Policy changes may be aimed at agency goals (for instance, what clientele the agency intends to serve), practice procedures (such as using crisis intervention rather than behavioral methodology, or vice versa), and personnel practices (such as workers' hours). Any time a worker decides to pursue an agency policy change, she should first answer two questions (Netting et al., 1998).

- Will the change result in improved service delivery and resources allocation for clients?
- Will the change result in improved working conditions for staff, enabling them to better serve their clients?

The bottom line is that, whatever the type of policy change, the ultimate beneficiaries of that change should be your clients.

Exercise 6.4: Applying IMAGINE to Agency Policy Change

Apply IMAGINE to the following case example by responding to the subsequent questions.[4]

---

[4] The idea and some details presented in this case example are taken from "The Appointment Letters," by G. H. Hull, Jr. In R. F. Rivas & G. H. Hull, Jr., *Case Studies in Generalist Practice* (Pacific Grove, CA: Brooks/Cole, 2000, pp. 166-70.) A condensed version of this scenario appears in chapter 4.

Hsi-ping is a worker for the Comeasyouare County Department of Human Services. She and most other staff disagree with many policies initiated by Marcus, the agency director. Workers commonly refer to Marcus as Mr. Scrooge. They frequently question his decisions, which they believe are based on financial variables rather than clients' welfare.

The latest problem is Marcus's decision to stop sending letters to clients without telephones. These letters announce that a particular worker will visit a client's home at a designated time. If that time is inconvenient, the client is asked to contact the worker to reschedule the visit. The letter then adds that the worker is looking forward to talking with the client. These letters have traditionally been sent out far enough in advance to allow clients to accommodate their own schedules or let the worker know beforehand that the time is inconvenient. Apparently, Marcus and his Chief Financial Manager, Millicent (often referred to as Ms. Scrooge), have figured out these letters cost the agency about five dollars apiece to send—including worker time, secretarial time, paper, postage, and any other agency efforts expended. Hsi-ping thinks Millicent read the five-dollar figure somewhere in a financial magazine and magically transformed it into a fact. She has a number of problems with the policy even if the figure is accurate.

- First, it ignores clients' right to privacy, respect, and dignity. Dropping in on people unannounced is inconsiderate and simply rude.

- Second, it violates clients' right to self-determination because it does not allow them any input in setting meeting times.

- Third, it complicates both workers' and clients' lives. There is no guarantee that workers will arrive at convenient times for clients or that clients will even be at home.

Hsi-Ping thinks about who might agree with her that this policy is unacceptable. She knows other staff in her own unit agree with her, but many of them are fairly new and would probably be hesitant to speak up. Hsi-Ping's supervisor Sphinctera follows regulations to the letter—even to the comma—without question. Nevertheless, Hsi-Ping likes Sphinctera, so she decides to share her feelings about the problem and see what reaction she gets.

Much to Hsi-Ping's amazement, Sphinctera is very supportive of Hsi-Ping's position. Apparently, Sphinctera is tired of the agency's many policy changes and has difficulty keeping up with them. This no-letter policy is just too much. Sphinctera even comes up with an idea. Why not send out postcards announcing home visits? The cards could be preprinted for a nominal cost, workers could then address them, fill in the proposed visiting time, sign them, and send them out themselves.

It's a fine compromise—but Sphinctera hesitates to make waves and wants more information and more support before she will propose her idea to Marcus. Hsi-Ping volunteers to talk to her other colleagues in the unit, and verifies that they generally agree with her. One worker, Ruana, emphasizes her relief that someone else is addressing the problem. She tells Hsi-Ping about a home visit she made the day before, an unannounced visit because of the no-letter policy. It took her about an hour to get to the client's home and back. Since the client wasn't there, Ruana's time was wasted—at a cost to the agency of about $11 in salary for Ruana's wasted time and about $12 in mileage reimbursement. Even if Millicent and Marcus are correct that letters cost the agency $5, Ruana's useless trip cost $23, so the agency lost $18 under the new procedure. Imagine multiplying this by the hundreds of home visits workers regularly make.

Hsi-Ping reports her findings to Sphinctera. Together they decide to address the issue with Marcus. Sphinctera suggests doing so at one of the agency's regular staff meetings when staff are encouraged to voice their ideas and concerns (whether or not administrators are paying attention). She encourages Hsi-Ping to raise the issue because it was originally Hsi-Ping's idea. Hsi-Ping thinks Sphinctera is really afraid to initiate it herself, but she agrees to do the talking and thanks Sphinctera for her support.

At the next staff meeting, Hsi-Ping expresses her concern about the no-letter policy. She takes a deep breath and is careful to speak with little emotion and no hostility. She presents the financial facts that support her proposal and emphasizes that she shares Marcus's concerns about the agency's finances. She then offers her suggestion and its rationale, adding that sending postcards was really Sphinctera's idea. Hsi-Ping adds that the postcards would not violate clients' confidentiality or privacy rights because they would carry no identifying information.

When she finishes, the eighty staff members in the room are dead silent for a few painful moments that seem like an eternity. Finally, six hands shoot up at once. One after another, staff support the idea. Hsi-Ping watches Marcus for some reaction. He looks straight ahead, says nothing, and pulls at his chin in his usual thoughtful gesture. Finally, he says, "You know, I think you just might have something here. Let's give it a try."

Hsi-Ping is overjoyed. She did it! She actually did it. She effected a substantive change in agency policy. Two days later Marcus sends a memo around the agency informing workers of the new change. Workers are generally pleased (although some old-timers still grumble that the letters were better). Marcus continues to seek new ways to cut costs—and, Hsi-Ping sometimes thinks, to make workers' lives miserable. However, the no-letter battle has been won and Hsi-Ping certainly is proud of that accomplishment.

Follow the seven steps in IMAGINE and respond to the questions below:

Step 1: IMAGINE—Start with an Innovative *Idea.*

    A.   Summarize the problem presented above.

    B.   Describe the innovative idea for a solution.

    C.   Explain the pros and cons of this idea.

Step 2: IMAGINE—*Muster* Support and Formulate an Action System. Identify the following systems portrayed in the case scenario above.

Macro client system:

Change agent system:

Target system:

Action system:

Step 3: IMAGINE—Identify *Assets*. Identify the assets in Hsi-Ping's favor and explain why each is important.

Step 4: IMAGINE—Specify *Goals* and Objectives.

    A.   Identify the major goal Hsi-Ping wished to accomplish.

B.   Identify specific objectives necessary for leading up to this goal. Use the *who did what by when* format.

C.   Identify action steps needed to achieve these objectives.

Step 5: IMAGINE—*Implement* the Plan. Evaluate and discuss the effectiveness of Hsi-Ping's implementation of her plan.

Step 6: IMAGINE—*Neutralize* Opposition.

A.   Explain how Hsi-Ping determined who would assume which roles in the change effort.

B.   Discuss the interpersonal dynamics determining who actually presented the issue and proposed recommendations.

C.   Explain how Hsi-Ping used persuasion to pursue her goal. What specific techniques did she use?

Chapter 7
IMAGINE Project Implementation and Program Development

Macro practice can be an exciting, rewarding part of your professional life. Targeting large systems for change can bring momentous benefits to large numbers of clients.

This chapter will:

- Identify some types of projects you can pursue and implement within agencies
- Examine and evaluate the usefulness of Program Evaluation and Review Technique (PERT) charts
- Introduce a role play for employing a PERT chart in a program development scenario
- Review the IMAGINE process and apply some of its steps to program development

Initiating and Implementing a Project

In Chapter 6, we worked with an example of an agency policy change. Now we turn our attention to another type of macro change you may choose to pursue in your agency setting—implementation of a project. Once again, you use the PREPARE process to decide whether to proceed with a macro change, then you apply the IMAGINE steps to get the project approved.

Projects by definition are relatively short-term, limited endeavors with specific goals, having measurable action steps and objectives. There are no limits to the types of projects you can dream up for your agency. It is up to you in your own agency setting to ascertain the agency's and clients' needs. After that, only your own imagination limits the type of project you can undertake. Personal creativity is the key to project development. Examples of project goals include the six listed below.[1]

1. *Meeting Clients' Special Needs.* Your clients might have needs that go beyond the resources or services you and your agency can provide. For example, suppose your clients are in drastic need of clothing, but your agency has virtually nothing to do with providing it. You might organize a one-time clothing drive in your community, and enlist interested citizens as volunteer helpers. Or suppose some clients have a special need unrelated to your social work practice. Maybe an adult with physical disabilities needs a new wheelchair but can't afford one. Or maybe a client needs special medical help that neither private insurance nor public resources will cover. You could propose a project aimed at raising the necessary funds.

2. *Fundraising Projects.* You might raise funds for anything from research on a specific physical disability to building a new office building. Fundraising lends itself to projects because it is limited, short-term, and goal-oriented in nature.

3. *Evaluation of Effects Due to Agency or Community Changes.* Sometimes changes in the agency or in the surrounding community will affect your ability to serve clients. In such cases, you could outline a project aimed at evaluating the effects of the change. You could also initiate a project that would assist the agency or its clients in adjusting to the change. For example, changes might include slashes in service provision due to budget or funding cuts. Conducting a research project to identify the effects of such changes could enable you to advocate on behalf of those who are affected.

---

[1] Many of these examples are suggested by Kettner, Daley, & Nichols in *Initiating Change in Organizations and Communities* (Monterey, CA: Brooks/Cole, 1985).

4. *Evaluation of New Intervention Approaches.* Suppose you become aware of new, more effective intervention approaches for clients—such as adopting a token system for child behavior management in a daycare center. This would help staff deal more effectively with the children in their care.[2] You might implement a project to evaluate the effectiveness of the proposed intervention approach. Testing the approach on a smaller scale first can help determine whether a major agency adoption of the approach is worth the effort.

5. *Implementing Internal Agency Changes.* Internal agency changes might include changing informal procedures (such as converting from handwritten notes to using personal computers), updating job descriptions, or converting from group to individual supervisory sessions. You might initiate a project to evaluate how agency procedures or structure might be improved.

6. *Providing Internal Services to Your Agency Staff.* Some projects can involve the development and provision of services to staff within the agency. For example, you might find a huge number of cocaine-addicted clients added to your caseload. If you talk to some of your colleagues and determine that they're experiencing the same problem, you might plan a series of in-service programs aimed at helping practitioners address problems related to drug addiction.

Exercise 7.1: Creative Projects

Read the following case vignettes and respond to the questions about potential project implementation.

Vignette #1: Manuela is a Protective Services Worker who works with legal authorities to investigate children who are at risk for child maltreatment, provide counseling, link families with needed services, and provide alternative placements for children when necessary. Most of her clients are very poor, and since Thanksgiving is approaching, Manuela worries that many of them will be unable to have much food at all, let alone a grand turkey celebration.

What types of projects could Manuela initiate? Specifically, how might she go about doing so?

---

[2] A token system or token economy is "a reinforcement system based on tokens;" "tokens are conditioned reinforcers such as poker chips, coins, tickets, stars, points, or check marks" that, after being earned by displaying appropriate behavior, may be exchanged for reinforcers such as desired "food and other consumables, activities, and privileges" (Kazdin, 1994, p. 139).

Vignette #2: Dougal is a counselor at a large urban YMCA. He organizes and runs recreational and educational programs for youth, functions as a positive role model, and provides informal counseling. Recently, he learned that the county social services agency had contracted with an expert on gang intervention to run a four-day in-service program for its staff. Dougal thinks it would be extremely helpful to the staff at the "Y" if they could somehow participate in such a program.

What sort of project might Dougal initiate to get in-service training for the "Y" staff? Specifically, how might he go about doing so?

Vignette #3: Jarita works at a Planned Parenthood organization where she does contraception and pregnancy counseling. She is also invited to give educational presentations to large groups of people. She finds that over the years her job has significantly changed: Whereas she once dealt primarily with contraception counseling, she now spends more time providing sex education, especially with respect to AIDS. Along with the changes in her job, many other changes have occurred in the agency over the past ten years. For one thing, it is much larger than it was when Jarita began working there. More restrictive state legislation has affected the referral process for abortions. Much more emphasis is now placed on sex education. Jarita observes that the agency policy manual has simply not kept up with the agency's progress and development. Even some personnel policies such as insurance coverage have changed significantly over time. Simply put, the policy manual is colossally out of date.

What sort of project might Jarita pursue in dealing with this concern? Specifically, how might she go about doing so?

Program Evaluation and Review Technique (PERT)

To initiate a project and follow the IMAGINE process described in Chapter 6, you need a specific plan. A project design or plan is like a map of the entire project from beginning to end. One useful way of formulating and illustrating a plan, or facets of the plan, is through the use of a PERT (Program Evaluation and Review Technique) chart (Federal Electric Corporation, 1963). PERT charts are flow charts or time charts "that show what steps need to be taken in what order"; "such charts can help [action] group members anticipate and reduce problems while providing a sense of direction for projects" (Rubin & Rubin, 1992, p. 402).

PERT charts illustrate a sequence of tasks or action steps in the order in which such tasks should be done to achieve a designated objective. When you create a PERT chart, you must first define your objective and then break it down into a series of steps. Figure 7.1 illustrates two PERT formats. Each has the same objective—being prepared to present informational findings at an agency meeting. This objective is one means to attain the broader goal of enhancing agency functioning. Specific action steps are depicted in the order they must be accomplished. For example, you need to gather information before you can complete a report on that information.

You can depict PERT chart tasks either horizontally or vertically by picturing necessary activities in boxes connected by horizontal or vertical lines. Each horizontal or vertical sequence of activity boxes connected by lines reflects a plan for achieving that particular goal.

PERT charts also establish a time frame, an estimate of how long it should take to complete each task and reach the primary objective. In figure 7.1 the horizontal format has a time line on the bottom of the charts. The vertical chart has the time line located on its left-hand side. The time lines in these charts illustrate weekly deadlines for achieving each of the four action steps necessary to attain the objective. The idea is to complete each action step and arrive at the objective by the indicated target completion date. When developing a PERT chart, be realistic about how much time it will take to complete each step. Each PERT format in figure 7.1 depicts completion of the following action steps in the following order: (1) gathering information by February 7; (2) completing the report by February 14; (3) reviewing the report with your supervisor by February 21; and (4) presenting the report findings at a designated meeting by February 28. The timelines can employ virtually any unit of time—hours, days, weeks, months. Figure 7.1 uses weekly units.

PERT charts may take a number of forms, and individual action steps can be illustrated in various ways. For example, you can use sequentially connected circles or simple statements instead of boxes. A very complicated chart could use a series of letter or number codes to indicate tasks or time frames instead of writing them all out. In such cases, whoever creates the chart adds a key to the code.

For purposes of simplicity and clarity, the PERT chart in figure 7.1 shows how action steps for one objective are achieved by *one* person. In reality, however, multiple action steps must often be accomplished simultaneously by different members of the action system, and some action steps may depend on the completion of others. For example, another member of your action system is developing a list of resource people for the in-service program, and you need that data to complete your report. PERT charts become more complex as tasks and participants increase in number.

Figure 7.2 is a PERT chart for initiating an agency in-service training program. Provision of in-service training is one objective under the broader umbrella goal of providing effective service. That objective is broken down into a sequence of action steps, and a time frame is established for achieving each step. When you decide what steps to take, you must consider a number of consecutive variables.

- First, approval from your immediate supervisor is necessary.
- Next, a staff interest survey will help you establish what direction the in-service will take.
- Subsequently, administrative approval is required for survey administration. Time must be allowed for distributing the questionnaire and for staff to complete it.
- Questionnaire results should then be communicated to administration.

- Arrangements for in-service speakers must be made.
- Finally, publicity and announcements should be used to notify potential participants of the in-service's time and location.

Figure 7.1: Examples of Amended PERT Chart Formats

Horizontal Format with Time Line at Bottom:

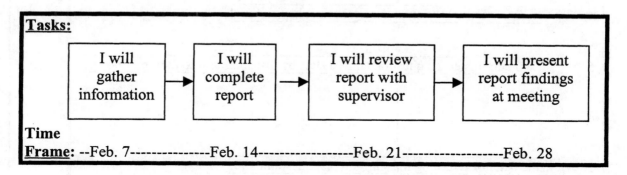

Vertical Format with Time Line at Left-Hand Side:

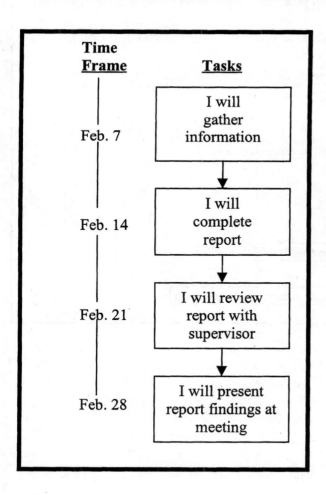

As illustrated here, PERT charts can assume either a horizontal or vertical format. Horizontal formats can depict a time line either at the bottom or top of the page. Vertical formats usually depict time lines on the left-hand side of the page. The important thing is that the time frame for the completion of each task is very clear. The other critical thing is that tasks be illustrated in their correct sequence. Generally speaking, the completion of one task depends upon the prior completion of the task listed sequentially before it. Hence, you can clearly illustrate your plan for completion of some designated goal in a step-by-step sequence.

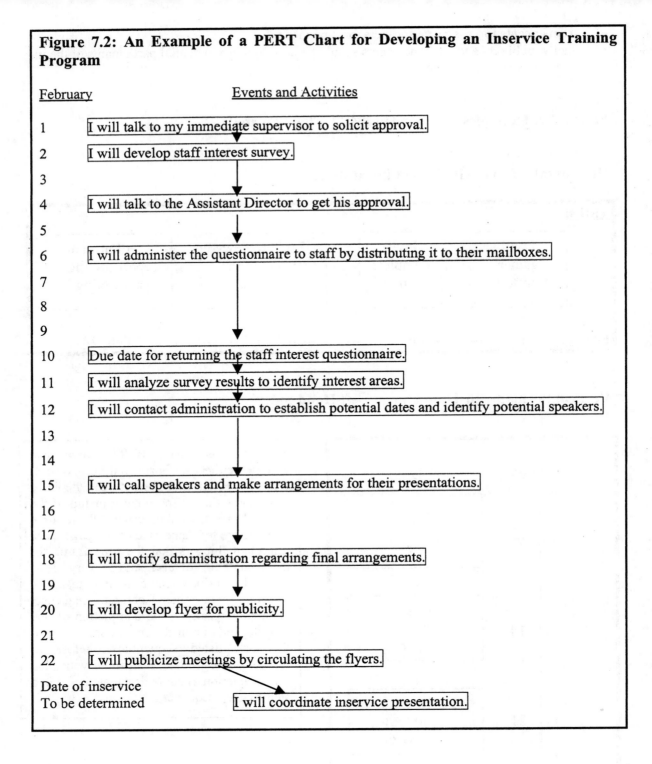

Figure 7.2: An Example of a PERT Chart for Developing an Inservice Training Program

February   Events and Activities

1   I will talk to my immediate supervisor to solicit approval.

2   I will develop staff interest survey.

3

4   I will talk to the Assistant Director to get his approval.

5

6   I will administer the questionnaire to staff by distributing it to their mailboxes.

7

8

9

10   Due date for returning the staff interest questionnaire.

11   I will analyze survey results to identify interest areas.

12   I will contact administration to establish potential dates and identify potential speakers.

13

14

15   I will call speakers and make arrangements for their presentations.

16

17

18   I will notify administration regarding final arrangements.

19

20   I will develop flyer for publicity.

21

22   I will publicize meetings by circulating the flyers.

Date of inservice
To be determined   I will coordinate inservice presentation.

156

Select a campus issue (for example, lack of adequate, inexpensive campus parking; difficulties getting into required course sections; or problems in the field placement assignment process) that you feel is significant. Think carefully about how you might implement a macro level change if you had the time and energy. Would you develop and conduct a survey to establish the significance of the issue and gain support? Which administrators would you approach about the issue? How would you present your position and your plan? Would fundraising or grant-writing be necessary to achieve your goal?

Develop a PERT chart below. Be sure to identify the primary objective, establish a sequence of tasks, and propose a time frame for task completion. You may choose to develop a PERT chart with other students. Brainstorming can be helpful. In that case you may establish a PERT chart with concurrent task sequences for each individual involved.

The role play below requires five characters: two unit counselors (change agents); the school's principal; a social work therapist; and the unit counselors' supervisor. In order to reflect real professional life, each character has a professional, an individual personality, and a personal agenda. The practice setting is Getalife, a residential treatment center for male adolescents with severe behavioral and emotional problems. To conduct the role play, follow the directions below:

1. Five students should volunteer for or be assigned the roles explained below. Remaining students should observe the role play and record their impressions on the Feedback Form included here. Role players should *not* record observations on Feedback Forms because that distracts from their role enactment.

2. Each role player should then read out loud his or her respective lines.

3. Review the organizational chart included below to understand the agency's chain of command.

4. Begin the role play and allow it to continue for approximately 20 minutes. The instructor should be responsible for halting the role play after the time has elapsed.

5. After the role play is halted, the entire class should discuss critical points, constructive techniques, and suggestions for improvement concerning what occurred. Use the feedback forms to aid in discussion. Role players may share their perceptions concerning their roles and what transpired.

Unit Counselor #1: Your job is to supervise daily living and recreational activities for Getalife's residents, to implement individual residents' behavioral programming, to keep records, and to participate in the residents' group counseling sessions. You also periodically attend staffings where individual case plans are established, implemented, and updated. You work in the Box Elder Unit which includes fourteen boys ages 13 to 15. You have worked for the agency for two years, like your job, and feel you can make valuable contributions to residents' well-being. You are especially concerned about residents' need for sex education. Many—perhaps most—of the center's residents have been sexually active. You know this from talking with residents, reading records, and attending staffings where such information is shared and addressed.

You can't think of anyone in the residential center—including child-care workers, teachers, social workers, or administrators—who has expertise in this area. You set up a meeting with the head child-care worker (your direct supervisor), the residential unit's social work therapist, and the school's principal to establish a plan. You have already explained to them your general idea so that they will have time to think about the issues prior to the meeting. You have discussed your ideas in greater depth with Unit Counselor #2 who seems to agree strongly with you and is willing to help you conduct the meeting. Together you hope to convince this group of the usefulness of your plan. You intend to establish a PERT chart for how to go about setting up a series of sex education sessions for your unit's residents.

You feel that sex education is tremendously important. You have a 14-year-old sister who is pregnant, and that adds to the significance of this issue for you. You are happy that Worker #2 agrees with you and is willing to help you pursue a sex education program for the Box Elder Unit. However, you believe that you are more committed to the issue than Worker #2, and you would like to apply some pressure on Worker #2 to take on more responsibility for planning and implementing the program.

Unit Counselor #2: You work in the Box Elder Unit with Worker #1 who has talked to you about the sex education proposal. You think that sex education is a very important need for the boys in the Box Elder Unit, but you are pretty busy with your job and you are going to school part-time. You'd like to get the sex education program going, but you don't have much extra time for planning or implementation. You like and respect Worker #1, and you realize that Worker #1 is extremely committed to the issue. It seems logical to you that Worker #1 should take on the most responsibility for planning and implementation. You are willing to expend substantial energy to get a PERT plan in place, but you would then like to minimize your involvement in the plan's implementation.

The Center's School Principal: You supervise six special education teachers and their six respective assistants in Getalife's on-grounds school. You have been with the center for three years, and you believe that anything related to education comes under the school's responsibility. Right now, the school is pressed for resources, and you consider sex education a frill that the school can't afford to address. What's more, in your opinion none of the current educational staff has any expertise in this area, and you wonder whether they would feel comfortable teaching about sexuality. All in all, you resent having to attend this meeting. You wish that the two workers would just drop the subject and mind their own business. You also don't much like the Box Elder Unit's social work therapist. You see the therapist as an ineffective employee in a cushy job. You believe that a good education will offer the adolescent residents more hope for their futures than is likely to come from talking about their feelings with some social worker in hocus-pocus, psychobabble therapy. In short, you have very little confidence that the social workers can accomplish much.

You don't plan to support this "sex plan," and you're coming up with a list of reasons that it's a dumb idea. If in the end the group decides to implement it anyway, you definitely want the programming to be provided by an expert from outside the agency. On this point you do not intend to budge.

The Box Elder Unit's Social Work Therapist: You are an MSW charged with providing the adolescents in your unit with one hour of individual therapy and two hours of group therapy each week, in addition to any family counseling that is deemed necessary. You also assist staff in developing behavioral programming, coordinate residents' individual plans through periodic staffings, write staffing summary reports, coordinate staff activity in implementing treatment recommendations, and monitor residents' progress. You have been with the agency for almost six months.

You are a relatively new "gung-ho" social worker, anxious to do your job and do it well. You have finally been able to get your bearings after six months of struggling to figure out how the agency operates and what you're doing with your clients. You have had some difficulty working with both the school principal and the head child-care supervisor. Both seem to resent any suggestions you make for treatment and your efforts to implement treatment plans in the unit and in the school. Without consistency and follow-through, it's hard to get your clients' behavioral programming to work. The principal is especially difficult to work with and very protective of school turf. The head child-care supervisor is more easy-going but appears to "know everything." You feel the supervisor treats you rather condescendingly and doesn't always come through after promising that something will get done. You think the supervisor is pretty passive-aggressive.

You really like the idea of implementing the sexuality programming. You took a sexuality course in college and have had some subsequent training, so with some brushing up on the content you think you could present a really good program. You also feel it would enhance your relationship with your clients.

The Unit Counselors' Supervisor: You supervise all the counselors (child-care) for the residential center's six units—a total of 58 full-time and part-time staff. You are responsible for scheduling their shifts, supervising their work, and arranging for training to meet ongoing treatment needs. You have an associate's degree from a local community college and have been in your current position for the past 17 years.

Since you have been at the agency an awfully long time, you believe that you really know what's going on. These young whippersnappers on the staff come and go, but you maintain continuity for ongoing treatment and care. You also feel that you're pretty much "a natural" with the kids. You don't need a lot of fancy degrees to work effectively with the residents and develop caring and consistent programs for them. You feel you've helped many, many young people get their acts together. You haven't as yet developed confidence in the social work therapist's ability to work effectively with the residents. The social worker seems to you to have promise, but still needs more experience. You think the school principal is rather cocky, but then you've seen half a dozen principals come and go. You're pretty easy-going and are willing to work with the principal's "eccentric" behaviors and needs.

You attend this meeting out of respect for your two Potawatomi Unit Counselors. You like to encourage your staff to develop new ideas. You also like to present opportunities for them to do so. You feel that it would be best for the agency if some in-house staff did the programming. After all, this idea is basically a fad or frill. Why should the agency expend its scarce resources to pay some expert to come in? Why not have some volunteer staff do the sex ed programming and, essentially, get it over with?

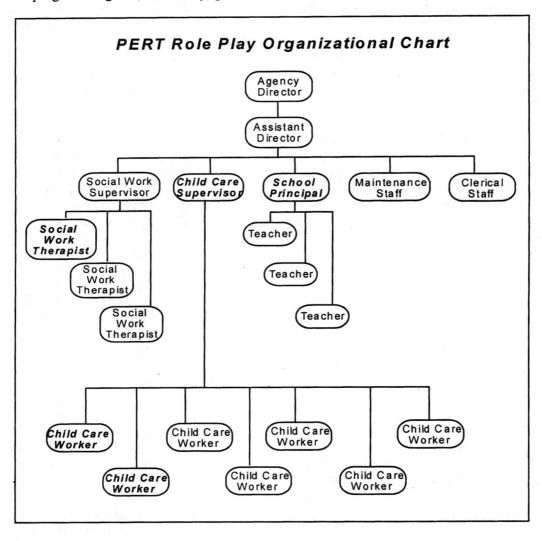

PERT Role Play Organizational Chart

Role Play Feedback Form

1.   What were the critical points or major issues addressed in the role play?

2.   What especially helpful techniques and approaches were used? Please be specific.

3.   What specific suggestions for improvement can you make? For example, how could issues have been addressed more effectively? What alternative responses might have solicited more information or cooperation? Please be specific.

Program Development

In addition to initiating agency policy changes and implementing projects, you may have the opportunity within your agency to set a whole new program in motion. A program is "an aggregate of actions directed toward accomplishing a single goal" (Rapp & Poertner, 1992). Program development can range from expanding services in an existing agency unit to developing a whole new organizational unit or even an organization itself. There are times in a worker's career when resources and services desperately needed by clients do not exist. At these times, workers must determine whether it is possible, practical, and worth their effort to pursue the development of some new program. Often workers are not alone in their concerns. There may be others—including clients, administrators, colleagues, and persons in the community and other agencies—who also support the establishment of badly needed services.

In most cases workers' job descriptions—established by others working for "The System"—will not include the pursuit of macro changes such as program development.[3] Nevertheless, it is part of professional responsibility to pursue macro change when necessary. You can't assume that the administration will always respond to a given need. It may be up to you to become the change agent.

As with policy change and project implementation, both the PREPARE assessment and the IMAGINE implementation processes can be applied to program development. In this case we will use IMAGINE.

IMAGINE's Step 1 is coming up with an innovative *idea* to address some programmatic need. During this phase, it is important to work with the client system. For example, if you want to start a homeless shelter program, input from the homeless people who will be involved is absolutely necessary, and so is a clear articulation of the program's purpose. For instance, you might want to renovate an unused building in a designated area of town to provide specified services to a certain number of homeless people who fulfill stated eligibility requirements.

Step 2 in IMAGINE involves *mustering* support for your efforts. Carefully choose action system members with the necessary motivation and expertise, and with the ability to work together toward your identified goal. An action system can solicit information and resources, clarify goals and action steps, and fight for community support for the proposed program (Hasenfeld, 1987; Kretzmann & McKnight, 1993).

IMAGINE's Step 3 is identifying *assets*. What variables will aid you in the program development process? Who else in your agency will assist and support you? Are there ways to enhance your own power and influence within the agency and community (e.g., by increasing your expertise in the area you've targeted or by ferreting out facts to support your proposal)? What potential and actual funding sources are available to you (Hasenfeld, 1987)?

Step 4 in IMAGINE is specifying *goals* and action steps to attain them. Using the *who* will do *what* by *when* format and formulating your plan according to a PERT chart can be helpful. Who will be served by your proposal? What services will be provided? What steps must be taken to accomplish effective service provision?

Actual program *implementation* is Step 5 in IMAGINE. During this phase it is important to monitor participating staff and solicit their support. Other suggestions for implementation include making a trial run before fully implementing your plan. This allows you to iron out any potential "bugs" and to start out small.

IMAGINE's Step 6 is the *neutralizing* of opposition. Carefully observe participating staff's reactions to the program as it develops and seek administration support for your plans.

Finally, Step 7 in IMAGINE is *evaluating* your progress and effectiveness. You accomplish this through day-by-day monitoring of the agency's performance to determine how efficiently and effectively services are actually being provided (Rubin & Rubin, 1992). This evaluation also requires you to discern who is really being served and how much progress has been made in helping these clients (Rubin & Rubin, 1992). An effective evaluation can lead to

---

[3]A job description identifies the specific tasks and responsibilities that make up your job.

the establishment of new programs to provide services on an ongoing basis (Brager & Holloway, 1983; Hasenfeld, 1987). How will the new program fit in with and be linked to other agency units and staff? How will permanent funding be established and maintained?

Exercise 7.4: Creative Program Development

The three vignettes below illustrate dilemmas that prevent direct service workers from providing needed services. Each sets the stage for program development from a generalist practitioner's perspective. Consider each situation, then answer the subsequent questions about program development based on the first three steps in the IMAGINE process.

Vignette A: You are an intake worker for the Sheboygan County Department of Social Services. The county is primarily rural with a smattering of small towns. Your primary job is to take calls from people requesting services, gather initial information about them and their problems, provide them with some information about county services, and make appropriate referrals to the agencies whose services they need.

You are alarmed at the growing number of calls concerning elderly people having difficulty maintaining themselves in their own homes. Most are calls from neighbors, relatives, or the elderly people themselves. Examples of concerns include: worries about falling and remaining stranded for days; forgetfulness (such as leaving the stove's gas burner on); lack of transportation to get to a critical doctor's appointment; difficulties in understanding complicated health insurance and Medicare reimbursements; and depression due to loneliness and isolation.

After you receive such calls, you typically refer the callers to the Department's Protective Services for the Elderly unit. However, you know that all that unit can usually do is make an assessment home visit and either refer the client to a local nursing home or terminate the case. That's depressing. Many of these people just need company and supportive help to maintain their independent living conditions. You have heard of such programs in other parts of the state. It would be great to have a program through which staff could visit similar clients, help them with daily tasks, transport them to recreational activities, and generally provide friendly support. Such a program would help these elderly people remain in their own homes. Can you initiate such a program?

IMAGINE Step 1: Develop an innovative *idea*.

Propose and describe a program that you feel would meet clients' identified needs.

IMAGINE Step 2: *Muster* support.

Who in your agency and/or community might be appropriate action system members for this macro change? Explain why.

IMAGINE Step 3: Identify *assets*.

What variables can you suggest that would support your change efforts?

In addition to the action system members you listed above, who in the agency might you call upon for support?

How can you enhance your own power?

What potential funding sources might you pursue?

Vignette B: You are a state probation officer. You notice a significant increase in your caseload (that is, the clients assigned to you) of men repeatedly committing acts that in your state are considered misdemeanors. A misdemeanor is a minor crime—less serious than a felony—that generally results in incarceration of less than six months (Barker, 1999). These men, for example, are speeding while driving under the influence, shoplifting items such as CDs, and even urinating when driving a car. (This last incident actually happened, although it's hard to picture.) As their probation officer, you see these "dumb" things getting them several-hundred-dollar fines and several-month jail sentences. You think this is senseless. There must be a better way to deal with this problem and to make these men more responsible for their behavior.

At a conference you hear about a "deferred prosecution" approach in an adjoining state. This program provides men arrested for such misdemeanors with alternatives to fines and jail terms. They can opt to participate in a 12-week group run by two social workers. Group sessions focus on enhancing self-esteem, raising self-awareness, improving decision-making skills, developing better communication skills, and encouraging the analysis of responsible versus irresponsible behavior. The program was initially funded by a grant (often referred to as "soft money," meaning temporary and limited funding), but it was so successful that the state now implements and pays for it in several designated counties with "hard money." ("Hard money" means relatively permanent funding that becomes part of an organization's regular annual budget.) Men who participated in the program had a significantly reduced recidivism rate. *Recidivism rates* in this context refer to the proportion of offenders who continue to commit misdemeanors. A recidivism rate of 25 percent, then, would mean that of 100 men, 25 committed additional misdemeanors and 75 did not.

You think, "What a wonderful idea!" You begin to investigate how you can initiate such a program in your agency.

IMAGINE Step 1: Develop an innovative *idea*.

Propose and describe a program that you feel would meet clients' identified needs.

IMAGINE Step 2: *Muster* support.

Who in your agency and/or community might be appropriate action system members for this macro change? Explain why.

IMAGINE Step 3: Identify *assets*.

What variables can you suggest that would support your change efforts?

In addition to the action system members you listed above, who in the agency might you call upon for support?

How can you enhance your own power?

What potential funding sources might you pursue?

Southlake Mall (shopping center)

East High School (high school)

Eken Park (public park)

Community Functions

Traditional communities serve a number of functions for residents, including socialization; production, distribution, and consumption of goods and services; social control; mutual support; and an opportunity for residents to participate with others (Warren, 1978). Table 8.1 highlights some of these functions.

Table 8.1: Community Functions	
Function	*Example*
Socialization	Transmission of values, culture, beliefs, and norms to community residents
Production, distribution, and consumption of goods and services	Provision of food, clothing, housing, and other services
Social control	Enforcement of community norms through laws, police, ordinances, etc.

Mutual support	Informal social supports and formal services such as social work and other human services
Participation of residents	Recreational opportunities, religious celebrations, and socializing

Every community is composed of multiple neighborhoods. Neighborhoods are usually defined as geographical areas whose residents have similar lifestyles, values, and expectations (Barker, 1999). One's sense of identity with one's neighborhood may be strong or weak. Sometimes it exceeds one's sense of connection to the community.

Neighborhoods provide some, but not all, of the functions of a community. Because of their smaller scale, they cannot provide everything a resident will need. For example, some neighborhoods lack food stores, adequate housing, and social control. Mutual support may be weak or nonexistent. However, others offer multiple opportunities for mutual support, participation, and socialization. The extent to which a neighborhood mimics the functions of a community may affect its attractiveness to potential and current residents.

Exercise 8.3: Socialization Functions

Using your hometown, describe the mechanisms of socialization used to help you learn the values, culture, beliefs, and norms of your community.

Exercise 8.4: Social Control

Again, using your own experience, identify one example of how the social control function of your community directly affected you.

174

Community Types

There are multiple ways to classify communities. One of the most obvious is according to size. We set relatively arbitrary definitions of communities. For instance, we say that the largest are *metropolitan,* but we apply this term to cities with several hundred thousand residents as well as to those with a million or more. The smallest communities are designated *nonmetropolitan,* and this category includes small cities, small towns, rural communities, Native American reservation communities, bedroom communities, and institutional communities. What's more, these subdivisions are not necessarily mutually exclusive. For example, a small town or city may also be a bedroom community for a large city, and thus part of a metropolitan area. Many Native American reservations are also rural communities. The "company town"—as some institutional communities are called—is probably also a small town.

All this means that, while size is an important means of categorizing communities, it does not always tell us much about an area. A more useful category than size is based on the degree to which a community provides the full range of functions referred to above, and on the degree to which everyone in the community benefits from these provided functions.

We also characterize communities on the basis of their heterogeneity or homogeneity. A community may be heterogeneous in the sense that many races, ethnicities, or classes are represented within its boundaries. It may be homogeneous to the extent that such diversity is absent. These factors can have important implications for a community's sense of identity and for its ability to serve the needs of its residents.

Likewise a community may be characterized by its wealth or resources. An economically disadvantaged community may lack sufficient resources to resolve basic social problems, while a wealthy city may provide a high quality of educational opportunity for its children. These ways of characterizing communities are a shorthand means of understanding the potential of a community to perform its functions and serve residents' needs.

There is one more use of the term community that we need to consider. We often refer to groups sharing particular characteristics as communities—the social work community or the medical community—because they share a sense of identity. This type of community does not function in the way that the geographical communities we have described do. Thus, we often call them "non-place communities."

Exercise 8.5: Typing Your Hometown and Your Communities

A.   Identify your hometown by type on the basis of its size and degree of heterogeneity.

B.   Identify any non-place communities of which you are a part.

Communities from a System Perspective

Chapter 1 discussed the importance of the system framework for understanding the macro environment. We may view a community as a system composed of a number of subsystems (for example, neighborhoods). Or we can look at a community as a subsystem of the state in which it is located. Human beings are systems in their own right, but are also subsystems of their neighborhoods and communities. A neighborhood or community can further the growth and development of an individual or family, or it can limit or even destroy that subsystem's progress. As social workers we must continually shift back and forth between attention to individuals, subsystems, and to the larger systems of which they are a part. This ability to look at both levels sequentially and/or simultaneously is a hallmark of social work practice.

Chapter 1 also introduced other systems terminology—client, change agent, target, and action systems—to designate the various roles involved in a change effort. For example, we usually refer to the social worker as the change agent, the person who undertakes to change the situation. The change agent may also be the person who identifies a problem or seeks a change opportunity—although this is not always the case. A client system (such as an individual, family, group, organization, or community) may bring the situation to the attention of the change agent. As the name implies, the target system is the one we seek to change, the target of our intervention. The action system includes all those who assist in bringing about change. If we are seeking the formation of a community task force to consider how best to deal with a recent drug problem, the task force is our action system and the drug problem our target.

As you can see, social workers are involved with a number of systems, and each system may be composed of a single individual or of many people, of a group or of multiple groups. Thus, a community (a large system) struggling with gang violence may be the client system. The gangs—which may individually or collectively be large in number—are the target. The action systems might include police, social agencies, and any other groups which take specific steps to remedy the situation. In our role as the change agent in a change-agent system (typically, an agency), we may also be part of an action system. Clearly, these roles are not mutually exclusive, so anyone can play multiple roles.

Exercise 8.6: Identifying Systems

In the following situation, identify the client, change agent, target, and action systems.

Livermore is a small East Coast city with a big problem. Situated along a major interstate highway, it has become a haven for street gangs and drug dealers because it has only a small police force and is less able than the nearby large city of St. Trump to arrest and prosecute these criminals. Mary Mercado moved to Livermore to escape the violence and crime in St. Trump. As a hospital social worker, she knew first-hand the effects of violence. Worried that her new city is going to end up like her old one, Mary talks with a few of her friends who suggest that she bring her concerns to the attention of her city council representative. Mary meets with Paul Hernandez and together they ask the city council to fund a small task force.

The task force (composed of Mary, Paul, another city council member, the city attorney, a probation and parole officer—a social worker, and the police chief) prepares a report recommending that the city take seven steps to reduce or eliminate the drug and gang problem in Livermore.

Identify the following systems:

2.	Identify two formal resource systems of which you are a member. List the kinds of assistance you might expect from them if you were in desperate need.

3.	Identify at least three public and three private societal resource systems with which you are acquainted. These agencies can be drawn from any community.

The Demography of Communities

The demographics of a community include the age of the population, its range of income and education, and its ethnic composition. For example, a community with low educational and income levels, and composed largely of the elderly, is very different from one in which most residents are young, middle-class, and have college degrees. The resources, both human and financial, available to solve community problems are likely to differ, as are the problems themselves.

The size of a community is another important demographic characteristic. A large city may have different problems than a smaller community. Metropolitan communities (those with over 50,000 residents) are likely to have different challenges than rural communities of 5,000. Resources may also differ significantly.

The United States has undergone a number of trends that affect the demographic characteristics of cities. The early years of the 20th century and the last half of the 1800s were characterized by urbanization, or movement from rural areas and small towns to the cities, because of the better paying jobs in factories and transportation systems. Often, this resulted in overcrowded housing and a host of social problems including child labor, poor sanitary conditions, and sweatshop employment conditions.

After 1950, the trend was significantly reversed as suburbanization drew millions away from the central cities.   The suburbs were essentially bedroom communities that offered residents more space, lower taxes, and fewer social problems. Mass transit systems, the automobile, and a new interstate highway system made the cities accessible from these outlying areas. Since the majority of those making this movement away from the city were non-minorities, the term white flight has been used to describe the results of suburbanization.

Of course, nothing is forever. Gentrification is beginning to reverse this trend as middle- and upper-middle-class individuals seek housing in the central city. Renovation of old buildings and construction of higher quality housing increases property values in these areas, forcing earlier residents to seek less expensive housing.   Naturally, this can and does produce overcrowding in more affordable neighborhoods which may already be struggling with high population densities and other social problems.

Exercise 8.10: Hometown Demographic Factors

Using your hometown as an example, identify the ways in which urbanization, suburbanization, white flight, and/or gentrification have impacted that community. Recognize that any community may be affected by one or more of these factors.

Rural Communities

Rural communities have been viewed from various perspectives at different times. Sometimes they are viewed as backwater towns offering little in the way of culture, job opportunities, or quality of life. At other times, they are portrayed as idyllic settings in which to raise children away from the hubbub of the city. They generally offer lower crime rates, lower taxes, and a more relaxed pace of living. Nevertheless, once former city dwellers move to rural areas, they often want the same types of services and amenities they had in the city. To achieve this, they may sacrifice those lower taxes and invite new social problems. On the other hand, rural communities do appear to provide an environment in which people know and care about one another and help in times of need. For the rural social worker, this can be a real benefit in terms of helping people use informal resources. Those resources must, however, make up for the lack of societal resource systems that might be available in larger communities.

A friend of yours is a social worker considering whether to practice in a rural community of 12,000 or in a nearby large city of one million residents. Help your friend decide by identifying at least three advantages of practicing in each type of community.

Social Stratification

Another important concept in understanding neighborhoods and communities is social stratification—categorizing people, neighborhoods, and communities by social class or economic level. Stratification can be used to delineate the types of employment available in a community. For example, a community with no factories or large companies might rely largely on service occupations for employment. These tend to pay less than industrial or factory jobs and offer fewer benefits. Similarly, stratifying a community on the basis of the age of its population can be helpful. On the positive side, social stratification is a simple shorthand description of a community. On the negative side, however, it may be used to discriminate against certain groups. For example, a bank may redline a portion of the community where the income level is very low and the quality of housing is poor. The bank will then refuse to lend money for housing in this area. (Redlining is illegal, but is still covertly practiced in certain places.)

Socioeconomic class is one of the most common types of social stratification. It is based on the income and educational level of residents. Because the decision about where to draw the lines between one class and another are subjective, you will often encounter different class descriptions. Thus, one document may refer to lower, middle, and upper classes while another breaks each of these classes into several subcategories. What is most important is to recognize that social stratification is simply a tool to help describe and understand a community.

Using your hometown as an example, identify two ways of stratifying or categorizing the community that would help an outsider better understand it.

Community Economic Systems

Producing, distributing, and using services and products are characteristic functions of all communities. All of us play some role in the economic systems of our communities as producers, consumers, or both. A healthy economic system is important for a healthy community so that people can earn money and spend it to support businesses and community functions.

Communities that lose businesses for whatever reason almost always suffer, and those that rely on a single large employer are always at risk of losing that employer. The absence of large businesses in a community affects employment possibilities for residents and places a larger property tax burden on homeowners. Of course, work remains a primary means of self-identity and economic mobility. Problems in a community's economic structure can impact both of these issues. At the same time, economic systems in any community are affected by many variables. Federal, state, and community laws and regulations affect businesses and industries. Competition, foreign subsidization of a particular industry, and changing tastes of consumers all affect what happens in your hometown. Many communities work very hard to retain and attract new industries and businesses by providing free land, offering tax incentives, and devising other inducements. These actions underscore the importance of a solid economic system to the well-being of a community and its residents. At the same time, we must remember that any economic system produces casualties. Loss of jobs, downsizing, and pay cuts are normal risks associated with our economic system. It is therefore critical that while we understand the importance of our economic system we also recognize its consequences for some members of our society.

Describe your hometown in terms of it success or lack of success in providing jobs to residents of the community.

Community Political Systems

Many decisions affecting social work and social welfare are political in nature. That means that governmental units at some level have a major role in deciding what programs get funded, which social problems should have greatest priority, and how much money can be spent to deal with a particular problem. It also means that many people have important input in making these decisions. Every community's political system includes both formal and informal political processes. For example, each community has some type of formal elected power structure charged with making decisions and spending tax money on identified problems. Of course, many decisions affecting social work are also made at the state or national level. At the same time, many decisions are made informally by individuals and groups who represent the informal political power structure but are not elected by voters. Their power and influence derive from their own resources (money, businesses, political involvement, academic credentials, etc.), relationships they have with others, or appointed positions they hold. This same pattern also operates at the state and federal levels.

Sometimes those with influence work so far behind the scenes that they are virtually unknown to the general public. At other times they may be prominent citizens one would expect to have political influence. Understanding the responsibilities and involvement of different levels of government is important to the generalist social worker. For example, if you are concerned about the enforcement of local health codes, you don't call your United States Senator to complain about the situation. On the other hand, a change in federal laws that reduce a community's eligibility for funding for low-income housing *does* require intervention on the national level. The federal government concerns itself with certain responsibilities and the city or county with certain others. Police protection is generally a local responsibility while many social service programs are state operated and funded. In some areas, there is significant overlap between local, state, and national governments roles. For example, the federal government may provide special funding to combat street crime, drug-related violence, and gang activity. This funding may be provided to local communities through grants or other means. At the same time, some programs involve multiple levels of government working together. For example, the federal government provides money and sets guidelines for operating various social service programs which are then carried out by state and local governments.

A.   Briefly discuss your hometown community in terms of how local, state, and federal governments affect it.

B.   Identify functions or services performed by each level of government.

Community Power Systems

Power is the "capacity to move people in a desired direction to accomplish some end" (Homan, 1999, p. 136). Power is either actual or potential. *Potential power* is the ability to influence others. *Actual power* is power in use. Sometimes there is no need to exercise actual power because others recognize and defer to an individual or group's potential power. For instance, the voting power of the elderly in our society is so significant that few political figures ever suggest cutting Social Security. To do so would likely result in an exercise of actual power: the elderly would vote against officeholders who supported such a plan.

Sources of power vary. Money has always been an important source of power in our society, but status, or position, also confer power. You can discover who the powerful people in a community are in one of three ways:

- The reputational approach relies on asking various people who, in their opinion, has power in the community. Popular people, respected and often talked about, are likely to be powerful.

- The issues approach examines critical concerns in the community and learns who is active on both sides of those issues. Those most involved in making decisions on these issues are considered powerful.
- The positional approach looks at the official positions people hold and assumes that the commissioners, the mayor, and the city council or county board representatives have power.

Each of these approaches is useful at certain times, but none is foolproof. You won't always recognize those who operate behind the scenes to influence those in official positions. What's more, power shifts from situation to situation. A powerful person in one arena or on a single issue might have no influence whatsoever in another situation.

Exercise 8.15: Power in My Community

Consider your hometown again. Identify at least two people who hold formal positions of power in the community.

List two other people who you believe are powerful, but who hold no formal positions. Explain why they are powerful.

The Neighborhood

Barker (1999, p. 324) defines the neighborhood as "a region or locality whose inhabitants share certain characteristics, values, mutual interests, or styles of living." Most of us grew up in something we referred to as a neighborhood and his definition tends to capture the most salient aspects of this term. For most of us, the term neighborhood usually refers to an area of land or a section of a community. Its boundaries are based on the perceptions of its residents rather than on any geographical marker. For example, a street separating two political districts in a city may have no bearing on one's sense of neighborhood. At the same time, a single political district or ward may be composed of several neighborhoods. The boundaries become most important when there is a threat to the neighborhood (as might happen when a nearby company wishes to expand its operation or a developer wants to build a shopping mall on the edges of the neighborhood). Boundaries can also become important when children are bused to schools outside their neighborhoods. Such boundary crossing activities are likely to arouse negative reactions from neighborhood residents.

Neighborhood Functions

Every neighborhood performs several functions for its residents. *Socially*, they provide status and friendships, and they are a potential resource in crises because of the relationships that exist among residents. *Institutional* functions—such as providing employment, education, or churches—are also commonly associated with one's neighborhood.

The *political* function of neighborhoods allows residents to become involved in the political process through seeking elective office or becoming active in neighborhood organizations. A neighborhood association fostering preservation and maintenance of the area can give residents considerable political influence. Finally, *economic* functions include such things as providing housing and shopping opportunities. The economic function of neighborhoods is always at risk as technology, changes in the business environment, and other factors influence events. As large malls replace neighborhood shopping centers and the corner grocery gives way to megastores located outside the area, the economic viability of the neighborhood is threatened. Redlining and gentrification can also affect the economic function of a neighborhood.

Neighborhood Types

Some neighborhoods are characterized by transiency—frequent turnover of residents—which can reduce cohesion and the sense of participation among those there. A high degree of transiency may result in feelings of social disorganization, reducing the social connection between residents.

Neighborhoods can also be understood by the names we apply to them. We refer to run down or deteriorated neighborhoods as slums, or we use the term ghetto to refer to an area in which a specific ethnic or racial group lives. Unfortunately, these terms tell us very little else about the area.

We can also characterize a neighborhood on the basis of the help it provides to residents. Neighbors can comprise a primary resource for other residents. Every neighborhood has some natural helpers on whom others rely for assistance, friendship, and support. Neighborhood organizations can help new residents feel welcome, protect the common interests of all residents, and encourage cooperation among residents. Because of the wide variety of functions served by such organizations, social workers should be aware of the existence of such organizations in the areas we serve. Conversely, the absence of a neighborhood organization may suggest a possible resource to be developed with the help of a social worker.

Neighborhood residents, particularly new ones, may be unaware of the large number of community resources available for dealing with a neighborhood problem. For everything from abandoned buildings to weed-infested yards, the community itself often has resources to assist neighborhoods. Typically these functions are performed by some branch of local government, and its a good idea to develop a list of such resources to assist residents with specific problems.

Exercise 8.16: Understanding Your Neighborhood

A.   Describe the neighborhood in which you were raised.

B. Discuss how well institutional functions and social functions were performed by the neighborhood.

C. Identify any opportunities for residents to become involved in the political functions of the area.

D. Briefly describe businesses or other organizations serving an economic function in your neighborhood.

E. Finally, discuss the degree of transiency of residents.

Assessing Communities and Neighborhoods

A more formal understanding of a community or neighborhood can be reached through the mechanism of a community assessment. An assessment is a detailed exploration of the community or neighborhood using a variety of data sources—census data, planning department records, newspapers, etc. It might also entail interviews with key residents of the area. An assessment might gather information on the location, population characteristics, social and economic influences, educational quality, and/or business and industrial climate in a community. It might also look at the history and attractiveness of a neighborhood along with such social amenities as parks, museums, and recreational opportunities. The availability of health and social service resources, income of residents, and distribution of power in the community may also be investigated. In the process of doing an assessment you might develop a database of the important people you met or learned about. The goal of an assessment is to achieve a better understanding of the community in which you work. It is a valuable tool for the generalist social worker.

Exercise 8.17: Assessment Tools

1.   If you wished to do an assessment of the community in which your college or university is located, what data sources would be relatively easy to locate?

2.   What kinds of data might be helpful in your assessment?

Generalist social workers often encounter community problems and change opportunities as they perform their various roles with individuals, families, and groups. Sometimes the prospect of intervening in the community seems overwhelming, especially to the new social worker. "How can I do anything about this situation? I'm just one person," you might say to yourself. The problems you confront are substantial. The situation is detrimental to your clients and diminishes the quality of life in the community. What can you do?

As a social worker you are in an extraordinarily good position to recognize community problems and their impact on social and economic justice issues and oppressed populations. The social problems you and your colleagues observe run the gamut from violence to drugs to education to health. If your job calls for you to tackle these issues, you have a responsibility to do something. Even if your actual job does *not* require you to confront these issues, you have a professional and a societal obligation to do so.

This chapter will:

- Highlight some of the ways generalists intervene to improve their communities
- Focus on using the PREPARE and IMAGINE strategies for assessing a community's potential for change and for carrying out a community change effort
- Identify individual steps needed to conduct a community intervention
- Discuss specific skills and approaches for use in the change effort

Change Efforts in the Community

Social workers' dual professional roles of working in and with the community offer multiple opportunities for macro change. At perhaps the lowest level, social workers participate in the political process by voting, running for office, and supporting the candidacy of others committed to furthering social work purposes and goals. We can also petition for changes in laws, policies, or procedures when this tactic promises to be effective, and we can become actively involved in social action efforts aimed at fundamental change.

Fortunately, the skills we have developed for working with individuals and groups are just as appropriate when undertaking change in the community. Verbal communication skills, for example, can be used to persuade others to change their minds. Writing skills can be used in letter-writing campaigns and to prepare educational materials. Group skills can be employed in social action designed to improve the overall quality of life by bringing people together to pursue a coordinated change effort.

The social worker's role in empowering clients extends to the community as well. Those we are trying to help must be perceived as partners in the effort. Otherwise, we promote dependency and a sense of incompetence on the part of the change effort's beneficiary. Also, professional values set limits on the kind of tactics and approaches we can employ in this effort. We cannot undertake change activities that clearly conflict with our professional values and ethical standards.

Viewing the Community

There are several different ways to view a community in the context of a macro-level change. For all of us, the community is the place where we practice social work. It is the context for our efforts and affects what we can and can't do. The community can also be the target of our change activities. Sometimes, the community is the client, in need of assistance from the social worker. At other times, it becomes the means or mechanism for change when it draws upon its own resources and those of its members to tackle community problems.

Match each of the following scenarios with the corresponding view of the community:

Scenario 1:   San Garcia is a community with many problems, primary among which is the absence of shelter for the homeless. The city council has repeatedly turned down a state grant that would help establish a homeless shelter. Julio Ruiz, the shelter's major opponent on the city council, is a very conservative individual who opposes all social programs. He faces reelection in a month and his opponent is a progressive former mayor of San Garcia, Miguel Gonzales. Mr. Gonzales has asked you to help him get elected because you are well known in the community, especially among the Spanish-speaking population. You both believe that residents will support a homeless shelter if for no other reason than to assure that the homeless will not begin sleeping on the streets of residential areas. If you decide to help in this campaign, would you consider the city of San Garcia the client, the target, the context, or the mechanism of change? Explain your answer.

Scenario 2: Franco City is a poor community on the edge of a mid-sized city, Beltville. Beltville has taken over most of the neighboring cities by annexation, a process of legally incorporating adjacent communities. A Franco City citizens' group is very concerned about this trend and wants the community to remain an independent community. At a community meeting they suggest that a task force be formed to plan a campaign against the loss of their independent status. You agree to serve on the task force. Is Franco City the target, client, context, or mechanism for change in this case? Defend your choice.

Scenario 3: Munchhausen Vale has been a wonderful community in which to live. Lately, several events have challenged the status quo in the town. The influx of immigrants from Southeast Asia has created tensions among many residents who have no experience with the benefits of community diversity. Residents have begun to lose the sense of community that once made living in "the Vale" so attractive. You live in the community and serve as an at-large member of the city council. The council decides to hold a series of community meetings to which all residents will be invited. The meeting will look at ways of recreating the positive feeling that previously characterized citizens' views of their town. You will serve as the convener for several of these meetings. Do you think that Munchhausen Vale is the mechanism, target, client, or context for your practice? Why?

Undertaking Change in Communities

The first step in the planned change model is engagement. It is the point at which you and the client system make initial contact, get to know each other, and make a decision whether you and your agency can be of help. It is also the point where the client is oriented to the helping process and you explain further steps that you and the client will follow.

Engagement in the Community

In the community setting, engagement occurs as you recognize that a problem exists. This often follows a period of observation and culminates in a clearer understanding of the history, experiences, and complexities of the community (Landon, 1999). During this period you will also make contact with others involved in the problem or change opportunity. You will build relationships with each client system using a variety of micro level skills discussed earlier in Chapter 2. Ideally, this relationship will be characterized by trust as others begin to recognize your commitment to a planned change process.

You will also begin using the social work principle, *professional use of self.* In other words, "you are using your knowledge, experience, and perceptions in the professional worker/client relationship in a planful manner" for several purposes (Kirst-Ashman & Hull, 1999, p. 72). For example, you will employ your knowledge of neighborhoods and communities to help understand the social environment with which the client is interacting. You will also share your understanding and perspectives with the client system. In addition, you will use both micro and mezzo level skills to further the goal of the macro intervention. Every action, decision, and communication should be guided by your professional knowledge, skills, and values. The engagement phase can be very brief or quite lengthy, depending upon the situation and your skill in forming relationships with others in the community.

Identify* Problems *to Address

Problems are relatively common in any community. They may be pointed out by news media, by victims, by social service providers, by politicians, etc. But not all changes focus on a problem. Sometimes you will seek to *prevent* a problem because you recognize a situation that could deteriorate and want to keep that from happening. Once a potential problem or opportunity has been identified it must be described clearly in sufficient detail that others can understand the issues involved. It is not sufficient to simply say that the community has a problem with homelessness. We need to know the extent of the problem, the characteristics of the homeless, and any other information that will assist us in bringing about change.

Exercise 9.2: Problem Identification

Consult a newspaper for your hometown or another community. Identify one problem affecting the community that is reported in the paper. From the information in the newspaper story, provide a succinct description of the problem and its extent, the characteristics of those affected by the problem, and any other appropriate information. What information is missing that might help you decide whether this problem is of sufficient importance to pursue an intervention?

1. Identification of Problem

2. Description of Problem

3. Extent of Problem

4.   Characteristics of Those Affected by Problem

5.   Other Pertinent Information

6.   Missing Information

Assess Your Macro and Personal **Reality**

Look first at the potential target. How powerful is it? Can it afford the changes you are pursuing? Next, find out whether the target itself shares your values and goals. If it does, it will be easier for you to "sell" your idea. Third, consider the consequences your projected change will have for the target. Is this target heavily invested in the status quo? Assess your own power to foster change. Finally, outline the general characteristics of the target: Is it susceptible to outside pressure? How will your change affect its sense of identity? Is it generally effective at achieving its own goals?

Exercise 9.3: Reality Check—A Force Field Analysis

Assume that your current social work program is considering raising the grade point average needed at the time of graduation from a 2.5 to a 3.5 because some faculty members believe that grade inflation has made the 2.5 meaningless. The social work program is your community. You spend considerable time in social work classes, many of your friends are in social work, and the social work program has become the context of your sense of who you are. You have a field placement set up for next fall, and you know that your own GPA of 3.1 will probably keep you from graduating if this new change is made. (The remaining exercises in this chapter will also focus on this example.)

As a social work student in this community, do a force field analysis. Review those variables that may help or impede your attempts to stop the implementation of this proposal. Answer the following questions:

1.   Who is likely to oppose this proposal?

2.   Who is likely to benefit from it?

3.   Who is unlikely to see the proposed change as a problem?

4.   Assess the power and influence of those who are most likely to support the proposal.

5.   Assess the power and influence of those who are most likely to oppose the proposal.

6.   Who is the potential target in this situation?

7.   Do you think the target shares your aspirations, values, and goals? Why?

8.   How susceptible is the target to outside pressure?

Establish *Primary Goals*

        Once the force field analysis or assessment is completed, it is time to establish your primary goals. The goals are derived from the problem or change opportunity you have identified. If there are multiple goals, prioritize them because you can't usually do everything at once. Be sure that your goals are clear, easily understood, and capable of motivating people. It is much easier to get people behind a project or change effort if the goals sound attractive and if they will make a major difference in the quality of life in the community.

Exercise 9.4: What Is Your Primary Goal?

1.   In the situation concerning raising the grade point requirement (in exercise 9.3), what is your primary goal?

2.   Do you have any other goals? If so, describe them.

Identify Relevant People *of Influence*

In this step you pinpoint those individuals who are (1) likely to agree with your goals, (2) capable of influencing others, and (3) willing to participate in the change effort. You also try to identify those who are likely to hurt your cause (such as someone who always achieves his goals, but only after bruising the egos of everyone else involved). Do you need someone who can address the city council or the state legislature? Then avoid anyone who gets tongue-tied in front of groups. But maybe that person would be effective as a grant writer. Your goals influence your choice of actors.

Exercise 9.5: Who Will Help?

1.   Referring back to exercise 9.3, list the individuals who are likely to agree with your goals.

2.   Identify anyone who is capable of influencing others to stop this proposed change and explain how.

3.   Who might actually help you stop the proposed change? Why?

Assess *Potential Financial Costs and Benefits*

Consider the various costs and benefits of your proposed effort. Benefits are usually clear—a new playground for children, bus service for the frail elderly, or some other worthy goal—so benefit assessment is relatively easy. Recipients of benefits can include specific client groups (such as gay men and lesbian women) or broader groups (such as a whole community benefiting from decreased gang violence).

On the downside, new programs cost money and must frequently compete with existing programs for resources. Tactics also cost you. You can offend coworkers, force people into uncomfortable positions, and lose friends. There is also a negative cost for failure. It is demoralizing to attempt a macro change effort and fail.

Exercise 9.6: What Are the Costs and Benefits?

Identify at least two financial costs and benefits if you try to oppose the GPA proposal. (Remember, in many real-life situations this step will either convince you and others to pursue the change or convince you to stop your efforts immediately.)

1.   Financial Benefits of opposing the GPA change.

2.   Financial Costs of opposing the GPA change.

3.   Are there any financial implications to the *tactics* you are considering? If so, try to estimate that cost.

Evaluate Professional and Personal Risk

Life is a risk. The goal of this step is not to scare you or discourage you from undertaking a change effort. It is silly and dangerous, however, not to consider the risks you face when pursuing macro-level change. You're not very likely to lose your job because you undertake to change something in a community, but you may very well become unpopular with target system members. You may be perceived as unprofessional if you select tactics that make others uncomfortable. Some people may wonder why you should make it your business to try to change the world (or the piece of it that you occupy). Your colleagues may think you're biting off more than you can chew, and your supervisors may wish you'd spend more time keeping your case records up-to-date instead of taking on city hall. In many cases the risk factor is negligible compared to the potential benefits, but consideration of risk is still a necessary step in the process.

Exercise 9.7: Determine the Risk

---

1. What possible personal risks are entailed in undertaking this change effort to halt the proposed grade point requirement?

2. Do you see any professional risks inherent in trying to stop this proposal? If so, describe them.

3. Do you consider the risks high in relation to the good to be achieved? Explain.

Evaluate *the Potential Success of a Macro Change Process*

Remember, you have still not committed yourself to pursue this change. The last step is to honestly reflect on the potential for success. You may conclude that success is more likely if you can shift tactically from a conflict approach to a more collaborative approach. Or you may decide that only a conflict approach will work because everything else has been tried. You already know the potential benefits and costs of trying to change something, so you might decide that the goal is so desirable that even a small chance of success is sufficient reason to move ahead. At this point, you can still decide to drop the idea entirely or postpone it until a more propitious time. Your final decision should be reasoned and unemotional, the result of critical thinking, not gut instinct or personal hubris.

1. Working toward the goal you described in exercise 9.4, list all the reasons this macro change effort is likely to succeed.

2. List all the reasons this change effort is *not* likely to succeed.

3. Is there sufficient potential for success to justify proceeding with the planned change? Why or why not?

Once a decision is made, you have more or less completed the planning process. We say *more or less* because new data can always come in—even during the implementation phase. Keep this in mind. You are now ready to consider the next phase and use the IMAGINE model as your guide through the implementation phase.

IMAGINE: A Process of Community Change

There are seven steps in this phase of the problem solving process. All were discussed in Chapter 6 and are briefly summarized below.

***Start with an Innovative* Idea**

You may actually have *several related ideas* that you intend to implement, either simultaneously or over time as the IMAGINE process unfolds.

Exercise 9.9: Restate Your Idea

Restate your *idea* regarding the grade point requirement.

Muster *Support and Formulate an Action System*

You muster support and establish an action system because you always need the help of others to achieve large scale goals. You have probably already identified likely allies, but it is important to get their unambiguous support. To increase the action system's potential influence, ask members to identify others in their immediate environment whom they could influence to support your project or idea. If your action system members are sufficiently influential, these significant others will increase the strength of your intervention. If you discover that collectively your action system has few influential contacts, take another look at your approach and the likelihood of success. Once your action system is in place, use a PERT chart or some other guideline to assign specific tasks.

Exercise 9.10: Mustering Support and an Action System

1.   Describe the steps you would take to muster support for your change effort.

2. Which of your potential action system members has the greatest influence and why?

3. Which of your potential action system members is likely to be least committed to your effort and why?

Identify Assets

Assets are resources that can assist you in the change effort. They include everything from money to people to time. The members of your action system are one of your largest assets, especially if they are committed to the goals you have identified. In macro change activities, people are usually your most readily available asset. Money is another important asset, though it is often less available. Other assets may include office space, use of a telephone, copier, computer, and similar resources. Substantial available assets can encourage members of the action system. A lack of assets makes your work that much harder.

Exercise 9.11: Asset Identification

Identify the following types of assets available to you:

1. Finances

2. People

3.	Time

4.	Other

Specify Goals *and Objectives*

Your primary goal already emerged from the PREPARE process but now it will need further refinement. Goals are general statements of intent which are made up of objectives. Essentially, we are separating major goals into their component parts or objectives. For example, your goal is to prevent any increase in the grade point average needed for graduation. You objectify this goal by stating that "we will marshal all of the objections to and evidence against changing the grade point average." If the original goal is broad enough, we can identify several objectives needed to achieve the goal.

Of course, marshaling evidence against changing the grade point average for graduation requires taking certain steps. These *action steps*, move you toward the objective. For example, making an appointment with the Program Director or meeting with the faculty could be steps in the process of achieving this goal. Each action step should be allotted a specified time frame and identified as the responsibility of a single person. Without such specificity, the steps are far less likely to be taken effectively.

Exercise 9.12: Spelling Out Goals, Objectives, and Action Steps

1.	Restate your primary goal of maintaining the current grade-point requirement:

2.	List two objectives that further specify the goal.

Objective one:

Objective two:

3.   List at least two action steps for objective number one:

Action Step:

Action Step:

Implement *the Plan*

      Carrying out the plan requires careful use of all resources. If the plan includes such things as petitioning door-to-door, holding public meetings, or other steps that require meeting the public, assign such tasks to people who are comfortable with this type of responsibility. The quiet person who prefers to remain behind the scenes developing a computer database of potential supporters (or donors) is equally valuable in that role. Build on and use the strengths of your action system and assets. Keep on top of the action steps by meeting regularly with everyone to monitor progress and evaluate success. Give people something to do as soon as possible. Otherwise your human resources will lose their motivation and wander off into other projects. Keep them busy.

Exercise 9.13: Implementation

      Indicate who will carry out each of the action steps listed above. Give your reason for assigning this step to this particular person.

1.   Action Step Implementer:

Reason:

2.   Action Step Implementer

Reason:

Neutralize *Opposition*

Neutralizing opposition means overcoming or outwitting those who oppose your goals and objectives. If the stakes—financial or otherwise—are large, you may face significant opposition. Sometimes the opposition turns out to be minor—or at least less substantial than you expected. Neutralizing tactics include bargaining, negotiating, mediating, persuading, and/or educating opponents. Most political decisions involve trade-offs, and negotiating can be a lengthy process. This is a drawback if your action system members lose interest or your goals get so watered down that you really accomplish very little.

Remember that collaboration is less polarizing than confrontation or conflict. On the other hand less confrontational approaches are not always effective. The effort required to neutralize opposition depends on your opponents' power, resources, and degree of intransigence, and on the influence of your action system.

While less confrontational approaches are often desirable, they are not always effective. Sometimes other approaches are needed, including lobbying, boycotts, marches, rallies, strikes, picketing, and lawsuits.

Exercise 9.14: Neutralize 'Em

This may sound like hitting someone with a phaser, but neutralizing the opposition is really benign.

1. In the space below describe the actions you would take to neutralize opposition to your change efforts. This might include bargaining, negotiating, educating, or persuading opponents, as well as other collaborative and conflictual approaches.

2.   Briefly indicate why you selected these tactics.

Evaluate *Progress*

    Clearly stated goals and objectives are readily evaluated. Well-articulated action steps can be monitored to ensure that each is completed in a timely manner. If the agreed-upon steps are not followed, the final goal may not be achieved. However, monitoring is concerned only with the *process*, not with the goal itself. Evaluation, on the other hand, focuses on whether we achieved identified goals and objectives and lets us know what is still needed to ensure that progress will continue. Sometimes called *stabilization of change*, it keeps our objectives from being lost after the change effort is completed. Changes in laws, policies, and regulations are often used to ensure stabilization of change.

    Negative consequences may also be revealed by evaluation. Unintended consequences may force us to work for additional changes. For example, a neighborhood complained bitterly to the city because its streets were in such poor repair. Large potholes the size of cows pocked the streets in the area until the city finally repaved them. Then traffic on the street increased, as did the speed of cars. Now the residents complain about this new nuisance. Sometimes you just can't win.

    Termination of a change effort is usually the last step after objectives have been achieved. We may have to end our efforts short of complete success if it is clear that we can't achieve the goal or if the unintended consequences are too damaging.

    Finally, follow-up ensures that the changes we attempted to stabilize remain in place. Promises made in the midst of negotiating can be forgotten or ignored after things have settled down. Organizations and people may return to their old ways of doing things when no one is watching. Follow-up helps reduce this possibility.

1.   Describe how you would monitor your proposed change effort to ensure that it stays on course.

2.   Describe how you would evaluate the success of your change effort.

Most of us like to think that the work we do is effective. Sometimes others tell us that we do good work, and sometimes we have a gut feeling that we have really helped. Unfortunately, neither our intuition nor testimonials from others is sufficient to justify the continuation of social work programs. Funding sources and common sense require that we use more systematic means of evaluating what we do. Macro practice poses additional difficulties in terms of evaluation because we often address complicated problems, and we cannot apply the most rigorous research tools available. Nevertheless, we must be familiar with the definition, purposes, and key concepts used in evaluation. We must also be able to anticipate potential difficulties we may encounter in carrying out various kinds of evaluation. Learning about methods of evaluation is just as important as learning the intervention skills needed to bring about macro level change. And, as in other areas of social work practice, our efforts must be guided by professional values and ethics.

This chapter will:
- Define evaluation
- Identify the purposes of evaluation
- Review key concepts in evaluation
- Describe barriers to effective evaluation
- Identify various kinds of evaluation and evaluation designs
- List and describe the stages of evaluation
- Review ethical principles that must guide macro practice evaluation

Why Evaluate?

Why do I have to evaluate my work? Over the past 15 years increasing attention has been focused on evaluation of social programs, because programs must demonstrate some degree of success if funding bodies are to continue to support them. Evaluation is a process of determining whether a given change effort was worthwhile. Evaluation can focus on everything from the amount of money or effort put into a project to the number of clients served to the results obtained. We hope that the outcome of our efforts—that is, a change in the quality of life—is evident and is sufficiently impressive to justify continued funding of our program. Failure to prove that a program "works" can result in the elimination of all financial backing for it. Which can mean the end of the program—and of your job. Fear of unemployment, however, is not the only motivation. Measuring the effectiveness of one's efforts is a professional responsibility, and evaluation is a normal part of the problem-solving or planned-change process.

Evaluation is also undertaken to prevent waste and duplication. Neither taxpayers nor clients should be asked to support inefficient programs when funding could be applied to more effective programs.

Evaluation Concepts

You have undoubtedly come across the term *baseline* in some of your other classes. A baseline is simply a measure of the amount or frequency of a variable. For example, if we implement a program aimed at reducing neighborhood violence, it is essential to know how much violence exists in the neighborhood before we launch our program. Our baseline data might include the number of domestic violence calls to the police, police reports of the number of shots fired in a given neighborhood, and other similar information. The baseline gives us the "before" picture with which we can compare our results after the intervention. In an ideal scenario, developing a baseline is the first step in the change process. Unfortunately, it is often impossible to gather data this way, so we must rely on different methods. Sometimes people are in such a hurry to begin a program that they can't take time to do a baseline, so old police records will be used. As useful as baselines are, the absence of such a measure does not preclude carrying out the change effort.

In laboratory research, we often are able to use *a control group,* a group more or less identical to that with which we are working. A control group allows us to evaluate our program outcomes by comparing the group we worked with to a group that did not receive any help. For example, we might find another neighborhood similar—in terms of race, age, gender, and socioeconomic class, for instance—to the one in which we want to launch our anti-violence program. A reduction in violence in our target neighborhood contrasted with continuing violence in the control neighborhood would support the effectiveness of our program. In such a comparison, the neighborhood we are working with is called *the experimental group.* We don't like to think we are experimenting with people, but in a sense every intervention *is* something like an experiment.

One of the most rigorous methods for testing program effectiveness is by using an *experimental design.* A true experimental design uses control and experimental groups and randomly assigns clients to one group or the other. Experimental designs are used frequently in laboratories—for example, when research scientists test new medications—but rarely in the human services because of problems with the random assignment of clients. In other situations, we may even lack a control group. To counter these problems, we employ *quasi-experimental designs.* Quasi-experimental designs copy some of the features of experimental designs but modify other components to accommodate the situation. For example, we might use a control group neighborhood, but we could not assign clients randomly to one neighborhood or the other.

The *independent variable* and the *dependent variable* are basically the cause and the effect. The independent variable is presumed to cause or otherwise influence some outcome. The dependent variable is caused or otherwise influenced by the independent variable. If we are trying to reduce school truancy rates, the rates themselves become the dependent variable. We hope that the rates will go down if our program works. In other words, the rates depend on (or are influenced by) our intervention program. Our intervention program, on the other hand, is the independent variable. Hopefully, the introduction of our program will produce changes in the dependent variable.

We use *sampling* to find out, for example, whether the new crime-watch program is making neighborhood residents more comfortable and less fearful of being victimized. It is difficult and expensive to contact every participant in every neighborhood involved in the program, so we turn to sampling and use a subset or sample of the total group. We say that our sample is *random* if each person in the population has an equal chance of being selected for inclusion. Stopping people on the street would not produce a random sample since only those on that particular street at that particular time could be selected. In fact, such a method could produce a biased sample. We would get more accurate results by making a list of all households (or addresses) and then randomly selecting those to be interviewed. Random sampling improves the overall quality of our evaluation and helps eliminate other explanations for the results we obtained in our program. We will discuss sampling in greater detail later in this chapter.

Such characteristics as the gender or income are called *descriptive statistics* because they describe the community. When we want to predict or infer—rather than describe—something about our community, we gather *inferential statistics.* Suppose we want to know the average age of community residents but don't have time to ask each of them. We randomly select a sample of residents and determine that their average age is 54. We then infer that the average age of residents in the entire community is 54.

Whether we are using descriptive or inferential statistics, we also employ *measures of central tendency*—shorthand ways of summarizing data. For example, in the previous paragraph we mentioned the average age of community residents. How do you calculate an average age? There are three options:

1. Simply add the ages of all residents of a neighborhood, then divide by the total number of residents to find the *mean* age. (Note: This is not to be confused with the other definition of the term *mean* which explains why the faculty made you take statistics.) Figure 10.1 presents one example of calculating a mean.

Figure 10.1: Calculating a Mean

The mean is calculated by adding up all the ages below and dividing by the number of family members.

Below are the ages of people living in the Smith household.

Grandmother Whiney:	91
Husband Waffle:	50
Wife Whimpy:	39
Son Rake:	17
Daughter Snooty:	<u>15</u>
Total	212

Number of Observations   5
Mean   212/5 = 42.4

Although it is commonly used, the mean can produce problems of interpretation. Too many extreme (very high or very low) numbers in a list can distort the data. For example, without Grandmother Whiney, the average age of the family shown above drops to about 30.

2. Another method for presenting data is through the use of the *median*. The median is the middle number in a range of numbers running from high to low or low to high. The advantage of the median is that it is much less affected by extreme numbers. The median is often used to describe such things as family income. Figure 10.2 shows how this might be calculated.

Figure 10.2: Calculating the Median

Look at the data on family income for clients participating in our first-offender intervention program:

Family A —	$ 20,000
Family B —	$ 25,000
Family C —	$ 30,000
Family D —	$ 31,000
Family E —	$ 45,000
Family F —	$ 90,000
Family G —	$ 150,000

The median family income of this group is $31,000 because that figure falls exactly at the half-way point in the distribution of incomes. (The mean for this group would be approximately $55,857, a much less realistic picture of this group of families' incomes.)

3. The last measure of central tendency is the *mode*—the number or observation which occurs with the greatest frequency. You might want to discover the most common problem cited by neighborhood residents concerned about the increasing criminal

activity in their part of the city. A survey of residents might produce the results shown in figure 10.3.

Figure 10.3: Calculating the Mode

A survey of neighbors in the San Miguel barrio identified the following concerns about criminal activity. Which problem represents the mode?

Problem	Number of Respondents Citing This Problem
Gang violence	34
Drug selling	76
Burglary	12

Drug selling is the most commonly cited problem in this barrio. As such, it is the modal response of residents.

Exercise 10.1: Calculate It Yourself

Using the following ages of students in a social work class, calculate the mean, median, and modal ages.

Marcia	20	Alicia	26	Fred	26	Sam	56	Chou	41
Andrew	30	Miguel	34	Noel	35	Maria	38	Nathan	26
Louis	23	Martin	24	Jose	26	Xavier	31	Kay	33

Mean age: _____

Median age: _____

Modal age: _____

Another commonly used statistical measure is the *standard deviation*. This measure is based on the mean and measures how much the scores or observations vary above or below the mean. Standard deviations are usually derived using computers or calculators. (When I was a child we did it by hand using an abacus.)

Suppose we are interested in the grade-point averages of students in our after-school tutoring program. The mean GPA for these at-risk adolescents is 1.89. The standard deviation is .03 which means that most of the students have grades very close to the 1.89 GPA. In other words, there is very little variability in this group. A larger standard deviation would mean just the opposite—that several students had much higher or much lower GPAs.

Reliability is the extent to which a given measurement will produce the same results at different times. We want to know if our Legal Education Group (LEG) is helping delinquent youngsters better understand the law and the consequences of criminal behavior. Unfortunately, while developing the test we find that the youngsters in our test groups score very differently on the exam. Scores seem to go up or down without apparent reason. If the test were reliable, the only thing that would affect scores would be new knowledge covered in the LEG program. Clearly, our testing system is not reliable, so we must find or devise new tests.

Validity is an instrument's ability to measure what it is intended to measure. If your social policy instructor gives you a test on the most effective interviewing approaches to use with resistant or involuntary clients, you will wonder what is going on. That test will not be a useful indicator of your knowledge of social welfare policy. There are many different kinds of validity. A certain degree of validity is assumed if an instrument appears to measure the right stuff. A social welfare history quiz covering the Elizabethan Poor Laws or the War on Poverty has *face* validity because it covers logical content from the course. The licensing examination for social workers in most states also has face validity because it measures what social workers should know about practice. Whether a high score on such exams means you will be a good social worker, however, is less certain. If an instrument can predict future behavior or performance, we say that it has *predictive validity*. This is a higher level of validity than simple face validity and requires more elaboration and testing to achieve.

Statistical significance is a measure of the relationship between two variables. For example, we might like to know whether the sample of neighborhood residents we used to study neighborhood attitudes toward crime is actually similar to the neighborhood population as a whole. If it is, we can have more confidence that the opinions we gathered truly reflect those of all neighborhood residents. We also use statistical significance to find out whether two variables are related to one another. For example, you have decided to explore whether grade point average was affected when adolescents completed an after-school peer tutoring program. If you discover that grade point averages were noticeably higher for students who completed the program, you can use this information to continue or expand the program. If your findings are challenged by opponents of the program, you can use statistical analysis to show that there is only 1 chance in 100 that the results obtained by students completing the program (i.e., improved grade point averages) could be due to chance. This bolsters confidence in the program because it shows that your results you obtained were statistically significant.

One of the most frequently used tests of statistical significance is the *chi-square*. The chi-square procedure allows us to compare expected frequencies with observed frequencies. Put slightly differently, the chi-square is a means of testing whether two observations are related. Let's say our new anti-violence program seems to be working. We notice that arrests for violence in our target neighborhood have dropped considerably. However, a report from the police department on violence-related arrests in the target neighborhoods indicates that the police have been arresting a larger number of people of color. That's curious because the neighborhood is very heterogeneous. You can't accuse the police department of uneven enforcement without some additional evidence, so you use the chi-square test to compare the actual numbers of people of color arrested to the expected number based upon the overall make-up of the community. For instance, people of color comprise 45 percent of the population in this neighborhood and in the community at large. All things being equal, we would expect to find about 45 percent of those arrested for violent crimes to be people of color. Instead, it appears that fully 90 percent of the arrests are of people of color. The chi-square test can help us verify statistically what our own common sense tells us, namely that something is rotten in Denmark.

Exercise 10.2: Keeping It All Straight

In the following exercise match each concept with its corresponding definition. (No cheating—don't look back.)

1. Baseline	_____		11. Median	_____
2. Control Group	_____		12. Mode	_____
3. Experimental Group	_____		13. Standard Deviation	_____
4. Dependent Variable	_____		14. Reliability	_____
5. Independent Variable	_____		15. Validity	_____
6. Sampling	_____		16. Descriptive Statistics	_____
7. Random Sample	_____		17. Inferential Statistics	_____
8. Experimental Design	_____		18. Outcome	_____
9. Quasi-Experimental Design	_____		19. Statistical Significance	_____
10. Mean	_____		20. Chi-Square Test	_____

A. A statistical procedure for comparing expected and observed frequencies.
B. The most frequently observed score in a group of scores.
C. A group used for comparison purposes.
D. Using a subset of all clients seen by an agency rather than surveying the entire group.
E. The group receiving an intervention.
F. A design using control and experimental groups but not random assignment.
G. The original amount or occurrence of a behavior or event.
H. The behavior intervention is intended to change.
I. The ability of an instrument to measure what it is supposed to measure.
J. The arithmetic average of a group of numbers.
K. A measure of the variability of a group of scores around a mean.
L. A quality of life change resulting from social work intervention.
M. The risk involved generalizing from a sample to the population as a whole.
N. Statistics used to draw a conclusion about a population based on a sample of that population.
O. The middle figure in a distribution of figures listed from highest to lowest or vice versa.
P. The likelihood that a measurement will yield the same results at subsequent times.
Q. The average age of a group of delinquent youth, for example.
R. A social work intervention is an example of this type of variable.
S. A subset chosen so that all members of the population have an equal chance of being selected.
T. An elaborate method for evaluating an intervention; includes control groups, experimental groups, and random assignment of clients to one group or the other.

Why Evaluations Don't Always Work

Many potential problems can arise before, during, and/or after a program evaluation, so it helps to be alert to the more common difficulties.

- First, program developers often fail to plan for evaluation at the time they begin their efforts. Later, when evaluation becomes necessary, there is insufficient data (lack of a baseline, for instance) and no efficient system for data gathering.

- Lack of program stability is another potential problem. Nothing is static in social work practice. Any program undergoes changes as personnel become more sophisticated and learn new approaches, and as the clientele changes. Evaluations, however, work best when the program is stable. Instability leaves evaluators in a quandary: Are they evaluating the original program or some modified version of it? The longer the program goes on before evaluation occurs, the greater the risk that such changes will confound the results. To overcome this difficulty, evaluators can focus on specific portions of the program that have *not* changed significantly or conduct the evaluation over a shorter time period. Nevertheless, all programs change and this problem cannot be entirely eliminated.

- The relationship between evaluators and practitioners can also create difficulties. As a social work practitioner, you probably prefer providing service to clients to attending to paperwork. The evaluator, on the other hand, is concerned with assessing program effectiveness, so records and data are of considerable consequence.

- There is also the implicit threat that an evaluation might prove that you aren't accomplishing your objectives or that your program should be eliminated or restructured. This scrutiny, although uncomfortable for you, is the evaluator's primary task.

- Evaluators are interested in such things as random assignment of clients, accuracy of records, and other details that may seem unimportant to the practitioner. Workers often rely on practice wisdom—the day-to-day knowledge and experience we gain by routinely doing our jobs—to assess whether progress is being made. This practice wisdom includes observations, assumptions, and intuition, but evaluators want hard data. How do we balance these two sets of priorities? We can focus the evaluation on the theory or approach that

B.   Discuss how each might be used in a social service agency.

Evaluation Approaches

Selecting the right method to evaluate a macro level intervention is as important as choosing the most appropriate change strategy. For example, you would not use an intrapersonal intervention such as cognitive restructuring to help clients dealing with substandard housing. You should be familiar with several different evaluation methods, including quantitative and qualitative, post-test and pre/post test, client satisfaction surveys, goal attainment and target problem scaling, case studies, group comparisons and quality assurance reviews.

Quantitative methods use objective and numerical criteria to measure change following an intervention. These methods typically use baselines, require a high degree of specificity, and focus on readily observable indices of change, such as a reduction in the number of reported burglaries to determine the effectiveness of a neighborhood watch program or the number of clients receiving public assistance who found employment following completion of a job training program. The use of such specific measurement devices makes it easier to identify whether change has occurred.

Qualitative methods do not usually use numeric indicators. Instead, they often rely on in-depth review of a small number of cases. For example, to learn about residents' concerns about housing, we might interview a sample drawn from target neighborhoods. Our open-ended interview would let respondents answer in their own words instead of giving them a list of problems to check off. The results of this survey would be subjected to a content analysis to find common themes in the responses. (A content analysis looks for patterns among responses, then counts the most frequently occurring responses.) Qualitative methods can also show how a program affected participants and what recommendations they might have for future interventions. These methods—which rely on interviews or logs, or journals kept by participants—can be used in conjunction with quantitative methods to get a fuller evaluation of a program. We might use a formal survey to ask residents of a public housing project about their perceptions of changes in drug and gang problems following an increase in police patrols. This quantitative measure could be combined with a qualitative study of residents' experiences with the police to learn whether the added police involvement produced any new problems.

The reference above to "changes" in perceptions suggests that we already have baseline data on residents' perceptions before the intervention took place. The ability to compare changes following an intervention is characteristic of a *Pre-test/Post-test design*. The "test" might actually be any baseline data such as police reports, attitude surveys, or any other information that allows a comparison over time. Frequently, this is termed an A-B design because it assesses change from time A (pre-intervention) to time B (post-intervention).

Without a baseline, the most common evaluation approach is a *One-group, Post-test design*. As the name implies, we are dealing with a single group and have no baseline available. We have to measure the impact of an intervention with very limited information about the situation prior to intervention. For example, we might want to know whether the new after-school recreation program for boys has helped them stay out of neighborhood gangs. We can show that fully 90 percent of the boys who participated never became involved in gangs, clearly a positive figure. But without a baseline to show the percentage of boys who became involved with gangs before the program was initiated, we cannot say with certainty that the recreation program worked. This design is often called a "B" design since we have only the post-intervention data from which to draw our conclusions.

Sometimes, we simply want to know program participants' perceptions. One of the most frequently used evaluation designs for this purpose is the *Client Satisfaction Survey*. These surveys gather opinions of those who used a service to determine clients' degree of satisfaction about such things as accessibility of services, fairness of policies and procedures, and what components of a program are viewed most favorably. A primary drawback of this design is that it measures only perceptions rather than actual changes in behavior. The fact that clients liked a program does not, ipso facto, mean that it was effective. The surveys can be used, however, to compare changes in perception over time if a baseline of previous survey results is available. Thus, the surveys can be used in both A-B and B designs.

Goal Attainment Scaling attempts to monitor progress in a client system to determine whether attainable and desirable goals were achieved. This design allows clients and workers to see actual case progress and to assess both the type and percentage of goals that were achieved. Goal attainment scales are considered qualitative designs since the goals and their achievement are specified and assessed by the client and worker. Generally, this design has good face validity and good reliability, and it can be combined with other designs when appropriate. The principle value of this measure at the macro level is the ability to combine the results of multiple goal attainment evaluations to get an overall picture of program effectiveness across all clients served. Figure 10.4 shows a goal attainment scale used to evaluate the success of a neighborhood watch program.

Figure 10.4: Goal Attainment Scaling

Levels of Predicted Outcome   *Primary Objective*

Levels of Predicted Outcome	Primary Objective
Least favorable outcome	No reduction in home burglaries
Less than expected outcome	Reduction in home burglaries is below 33%
Expected level of success	Reduction in home burglaries is 33%-40%
More-than-expected level of success	Reduction in home burglaries 41%-50%
Most favorable outcome	Reduction in home burglaries above 51%

Another qualitative design is *Target Problem Scaling*. The principle behind this design is that a problem is carefully identified, intervention occurs, and the existence and degree of the problem are measured over some time period. By using repeated measurements, the worker is able to determine what changes are taking place with respect to the identified target problem. For example, if the problem is lack of park facilities in a community, the results of a community-wide drive to develop parks could be assessed across several months or years.

We use *case studies* when we want to know a great deal about a single case or a small group. Using the earlier example, we might want to know, for example, why the 10 percent of boys who ended up in gangs did not benefit from our after-school recreation program. We would probably use unstructured interviews to find out what factors made the program less effective for this group. Depending upon the participants' answers, we might need to ask additional follow-up questions. The case study might also consider such demographic data as age, race, or other factors.

Group comparisons are designs that compare two or more groups (such as a "treatment" and a "control" group). It can also be used to compare different interventions used on different groups. Group comparisons may be either of the post-only or pre-post design. We might like to measure how two groups of at-risk children differ in terms of drug usage. One group may have received an education-focused intervention while the other participated in an activity program designed to strengthen their involvement with their parents. With quasi-experimental designs such as group comparisons, we never know for certain that the intervention produced the observed change. Without random assignment of members to the intervention group we cannot rule out other explanations for the outcome.

Quality Assurance Reviews focus on ensuring a uniform quality of service in an agency or organization. The quality assurance review is typically a comparison of actual agency operation to a standard of performance. For example, an agency policy may require that each referral be followed up within 24 hours. A quality assurance review will verify whether this standard of service is being maintained. Similarly, regulations or policies may require that each case file contain a plan for service and a record of worker contacts. These items can be assessed during a quality assurance review. This type of evaluation design can be done on an ongoing basis or when problems arise. As noted, the purpose of the review is to help the organization determine if its own standards are being maintained.

As you can see, each of the evaluation designs described above helps us monitor and evaluate our interventions. Some are focused on process and others on outcomes. Each differs in its degree of rigor and selection is based upon the purpose and capabilities of the design.

Exercise 10.6: Designing an Evaluation Program

For each of the scenarios described below, discuss how you would evaluate the program.

A: *Evaluating Hospital Discharge Planning:* You are the Director of Social Services at Our Lady of Perpetual Misery Hospital. Your unit is primarily involved in doing discharge planning, with three BSW social workers assigned to this function. Discharge planning involves working with the hospital medical staff to facilitate patients' transition following discharge. Typically, your unit helps clients return to their own homes, go to nursing homes for temporary care or on a permanent basis, or go to live with relatives. Your unit uses a variety of community services including transportation, medical equipment for use in the home, visiting nurses, home health care, and similar services. The hospital administrator has asked all directors to begin to consider how they might evaluate the effectiveness of their units. You want to develop an evaluation program that can be done with existing staff, does not intrude on your work with patients, and is relatively simple to implement. Explain the methods you will use to evaluate your unit's effectiveness.

B: ***Evaluation of a Hospice Care Program:*** Your hospice program has been funded by the county for its first year of operation. As a condition of continued funding, you must develop an evaluation component that will allow the funding source to determine whether to continue your program next year. Patients come to you from area hospitals, nursing homes, and from their own homes. All are suffering from terminal illnesses ranging from AIDS to cancer to other life-ending diseases. Your hospice provides services to in-patients and to people in their own homes. Your evaluation plan should provide the county with data to justify your continued funding.

C: ***Evaluating an Assertiveness Training Group:*** Your agency operates assertiveness training groups for women who are survivors of domestic violence. Each group lasts four weeks and consists of 6-8 women per group. You lead this group and are curious about whether members really become more assertive after leaving the group. Design an evaluation system that would help you answer this question.

D: *Evaluating a Neighborhood Watch Program:* You have helped the Green Oak neighborhood develop a neighborhood watch program to combat the many burglaries and auto thefts suffered by area residents. The police department was very cooperative in helping you establish this program, but your agency director isn't convinced that these kinds of programs are worthwhile. He questions why you spend your time on such activities. How would you design an evaluation program to show whether this type of program is effective in reducing crime?

Stages in Evaluation

Like the problem-solving process, conducting an evaluation consists of specific steps. The most rigorous evaluations require you to think about what will be needed before you begin the intervention or program. Finding out afterward that you should have kept certain records can doom you to a substandard evaluation.

The first stage in evaluation is *conceptualization* and *goal setting*. You would not begin an intervention until you had considered where you were going and what you hoped to accomplish. The same is true in an evaluation. A goal is an observable outcome that will occur as a result of our efforts. If an agency's goal is to serve ten new low-income clients each month, the outcome is easily measured. If the goal is to develop a transition facility to house families moving from the homeless shelter to independent living, evaluation is easy. Either the facility has been developed or it has not. The more clearly specified and articulated the goals, the more readily they can be assessed. Ideally, some sort of feedback or management information system will be in place to record data on goal achievement. Let's say we wanted to determine what percentage of clients successfully completed the agency's outpatient drug treatment program. Agency records should give us this information, but if those records are not kept or are not accurate, we'll have a problem. If records don't detail each worker contact with a client, we can't determine whether the agency's goal of prompt service is being achieved.

The second stage of evaluation is *measurement*—identifying the measures to be used in the evaluation, such as worker records, other agency or organization data, results of surveys undertaken specifically for this evaluation, etc. We might want to measure the number of clients seen by a worker, the number of reports of elder abuse, or the number of homes receiving energy reduction treatments such as insulation and storm windows. We must decide what data to collect and how to collect it. It is critical that the data we collect be appropriate to the research question we want to answer. Program records provide some information, but other data must be acquired elsewhere—through case studies or client interviews, for instance.

In the next stage, *sampling*, we must decide whether to include the total client population or create a subset (sample). Gathering data for an entire population can be expensive and unnecessary if the population is sufficiently large and rigorous sampling procedures are followed. The size of the sample we use is generally a function of the size of the population: A large population may allow a sample size as low as 10 percent while a smaller population may require a 50 percent sample. Once the decision is made to use a subset of the population, several types of sampling are available. We have already discussed random sampling, in which every member of the population has an equal chance of being included. A modification of the random sample, the *systematic random sample*, allows us to simply divide the population by the desired sample size and select every *n*th client for inclusion in the research. Absent any naturally occurring bias (such as every tenth person just happening to be a woman), this approach offers most of the benefits of a random sample. Sometimes, however, random samples can cause problems. If your agency wants to know whether outcomes for gay men and lesbian women served by the agency are different from those of straight men and women receiving the same help, a typical random sample of clients served might not include any gay men or lesbian women at all because they constitute a very small portion of the entire client pool. The solution is the *stratified random sample*. Using this method, you divide your population into two groups, gays and straights, and assign numbers to all members of each group. If 5 percent of your population is composed of gay men and lesbian women, you select 5 percent of your sample from this group and 95 percent from the other group. Random sampling will predict with some accuracy whether the results found in the sample are typical for the population.

The fourth stage of the evaluation process is *design*. The goals of this stage are to select an appropriate design and to rule out other possible explanations for our findings. For example, without a comparison group or control group, we might erroneously conclude that our new first offender diversion program is ineffective because only 50 percent of the participants stayed out of trouble. With a control group, we might discover that our 50 percent success rate is twice that of first offenders not receiving the intervention. The design stage also helps us eliminate other problems. Research results can be called into question when the success of a program appears to be the result of factors such as the developmental maturation of participants or the fact that only the most promising clients were selected for inclusion.

The fifth stage of the research process is *data gathering*. Sources of data can include observations by the worker, client, or others in the environment; written survey results; official records (such as census or agency records); and case notes. Data may include opinions, test scores, and ratings completed by workers, clients, or others.

The sixth stage is *data analysis,* the process of reviewing the nature and significance of the data you have gathered. If the goal is to determine how many clients' files are marked, "closed, improved," simply count them. Data analysis can be simple if we report only means or modes (such as the average income of clients before and after receiving job training services). Other levels of analysis involve two or more variables. Computers are frequently needed to analyze such findings.

The final stage in designing an evaluation is *presentation of the data*. Data analysis provides results, but they are only as useful as the presentation method employed. The intended audience for your evaluation determines how your report is constructed. Clarity is critical. A single-page executive summary of the results should be included identifying the most important findings, though the report itself typically contains several sections including an introduction, literature review, methodology, results, discussion, references, and appendices.

Exercise 10.7: Sample or Population?

Read the following case example and propose a sampling method:

Your dispute resolution agency helps community residents involved in disagreements by providing a mediator to help work out their differences. The agency has assisted in this manner with custody disputes, landlord-tenant issues, and employer-employee disagreements. You serve about 250 people per year, including members of the community's small Latino population. You wish to learn the opinions of those who have used your service during the past year and are especially interested in how Latinos see your agency. You decide to use a client satisfaction survey to gather this information. Indicate whether you would select a sample of your potential population or survey everyone who used your service. Give your reasons for this decision.

226

Next to each evaluation stage listed below, write the letter of the activity that belongs at that stage:

Stage		Activity
1. Conceptualization/goal setting	a.	Preparation of written report on findings
2. Measurement	b.	Collecting information on outcomes from client records
3. Sampling		
4. Design	c.	Specification of outcome
5. Data gathering	d.	Reviewing the nature and significance of information acquired from various sources
6. Data analysis		
7. Presentation of data	e.	Deciding how information will be gathered
	f.	Deciding whether to include all clients or a subset of them

Ethics and Values in Evaluation

The principles of ethical research suggest several general rules:

- First, participants must have the right of self-determination and the right not to participate.
- Second, risks to participants should be described honestly. No harm must come to participants who participate or choose not to participate.
- Third, confidentiality is maintained as scrupulously as in practice.
- Finally, recognize that there may be clashes between the implications of our research findings and our desire to help others. If the results of our research show that a program is not efficient and/or effective we must accept the fact and move on. A generalist social worker should not fail to be guided by research.

You are part of a community-school task force focused on identifying adolescents at risk of dropping out of school. To get a better estimate of the incidence of behaviors which might place adolescents at greater risk of dropping out, Horace, a member of the task force, proposes that the group survey all junior high students. He suggests that the students be told they will be anonymous but suggests the surveys should be coded in such a way that the task force can later identify the most at-risk respondents. With this information in hand, school social workers, guidance counselors, and others can begin to work with each of these youngsters. Evaluate this proposal, then state and explain your reactions.

Social workers are well aware that certain population groups are at risk of being disadvantaged in our society. These at-risk groups experience social and economic injustices that require social work interventions. Typical macro interventions include social action, advocacy, and empowerment. The effective generalist practitioner must clearly understand two things:

1. The nature of the risk faced by certain groups.
2. The knowledge and skills needed to ensure social and economic justice for these groups.

This chapter will:
*   Define key concepts important to macro practice
*   Review macro strategies of advocacy, social action, and empowerment
*   Discuss what places a population at risk and give examples
*   Describe the social worker's role with populations-at-risk
*   Discuss advocacy, its use and principles
*   Consider legislative advocacy and the social work role
*   Review social action
*   Discuss empowerment

Key Concepts in Macro Practice

In social work, *advocacy* means representing, championing, or otherwise defending the rights of others. It is a normal part of social work practice and may include either case advocacy or cause advocacy. As the title implies, case advocacy is advocating for individuals or families, and arises in micro practice situations. Workers, however, often find many client systems with similar problems. For example, you are advocating at the micro level for Mrs. Lopez whose children are being taunted on the playground about their ethnicity. In the process, you discover that many children of Hispanic descent are experiencing the same harassment. When multiple client systems share a similar problem, cause advocacy is an appropriate response. As a cause advocate the worker represents and works on behalf of groups of people rather than individuals.

Much early social work was based on cause advocacy as practitioners fought for civil rights, better housing and health care, and educational opportunities for various populations-at-risk. The underlying assumption is that helping individuals one by one is less efficient than working on behalf of an entire group that shares a similar problem.

Social action, another avenue for the generalist practitioner, is "a coordinated effort to achieve institutional change to meet a need, solve a social problem, correct an injustice, or enhance the quality of human life" (Barker, 1999, p.446). Social action may be employed by social workers as well as by other professionals, agencies, and organizations. For example, a group of local churches in a violence-threatened city combined their efforts to curtail drive-by shootings and drug sales in residential neighborhoods. They organized several hundred people to march on a notorious crack house. The march produced new commitments by area officials to deal with criminal behavior in the community. The ability to combine the resources of many churches immeasurably increased the influence that any single religious organization could have had. Such coordination is important to the success of social action.

Empowerment is based on the social work principle of self-determination: Empowered people can exercise their ability to achieve their own goals. Empowerment is the use of strategies that increase the personal, interpersonal, or political power of people so that they can improve their own life situations. Empowerment is achieved when social workers find ways to enhance the natural rights, skills, and competencies of clients. It does *not* mean that social workers give power to the client system. The power already belongs to the client system, inherent in self-determination and basic constitutional rights to life, liberty, and the pursuit of happiness. The social worker simply finds ways to encourage client systems to recognize, increase, and use more effectively the power they already possess. *Populations-at-risk* are groups likely to suffer the consequences of, or be at risk of, discrimination, economic hardship, and oppression (such as women, lesbian and gay people, and persons of color). These groups have historically suffered discrimination and social and economic injustice. At the same time, other factors can put a population at-risk. People with disabilities, people with different religious or political views, and others with little or no power in our society can be at risk.

Exercise 11.1: Recalling Key Concepts

Miguel Gonzales is a social worker with A Family Affair, a counseling service for couples and families. During one of his sessions with the Chou Vang family, recent immigrants from Southeast Asia, he learns that the Vang children have been prevented from using the community swimming pool. According to Mrs. Vang, one of the lifeguards has called her children names and said they should go back to their own country. Miguel offers to help the family deal with this situation and agrees to talk to the city's recreation director who oversees the pool. Using the information given you, answer each of the following queries.

1. Is Miguel engaged in cause advocacy or case advocacy as he seeks to help the Vang family? Explain your answer.

Miguel discovers that the director of recreation believes that the Vang children and other Hmong refugees should not be using the pool because they are not yet U.S. citizens. Miguel decides to challenge the director's decision by enlisting the help of the local Urban League. Together, they picket the swimming pool and invite the media to cover the event.

2. Does Miguel's strategy fall under the classification of social action? Why or why not?

3.   What would be needed to empower the Vang family to solve this problem by themselves?

4.   Do you consider the Vang family a population-at-risk? Explain your answer.

What Puts a Population at Risk?

Factors that help put a population at risk include physical differences, values and beliefs at variance with other dominant groups in society, and economic conditions. Some populations are at risk because they look, act, or believe differently from the majority, and this difference makes the majority uncomfortable or fearful. This reaction may be based on ignorance or on lack of experience with the at-risk group, so it can often be ameliorated by increasing contact between groups.

When a population is at risk because its members do not hold the same beliefs as the rest of society, the situation can be more difficult to remedy. People who misquote or misuse the bible to define homosexuality as sinful justify their discrimination toward and oppression of gay men and lesbian women. Unrealistic fears about homosexuals in the armed forces are also based on views that highlight differences rather than commonalities.

A group's economic condition also can place it at risk. People of marginal economic standing tend to be less valued in a capitalist society, but economic marginality may be created by institutional behaviors. For example, both government policy and economic goals led to such atrocities as the banishment of Native Americans from their lands and efforts to exterminate tribes and their traditions. The land was considered more valuable than its owners. African Americans were enslaved for economic purposes. Asian Americans were prevented from owning land and discouraged from immigrating here for both social and economic reasons. Finally, women were denied the right to vote and otherwise participate in the political process in part because they were not an economic force in society.

Today, clients receiving public assistance are similarly perceived as economically insignificant except as a drain on tax dollars. This places them at risk. When employers hire two part-time workers rather than one full-time employee to avoid paying such mandatory benefits as health insurance or retirement pensions, they increase the risk to these individuals.

Common Populations-at-Risk

According to Ginsberg, (1992) the groups described below are some of the most-at-risk.

African Americans, for example, have infant mortality rates 80 percent higher than whites. Black males are seven times as likely to die from homicide as white males. Blacks are arrested more frequently for criminal behavior and comprise about one-half of the U.S. prison population, well beyond their representation in the general population. They routinely experience discrimination in employment, education, and other areas of opportunity, nondiscrimination laws and affirmative action policies notwithstanding.

Hispanics (Latinos) are also at risk. They comprise over 25 percent of those in federal prisons, and Hispanic juveniles are being incarcerated at a greater rate than youngsters from other ethnic groups. Trends indicate that Hispanics are moving increasingly to one-parent household status and are less likely to have completed college than either African Americans or whites. Recent efforts to reduce or eliminate welfare benefits for immigrant groups are also affecting Hispanics disproportionately.

Some of the most serious social and health problems in the United States are faced by *Native Americans* and *Alaskan Natives*. Both groups suffer a higher than average incidence of death from causes ranging from cancer to accidents and suicide. In fact, deaths from alcoholism and tuberculosis are five to seven times as high among these groups as among whites.

Asian Americans have often been called the model minority because many of them have made great strides in pursuing education and economic success. However, what is true of many Chinese and Japanese, is not true for other groups from Southeast Asia. Those who came to the United States after the end of the Vietnam War arrived with few language skills, an agrarian background, and values and behaviors at odds with those of Western society. Their customs sometimes clash with those of whites or African Americans, and they may be seen as rivals for certain types of employment.

Women have always experienced conditions that place them at risk. Early debates about whether women should be able to vote have been supplanted by arguments over a woman's right to control her own body. Women are the primary victims of sexual harassment in the workplace and domestic violence in the home. They receive lower pay for the same jobs, discrimination in certain types of employment, and stereotypes about their performance on the job.

Gay men and lesbians constitute another group at risk. Legal barriers to certain jobs, discrimination in areas as diverse as insurance coverage and child custody, and homophobia constitute just some of the problems facing this group. The anti-homosexual religious and political agendas of some groups represent a major threat to the ability of gay men and lesbians to enjoy the same rights and opportunities available to the rest of our society.

232

1.　　Think about the place where you grew up. List any groups living in your community that you would classify as at-risk and give a brief explanation of why you listed them.

2.　　Now think about where you are living today. List any groups in your present community that you would classify as at-risk. Again, give your reasons.

3.　　Is every member of these groups at risk? Explain your answer.

What Is the Role of Social Workers with Populations-at-Risk?
　　　The social work profession is both aware of and well placed to help populations-at-risk. Social workers are likely to witness the devastation caused by prejudice and discrimination. Social workers are aware that institutions such as social agencies can be guilty of insensitivity, poor planning, and outright discrimination against these groups. Agencies purporting to serve an entire community, for example, should be evaluated based on this claim. If an agency fails to live up to its claim, its own workers should pursue remedial action. A community that fails to address problems facing a particular group can also be the target of an appropriate intervention.
　　　Social workers have the skills to help bring about macro system change by preventing conditions that place populations at risk and by advocating on their behalf. This can be done by

closely monitoring what goes on in your agency, community, and state—keeping your eyes and ears open, reading the newspaper, attending community forums and public meetings, and looking for evidence of problems. Of course, you don't have to wait for a problem to arise. If you see a change opportunity that will improve the quality of life of populations-at-risk, determine how you might intervene.

Exercise 11.3: Keeping Your Eyes Open

1.   Read your local newspaper for three days. Look for examples of populations-at-risk and the problems they are experiencing. Describe the groups you found in the paper and briefly summarize their problems.

2.   Look in your community newspaper for an interesting article about a human service-related program.

      A.   In what ways, if any, does the article discuss the program's services to populations-at-risk?

B.   What services are provided?

Advocacy

Social workers have long used advocacy to bring about large-scale change in organizations and communities. Advocacy is clearly consistent with the values of the profession, especially those that support the basic worth and dignity of people and their rights to make their own decisions. In fact, advocacy has been the primary road to achieving civil rights for people of color, those with mental illness, and others with various physical and mental disabilities. Advocacy won minorities and women the right to vote, and it is needed today to ensure that those who have this right exercise it.   Of course, advocacy is difficult when economic times are tough. New and expensive programs are usually viewed with skepticism when money is tight.

Exercise 11.4: Assessing Your Experience as an Advocate

In the past you've probably come across situations when it was necessary to advocate for yourself or others.

A.   Describe one such situation you encountered and list the actions you took.

B.   If you took no action, what considerations led you to decide *not* to act?

C.   What was the eventual outcome?

235

D.   Looking back, what do you think you could have done to increase your effectiveness?

Agency Commitment to Advocacy

Not every social work agency is committed to advocacy. Domestic violence shelters are often at the forefront of efforts to protect and enhance the lives of their clients, but other types of agencies have little or no such commitment. Some organizations engage in modest efforts to expand their services to underserved populations, but others do not even inform existing clients about available services. Without an agency commitment to change, it is very difficult—though not impossible—for an individual worker to undertake large-scale efforts. In such cases, your sanction and motivation for advocacy must stem from your own professional values rather than from agency support.

Exercise 11.5: Organizational Commitment to Advocacy

Identify one organization with which you are familiar that appears committed to advocacy. What does this organization do that makes you believe it supports advocacy?

Identifying Opportunities for Macro-level Advocacy

Opportunities for advocacy are virtually endless. They include extending services to underserved populations, placing clients on the agency's board of directors, hiring staff from populations-at-risk, or changing agency policies that do not support social work values. Public information and education can help combat stereotypes and overcome irrational fears (such as the fear that talking about sex or homosexuality will actually produce sexually active teens or gay men and lesbians). Legal advocacy may be appropriate when legislation is needed to enhance or protect the rights of groups victimized by discrimination.

Identify one situation which you perceive as an opportunity for macro-level advocacy. Explain why you think this situation represents (1) a problem and (2) an opportunity for advocacy.

Principles of Macro-level Advocacy

The first principle of macro-level advocacy is that it should be designed to increase the accessibility of services to clients. This requires that we look not only at *whether* we serve a population but at *how well* we do so. Offering services that are physically inaccessible, tangled in red tape, or beyond the client's capability to pay denies access.

A second principle is that we advocate for services that enhance and do not detract from people's dignity. Many clients find the conditions and treatment they experience in seeking help humiliating and degrading. Lack of privacy, insensitive treatment by staff, and similar problems undercut efforts to help.

The third principle of advocacy is that it should be aimed at developing services that are available to all who are eligible. Services that assist only one group or that ignore or downplay others' needs should be re-evaluated.

237

1.   What kinds of conditions or treatment do you define as humiliating, degrading, or damaging to a person's dignity?

2.   Can you think of an experience in which *you* were treated this way? Describe the situation and how you felt at the time.

Guidelines for Macro-level Advocacy

The principles above provide useful direction but they are insufficient to guide the pursuit of macro-level advocacy. Several guidelines can help improve your chances of success in macro advocacy.

- First, be reasonable in what you undertake. Changing an organization often means challenging the beliefs, values, assumptions, or behaviors of those who make up the organization. This can be daunting especially when there is much that needs to be changed. It is usually best to focus on the most achievable objectives and postpone the greater challenges. For example, if you advocate that the agency stay open one evening a week to serve clients who work during the day, you are less likely to meet resistance than if you suggest the agency should stay open until 10:00 p.m. Monday through Friday.

- Second, use teamwork whenever possible. Working in teams takes advantage of the expertise and energies of different groups and agencies, thus maximizing the resources directed at a problem. One person working alone can achieve great things, but a group can usually advocate more effectively than a single person.

- Third, recognize that advocacy sometimes requires being assertive. This can be unpleasant, because most of us want to be liked. Constant niceness, however, may require us to ignore very real problems. Being cooperative and ready to compromise may seem a sign of weakness in certain situations. Standing up for those without power is not likely to be popular, especially when you are asking people to change their behavior or to expend resources.

- Fourth, see flexibility as a strength, not a weakness. Sometimes it's best to accept half a loaf if that's all we can get this time around. Advocates must know when they have achieved the maximum benefit from an approach and be willing to change direction as needed.

- Fifth, remember that you win some and you lose some. Even the best advocates sometimes encounter too many barriers or decide that a given end does not justify the means needed to achieve it. Know when to "fold 'em."

- Finally, use a variety of strategies whenever possible. Have both adversarial and cooperative approaches at your disposal, and use them simultaneously or sequentially. If possible, use collaborative strategies first in order to achieve a win-win outcome for both parties. Be prepared, however, to use other advocacy approaches as needed.

Exercise 11.8: Understanding the Guidelines for Advocacy

Select any three of the six guidelines discussed in the section above. For each guideline, describe at least one situation in which it would be helpful to your advocacy efforts.

A.   Situation # 1:

B.   Situation #2:

Advocacy Tactics

Advocacy can include a number of approaches in the repertoire of the generalist social worker—persuasion, fair hearings, grievances and complaints, embarrassing the target, political pressure, and petitioning.

Persuasion is a matter of getting the target system to alter its decisions and/or actions in a way that reflects your goals. This can be accomplished in some cases simply by providing information, especially if the information is new to the target.   You can also persuade by questioning your adversaries in a way that forces them to rethink previous positions or decisions. Persuasion is quite effective if you can articulate the arguments on both sides of an issue, because that forces you to anticipate an opponent's arguments and prepare appropriate counterarguments. Persuasion is enhanced by persistence: Persistent people don't forget promises that were made. They follow up to see that what was promised was delivered. What's more, they don't give up when confronted with a setback or when an issue is not quickly resolved.

Fair hearings are administrative procedures available to those who believe they have been denied a benefit or right. Most agencies that receive federal or state money have fair hearing processes in place to consider the appeals of those who have been refused assistance. An outside evaluator (fair hearing examiner) is brought in to hear arguments on both sides. The examiner's decision can uphold either the agency decision or the petitioner's position.

Grievances and *complaints* also challenge decisions made by administrators and others. Grievance and complaint procedures may be outlined in agency policies, union contracts, or laws governing the organization. For example, denial of either civil rights or rights of people with physical disabilities can be met with a complaint filed with state or federal agencies. Sometimes the mere threat of filing such a complaint will force decision-makers to reconsider their positions.

Embarrassing the target is another effective tactic. An advocate can point out in a public forum that the decision-maker's actions are not consistent with previously expressed intentions. In effect, the advocate holds the target up to public ridicule, sometimes by calling media attention to a problem. Letters to newspapers, picket lines, and press releases can all embarrass a target.

Political pressure can also force necessary changes, especially if the advocate is dealing with tax-supported (public) organizations and or people in political office. In some cases, political office holders themselves can be persuaded to intervene and pressure a public agency to change its policy or practice. Since public organizations draw most of their support from tax money, petitioning (collecting signatures on a form asking an organization, agency, or individual to act in some specified manner) can be effective. Petitions have been used by city residents to oppose massage parlors, request changes in the way property taxes are computed, and demand better police protection. Signatures on petitions can be gathered by going door-to-door or by soliciting them in public spaces such as shopping centers. While petitions are relatively easy to use, their impact on the target system may be less noticeable. To enhance their effectiveness,

There is nothing magical about legislative advocacy. Legislators are responsible to those who elected them and must stand for election on a regular basis. Thus, they are interested in the views of those they represent. At the same time, legislators often have inadequate information on which to base their decisions. If they never hear from their constituents and the only views expressed to them come from professional lobbyists, who is to blame if we disapprove of their votes? (Many lobbyists work for organizations whose agendas we agree with and even support, but they may nevertheless be unaware of their legislation's effects on our clients.) Bills are sometimes so complex that even legislators don't understand all aspects of a proposed law. The need to supply legislators with important information is a major point of access for social workers. It is well known that legislators are often influenced by a handful of letters about a bill. Some legislators are reputed to count the letters they receive on each side of an issue and use this information to determine how to vote. Let your legislator know what you think about a bill. Enlist colleagues or clients to share their opinions. Clients, the ones directly affected by a bill, are too often the last ones to know about it and are unlikely to contact lawmakers. Don't ignore this potential source of support.

Skills needed for legislative advocacy include sensitivity and awareness of the factors that affect the legislative process: What will it cost to implement a bill? How popular is it with the public? Bills that benefit obscure groups or are expensive are less likely to find legislative support. A bill that requires authorities to notify neighbors if a convicted child sex offender moves into the neighborhood is more likely to pass than one that provides expensive treatment for the offender.

Once a bill has been drafted, become an expert on it. Find out who has taken or is likely to take a stand on the bill, how much implementation of the bill will cost, and what advantages or disadvantages passage will have for your clients. Identifying, obtaining, and maintaining sponsors for a bill is the next step, and you need to know whom to contact for support.

List those supporting your bill, those opposed, and those who are neutral to the idea. Both neutral legislators and opponents can be persuaded, so don't ignore them. Recognize that support for a bill may come from outside the legislature. Professional organizations such as NASW, social service providers, and other community groups may support (or oppose) a given piece of legislation, and these groups may employ lobbyists who are familiar with both the process and the legislators. In addition, the governor or president and the various federal or state agencies affected by the bill may be actively working for or against its passage.

Lobbying for passage of the bill can include writing, telephoning, e-mailing, telegraphing, or speaking directly to legislators or their staffs. Try to work with other interest groups who support the law.

Educating the public is another facet of legislative advocacy. While the public is not interested in many bills, the perspectives of the average citizen should not be ignored. Opposition to certain bills can be increased, especially when the general public has strong views that are not being heeded by their legislators. Public support for bills can be garnered if people know about a proposed law and are helped to express their opinions. For example, a social worker could stimulate public awareness of a bill by writing letters to the newspapers, holding public meetings to discuss a topic, and, if appropriate, going door-to-door with leaflets that provide additional information. One social worker who was concerned about proposed welfare reform legislation pending in the state legislature, spoke on the topic at the public library. He and his colleagues advertised the meeting by word of mouth and by posting flyers in area churches and restaurants. Those who attended learned much more about the welfare reform proposals, had an opportunity to share their views, and left with additional written information including the names, addresses, and phone numbers of their elected representatives.

Influencing legislative committees is crucial. These bodies discuss, often modify, and hopefully act on the bill. A favorable decision by the committee or subcommittee means that a bill will be sent to the entire body for a debate and a vote. Of course, a committee can decide to kill a bill by voting against it or by simply not getting around to discussing it.

If you write to your legislators, use the correct form and address for such letters. Some common addresses and the accompanying salutations appear below:

Letters to the president:
    The President
    The White House
    1600 Pennsylvania Ave., NW
    Washington, DC 20500
Salutation: Dear Mr./Ms. President:

Letters to U.S. Senators:
    The Honorable (insert full name)
    United States Senate
    Washington, DC 20510
Salutation: Dear Senator (insert last name):

Letters to members of the House of Representatives:
    The Honorable (insert full name)
    U.S. House of Representatives
    Washington, DC 20515
Salutation: Dear Representative (insert last name):

A current list of your elected representatives at all levels from local to national can be found at most public libraries or by checking with city hall. If possible, open your letter by telling the official that you are pleased with some action they have taken. Starting on a positive note is more persuasive than berating the person for disappointing you. State your purpose clearly and explain precisely what you would like the recipient to do. Give reasons for your position and request. Be polite and respectful of the person's position even if you disagree 100 percent with all of that person's decisions. Always thank legislators or executives for considering your views and invite them to share with you their perspectives.

Exercise 11.10: Advocating with Legislators

1.   Give two reasons why legislators are interested in the views of their constituents.

2.   Respond to Jack, another social worker, who says that the proposed new licensing bill for social workers is so well written that there is no need for any amendments. He argues that your coalition of social work groups should convey this message to the bill's sponsor. How would you respond to Jack?

3.   Your friend Melanie is very unhappy about the new welfare bill going through your state legislature. She confides to you that she is writing a letter to the President really blasting this bill. What would you say to Melanie?

4.   Write a letter to your U.S. Senator, Mortimer Snerd, asking him to support changes to the welfare bill that would provide two full years of child care for every client going off public assistance and taking a job that pays less than $9 per hour. Senator Snerd is an influential member of the senate public welfare committee currently considering the bill. Suggest changes and present your arguments. Keep your letter under one page in length.

Social Action

Social action, as defined earlier, typically involves more difficult, complex, and confrontational approaches to problem solving. It may be used in combination with advocacy or when more collaborative efforts fail. Because of its more confrontational aspects, social action raises ethical issues and differences of opinion.

One of the more militant approaches to social action was formulated by Saul Alinsky (1971). Alinsky believed deeply in the concept of power as a key to social change. Only those with power are in a position to control their environment. Power may come from money or from people (because when enough people support an idea, they have power). Alinsky's strategy was to acquire power by organizing people in their own interests. He also argued that sometimes the illusion of power is enough, since it is the appearance of power that matters. Thus, it can be important for others to think that you have more power than you actually do.

According to Alinsky, power is not given to people but is acquired when they take it from those who have it. He believed that people with power do not give it up willingly, and therefore the more confrontational aspects of social action are necessary. Alinsky observed that all organizations have rule—policies, laws, or other regulations—by which they *say* they abide. He taught that by making organizations operate in accordance with their own rules, an activist could ensure fairness and improve the quality of services provided. He achieved his goal by embarrassing the target—by showing that people were not following their own rules. Another Alinsky rule was to organize around issues that are vital to people. If an issue is not considered very important, it is not a suitable cause for social action. He also firmly believed in using political pressure to create change.

Perhaps the most controversial Alinksy rule was to paint the issues as a conflict between good and evil, or the haves and the have-nots, thus positioning yourself as moral and good and suggesting that your opponent is immoral and bad. The final Alinsky suggestion is to propose an alternative. It is not sufficient to simply complain—you must suggest a better way of doing things.

Concerns about Social Action

More recent writers have suggested that Alinsky's ideas are somewhat dated (Zippay, 1994). Zippay notes that enemies are harder to identify today, situations are more complex, and technology and media are more influential than they were 30 years ago. Community problems can rarely be solved solely by local resources. External resources are needed in many situations because cash-strapped communities lack the ability to create massive programs. Zippay urges working collaboratively with business and civic leaders to bring about change. Skills such as fund-raising, lobbying, legislative advocacy, and the ability to work with local groups are the route to successful social action.

1. Saul Alinsky believed that power and the appearance of power are critical elements to the success of social action. Do you agree or disagree with his perspective? Give your reasons.

2. Another Alinsky rule was that you always paint issues as a conflict between good and evil or the haves and have-nots. Do you agree with this argument in a current context? Give your reasons.

Legal Action

Legal action involves using the court system to resolve issues or to force changes that otherwise would not occur. Recent history shows the influence of legal action on a number of issues from a woman's right to an abortion to the now discredited "separate but equal" school system. Similarly, Native Americans have used the court system to force restoration of tribal lands stolen many years ago. Courts are also the place where those who refuse to obey the law are called to task. For example, those who discriminate against protected classes or people with disabilities may find themselves in court. Courts are used to force obedience to specific laws, to requirements of the U.S. Constitution (such as due process), or to settle disputes of a contractual nature. The civil courts provide an alternative to criminal courts in some cases, and the class action suit is a frequently used tool in civil court. This type of suit argues that an entire group of people has been harmed. For example, women paid lower wages by an employer may file suit charging sex discrimination and naming all women employees (past and present) as part of the class seeking the court's help. Courts can also be used to challenge a law that you believe is unconstitutional or overly vague (and therefore unenforceable).

Sometimes, courts are used to force organizations to obey their own rules and policies. For example, an agency might be taken to court for firing a worker without letting him know why. If the agency policies require that workers be given the opportunity to correct poor performance, the court may find that the organization has failed to live up to its own rules.

Even the threat of using the courts to settle disputes or create change can prove effective. The expense, bother, and embarrassment of going to court are often sufficient to bring the other side to the bargaining table. Finding that the courts can be used to help achieve group goals can be very empowering. Generally speaking, courts are less susceptible to the political process than are other elected officials, so they are unlikely to be swayed by phone calls, letters, contributions, and other means that might persuade other political leaders. This can be both an advantage and a disadvantage. On the one hand, the decision of the court will be based as much as possible on legal issues, and your opponent will be less able to use political clout. On the other hand, you also lose the ability to influence the judge.

A very real disadvantage to using the courts is the time involved. Court decisions may not come for several months or years. Of course, if your group benefits from the delay the time issue may be moot. You may be able to use the time to get a law changed or to force your opponent to expend more resources. Residents of the City of Yarg were opposed to the newly proposed nuclear power plant to be built on the edge of the community. Not only would it consume a sizeable chunk of lake-front property known for its scenic beauty, but many residents were opposed to nuclear power for environmental reasons and out of ordinary fear. Residents and environmentalists together went to court to block construction of the power plant citing several federal laws as the basis for their lawsuit. The court case took so long to resolve that the electric power company scrapped the project. The time delay had added unacceptable costs to the project and the company suffered a black eye in public opinion because of all the publicity. In addition, new regulations on nuclear power had been developed while the case dragged on and greater attention was focused on the problem of disposing of nuclear waste.

Another potential disadvantage to using the courts is the cost. Attorney fees can mount up quickly for both sides, and it is not always possible to get attorneys who will work pro bono (free). On the other hand, your opponent is also going to have to pay for an attorney.

Using the courts is very confrontational and can label you a troublemaker, but if you are certain this is the most effective means at your disposal, don't be intimidated.

Exercise 11.12: Taking Legal Action

1.

    A.   Identify at least one social issue that has been affected by court decisions in your lifetime.

B.   Specify the court decisions that were made.

C.   What is your opinion about each decision?

2.   Assess the advantages and disadvantages of using the legal system to bring about social change.

Empowerment

We indicated earlier that using the court system can be an empowering experience, especially for those who are typically powerless in society. Empowerment, as Hartman (1993, p. 365) notes, is "the right to power, ability, and authority to achieve self-determination." Although empowerment is supported by social work values, practitioners cannot always achieve it in work with client systems. Those with less power in society are often the most in need of being empowered. There are many ways to empower clients. We can demystify what we do by explaining precisely how our agency works and what needs to be done, and by encouraging the client system to carry out tasks rather than doing it for them. Allowing client systems to make their own choices and keeping them informed of their options and their progress will increase their sense of power.

Group approaches to problem solving that emphasize collaboration are also potentially very empowering. Participating in a group creates a sense of connection, and finding that other people share one's problems and concerns lessens the sense of isolation. It also multiplies the energy, time, and other resources directed at a problem. Effective empowerment unlocks the natural ability of client systems to solve their own problems, use their unique skills and abilities, and make their own decisions.

Exercise 11.13: Arguing Empowerment

Sam Woodson, a worker in your agency has just come back from a workshop on empowerment. Grousing about the new emphasis on empowerment, he says, "It's really crazy, you know? There are *no ways* to empower our clients. For crying out loud, this is a *nursing home* and now the Director of Social Services wants us to empower our clients." You disagree with Sam. Offer at least two arguments and two examples of how it is possible to empower nursing home residents:

1.   Argument:

        Example:

2.   Argument:

        Example:

Practitioners always work within the greater macro contexts of the organization and the community. Consequently, the surrounding macro environment inevitably impacts their decisions about what to do, what not to do, what is right, and what is wrong. Public laws and agency policies regulate what practitioners are supposed to do and how they're supposed to do it, but what happens when you conclude that the right thing to do is in serious conflict with these laws and policies? What if the existing laws and policies ignore or don't allow for services your clients or other people need? What if you see colleagues, administrators, or community leaders doing things you consider unethical? This chapter deals with making ethical decisions within macro contexts, focusing on the decisions *you* must make when there is no absolutely clear *right* thing to do.

This chapter will:

- Explain the meanings of values, ethics, and ethical dilemmas in macro contexts
- Identify the core concepts in the National Association (NASW) Code of Ethics
- Address some selected principles in the NASW Code of Ethics
- Propose a seven-step model for making ethical decisions based on Loewenberg & Dolgoff's (1996) Ethical Principles Screen
- Suggest a range of ethical dilemmas commonly observed in macro contexts for you to analyze, discuss the application of ethical principles, and make recommendations for action

Professional Values and Ethics in Macro Contexts

Along with knowledge and skills, professional values comprise the foundation of generalist social work practice. Values are *beliefs* about what is good or desirable, and what is not. They require you to make judgments or decisions about relative worth—that is, what is more valuable and what is less valuable. Ethics, on the other hand, are *principles* that specify actions to uphold our values. They clarify what should and should not be done in practice. Values deal with beliefs and ethics with the application of those beliefs in actual situations. As you should know very well by now, social workers have a specific *Code of Ethics* based on professional values (National Association of Social Workers [NASW], 1996).

The Code of Ethics is based upon six core values that include:

1. Service: Providing assistance and resources to help people reach their potential.
2. Social Justice: Commitment to a society in which all people have the same rights, opportunities, and benefits.
3. Dignity and Worth of the Person: Belief that each person is to be valued and treated with dignity.
4. Importance of Human Relationships: Valuing the connections between social work and client as essential to creation and maintenance of a helping relationship.
5. Integrity: Commitment to honesty and trustworthiness.
6. Competence: Commitment to the necessary knowledge and skill to work effectively with clients.

The NASW *Code of Ethics* also addresses six aspects of professional responsibility. In other words, ethical guidelines for how to make decisions and practice social work are given in six general areas. These six areas include the social workers ethical responsibility to: clients, colleagues, in practice settings, as professionals, to the social work profession and to broader society (NASW, 1996). Most social work-related organizations have similar themes which underpin their ethical codes including the Canadian Association of Social Workers.

In effect, social workers have ethical responsibilities to clients, to colleagues, in practice settings, as professionals, to the social work profession, and to the broader society. Thus, social workers should make decisions that comply with the basic values and ethical principles identified above concerning any of these practice dimensions.

Social work practitioners often encounter ethical dilemmas, problematic situations in which ethical principles conflict and a decision must be made concerning the best or most ethical course of action. All possible solutions, in such cases, are imperfect or not fully satisfactory—otherwise it wouldn't be a dilemma. The potential variety of ethical dilemmas is endless, so we will arbitrarily select and address a range of macro practice ethical dilemmas that deal with specific aspects of the Code.

Ranking Ethical Principles to Solve Dilemmas

Loewenberg & Dolgoff (1996) propose a hierarchy of ethical principles with which to evaluate the potential courses of action possible in ethical dilemmas. A hierarchy is a ranked order, so a hierarchy of principles shows that one principle takes precedence over the ones below it. In other words, it is more important to abide by the first principle than by principles two through seven, by the second principle than by principles three through six, and so on. Thus, the Ethical Principles Screen, a prioritized list of seven ethical principles, is summarized in figure 12.1 (Loewenberg & Dolgoff, 1996, p. 63) and explained further below.

Figure 12.1: A Hierarchy of Ethical Rights*

Principle	*Ethical Right—People Have the Right to:*
1	Life
2	Equality
3	Autonomy
4	Least Harm
5	Quality of Life
6	Privacy
7	Truthfulness

*Adapted from Loewenberg & Dolgoff's (1996) "Ethical Principles Screen" (p. 63).

Principle #1: People have the right to **life**.

Therefore, when an ethical dilemma involves a life-or-death variable, you should choose the action that will save the life, even if this means breaking confidentiality with a client or interfering with the rights of others. For example, a health maintenance organization (HMO) might decide to stop covering drugs that keep patients with AIDS alive. A number of such patients are your agency's clients. Undertaking a macro change effort to change that policy would be ethical, because the patients' right to life takes precedence over the HMO's right to decide what medical costs it will cover.

Principle #2: People have the right to **equality**.

This means that people should be treated fairly and equally. A social worker should abide by this principle except in life-or-death cases. (That is, only, ethical principle #1 could take precedence.) Suppose your agency's food distribution program is not reaching everyone who is eligible, but the resource is limited so there is not enough for all. The people who *are* receiving food are by far the most needy. They depend on this food to live. Under most circumstances, you would act according to Principle #2—treat all people equally—by trying to expand the reach of the your surplus food program. In this case, however, doing that would deprive those already receiving food of their only means of survival—so Principle #1 would take precedence. Maybe you could increase the amount of food available to protect the lives of the most destitute and still offer fair and equal access to other needy people.

Principle #3: People have the right to **autonomy**.

People have the right to be free. Social work emphasizes the principle of self-determination—a person's basic right to make his or her own decisions. According to the Ethical Principles Screen, only people's right to survival and their right to equal treatment take precedence over their right to freedom.

Principle #4: People have the right to experience **least harm**.

People have the basic right to be protected from injury. If injury is unavoidable, they have the right to experience the least injury possible, the least lasting harm or injury, or "the most easily reversible harm" (Loewenberg & Dolgoff, 1996, p. 64). For example: A community decides to build a recreation center for its residents. Two properties are available for development. One is an open three-acre area used almost daily by community youth for sports activities. The other is an abandoned, run-down warehouse no one really cares about. Principle #4 suggests that the community should develop the warehouse property because that will have the least negative impact on community residents. Using it won't deprive the young people of their recreational area.

Principle #5: People have the right to a decent **quality of life**.

People have the right to seek and attain a "better quality of life" than they currently have (Loewenberg & Dolgoff, 1996, p. 64). This applies to individuals, groups, neighborhoods, communities, states, and nations. Only principles one through four take precedence over this right. Consider a county unit that offers job training for single mothers on public assistance. The program's stated intent is to help these women become self-sufficient and to improve their quality of life, so public assistance is discontinued when they complete the program. But what if the women can't get jobs at the end of the training program because such jobs don't exist? In that case discontinuing public assistance will interfere with the women's ability to survive, so according to Principle #1 the program should be discontinued.

Principle #6: People have the right to **privacy** and confidentiality.

People have the right to privacy and confidentiality, the right not to have their private information made public. Such information might include the names of clients, information that clients divulge, the professional beliefs and findings of the social worker, and anything the worker has written about a client.

Principle #7: People have the right to the **truth** and all relevant information.

People have the right to know the truth, which means they have the right to accurate information. It would be nice to get the truth and nothing but the truth all of the time. However, what if you are legally forbidden to disclose certain information to clients? Should you be forced to tell clients everything you think about them, even when your thoughts and ideas are negative? Must you always show people—including clients—all of your notes about them and the issues concerning them?

As you can see, ethical screens can be useful in helping resolve dilemmas. They allow you to weigh various considerations against one another before making a professional decision involving social work ethics.

Types of Ethical Issues Confronting Agency Workers

You may encounter ethical issues in any area of practice including direct service to clients, social and agency programs or policy, and interactions with other service providers. Each poses complex and difficult ethical challenges which you must resolve in order to practice ethical social work. The issues addressed below reflect a combination of these three areas. As we have established, ethical issues in direct practice do not occur in a vacuum but within organizational and community macro contexts. Social welfare policies and programs impose both responsibilities and constraints on your direct practice. Ethical issues involving colleagues are different from those involving client systems, regardless of whether the system is an individual, family, or group. Dealing with collegial and even administrative ethical issues requires a broader macro focus.

Exercise 12.1: Making Decisions about Limited Resources

Resources are consistently limited, and often appear to be shrinking. Hard decisions must frequently be made regarding what is more necessary and what is less necessary. Choosing some things probably means giving up others. Read the following vignette and answer the questions that follow.

The family services agency where you work counseling survivors of domestic violence has suffered significant budget cuts. The agency administration has indicated that it will eliminate some services in order to stay afloat. Potentially targeted programs include day-care for working parents, sex education and contraception counseling for teens, or the thriving but expensive foreign adoptions program. The agency's other alternatives might include elimination of your own domestic violence program, decreasing staff for all programs including your own, or significantly cutting workers' salaries (including your own) across the board.

The community has depended on your agency's provision of its various services for many years. Thus, adequate alternate services do not exist in your community.

1.   Which principles might apply to this situation? Explain how.

2.   How can you use the Ethical Principles Screen in deciding how best to cut expenses?

3.   As a social worker, what would *you* do in this situation?

Exercise 12.2: Unethical Behavior on the Part of Colleagues—Sexual Involvement with Clients

On one hand, the NASW Code of Ethics dictates that professional social workers "should treat colleagues with respect" (NASW, 1996). On the other hand, it emphasizes that "the worker's primary responsibility is to promote the well-being of clients" in addition to strictly forbidding engagement "in sexual activities or sexual contact with current clients" (NASW, 1996).

Read the following vignette and answer the questions that follow.

You see a professional colleague engaging in what you consider unethical behavior. Twice you have seen him out in the community on dates with women you know to be his clients. It would be very uncomfortable for you to confront him about this behavior. Informing your supervisor seems like tattling.

1.   Which ethical principles might apply to this situation?

2.   How can you use the principles' ranking in deciding what to do in this situation?

3.   As a social worker, what would *you* do in this situation?

Exercise 12.3: To Blow the Whistle or Not to Blow the Whistle? That Is the Question

Whistle-blowing means "informing those people in positions of influence or higher authority outside an organization about the existence of an organization's practices that are illegal, wasteful, dangerous, or otherwise contrary to its stated policies" (Barker, 1999, p. 517). It means taking the problem outside the organization and making it known to others, possibly the general public.

Whistle-blowing carries a degree of risk that varies in direct proportion to the seriousness of the allegations. Airing "dirty laundry" outside an agency can be very threatening to people who run the agency. All agencies have problems of one sort or another, just as all individuals have problems. People responsible for agency activity do not like the negative aspects of this activity to be displayed for all to see. Such exposure reflects badly on the agency and its administration because the implication—perhaps rightly—is that the administration is at fault. As a result, whistle-blowers have been fired, reassigned to insignificant responsibilities at remote locations, harassed into quitting, and even blacklisted as troublemakers in the professional community. In short, administrators and other people in power can make a whistle-blower's life extremely miserable.

Nevertheless, sometimes whistle-blowing is necessary, especially after other less extreme measures (such as discussing the problem with the agency administration) have already been tried and failed. It may be an ethical imperative "when the violations of policy or law seriously threaten the welfare of others" (Reamer, 1990, p. 219).

There are several factors to consider before blowing the whistle: How serious is the actual threat to potential victims? What type and quality of proof do you have that wrongdoing has occurred? Could the problem be addressed and solved in some other way? To what degree will whistle-blowing put you at risk of such negative consequences as ostracism by other staff or loss of your job (Reamer, 1990)? It is critical to weigh the pros and cons of each alternative to determine your most viable course of action.

If you do decide to blow the whistle:
1. Clearly define the variables: the proof of your allegations and the specific rules being breached.
2. Know your rights and the agency's grievance procedures.
3. Prepare yourself for possible consequences such as reprimands and ostracism.
4. Follow all steps specified by agency policy for raising issues and follow the chain of command.
5. Establish a clearly defined plan of action: whom you will tell, whom you will solicit as allies, and what you will say.

Read the following scenario and respond to the questions that follow:

You are a public assistance worker facing an ethical dilemma concerning whether or not to blow the whistle on a newly promoted supervisor (Reamer, 1990). You have worked at the agency for almost two years, and you are increasingly frustrated by the attitudes and work habits of a number of your immediate colleagues. They seem to spend as little time as possible with clients, even denying them necessary and appropriate assistance if the worker doesn't have time to complete all the necessary paperwork. In other cases, workers bend the rules to give clients benefits to which they are not entitled. For instance, many clients work as domestic help and are paid in cash, and workers do not always report all the clients' income. Workers simply make decisions according to their own discretion. Additionally, you note that workers consistently pad their travel expense accounts.

You are appalled by this behavior, and although you don't like the thought of "making waves," you finally confide your concerns to your friend and colleague Zenda. Zenda "pooh-poohs" your concerns condescendingly, remarking that such violations bend rules that aren't very good to begin with. She explains that such worker discretion is really an informal agency policy and adds that padding travel expense accounts is universally accepted as a means of increasing workers' relatively meager salaries. Zenda tries to soothe you and arrest your concerns, but it doesn't work. You decide that from now on you had best keep your concerns to yourself until you can figure out what to do about them.

Abruptly you find out that Zenda has been promoted and is your new unit supervisor. You are stunned. How can Zenda maintain order and help supervisees follow agency and other regulations when Zenda herself typically violates them?

What can you do? Ignore the whole situation? Confront your colleagues about their behavior? Confront Zenda again, even though it did no good the first time? Report your concerns to someone higher up in the administration? If you do and Zenda considers you a traitor, how miserable can Zenda make your life as an employee? Should you report the problem to NASW or the State Licensing Board? Should you blow the whistle to the press? How long do you think you'll keep your job if you take the problem outside established agency channels? Should you quit?

1.   Discuss which principles might apply to this situation?

2.   How can you use the principles' ranking to come to a decision?

3.   As a social worker, what would *you* do in this situation?

In addition to dignity and worth of the person, the NASW Code of Ethics emphasizes social justice and the need for "cultural competence" in terms of understanding cultural and social diversity (1.05). It asserts the importance of workers acting to prevent and eliminate discrimination (6.04d) and stresses that "social workers should not use derogatory language in either written or verbal communications to or about clients" (1.12). It also states that "social workers should not practice, condone, facilitate, or collaborate with any form of discrimination on the basis of race, ethnicity, national origin, [or] color . . ." (4.02). Instead, they should "act to prevent and eliminate discrimination in the employing organization's work assignments and in its employment policies and practices" (3.09e).

The private social service agency you work for does not have a formal affirmative action policy for hiring personnel. You have heard the agency director make several lewd racial remarks and jokes. You cannot believe he has gotten away with it. You have only worked for the agency for three months of your six-month probationary period, so you could be dismissed in the blink of an eye. The agency has no people of color on staff though it has clients who are. You believe that recruiting staff who are people of color is essential to the agency's ability to perform its functions. You also think the staff and the agency director need feedback in order to change their prejudicial and discriminatory behavior.

What is your role? Should you look away and pretend you don't know anything is wrong? Should you charge into the Director's office like a bull in a china shop and complain? Can you talk to other staff to see what they think? Should you contact the agency's board of directors? Should you contact the press or some external regulatory agency and blow the whistle? Should you quit your job?

1.   Which principles might apply to this situation?

2.   How can you use the principles' ranking to come to a decision?

3.   As a social worker, what would *you* do in this situation?

We have established that the NASW Code of Ethics maintains that service, social justice, and dignity and worth of the person are core concepts in making ethical decisions. The Code also states that "social workers generally should adhere to commitments made to employers and employing organizations" (3.09a). Additionally, the Code provides guidelines for social and political action (6.04). It emphasizes that "social workers should engage in social and political action that seeks to ensure that all people have equal access to the resources, employment, services, and opportunities they require to meet their basic human needs and to develop fully" (6.04a). Social workers are responsible for expanding the "choice" and "opportunity" available to all people, especially those who are vulnerable and disadvantaged (6.04b). Read the vignette below and respond to the questions that follow.

The community in which you live and work provides no services for homeless people, despite the fact that their numbers are escalating. Every day on your way to and from work you pass at least a half dozen people roaming the urban streets. Many times you see children with them, dirty, probably hungry, and obviously not in school. Most people at your agency don't really want to talk about it. You get the feeling that colleagues, supervisors, and administrators think they have enough to do already. Work demands continue to increase while funding resources shrink.

1.   Which ethical principles might apply to this situation?

2.   How can you use the principles' ranking to come to a decision?

3.   As a social worker, what would *you* do in this situation?

Exercise 12.6: Community Support (or Lack Thereof) for Service Provision

The NASW Code of Ethics maintains that social workers should "respect and promote the right of clients to self-determination" and help clients work toward the identification and clarification of their goals (1.02). Social workers should seek to educate themselves about social diversity including sexual orientation (1.05c). Furthermore, they should "engage in social and political action" aimed at providing all people with equal access to resources and opportunities (6.04). Finally, social workers should pursue the elimination of discrimination against any person or group based on sexual orientation (6.04d).

Read the following scenario and respond to the questions that follow.

You are a worker at a rural county social services agency. You, other colleagues, and agency administration have identified a significant lesbian and gay population in the area. You and the other professionals would like to implement a new program providing support groups for lesbian and gay people dealing with several issues, including single parenthood, legal difficulties such as housing discrimination, and other issues. Several relatively powerful members of the County Board get wind of your idea and react with almost violent frenzy. They band together with a number of citizens who adamantly refuse to allow expenditure of public resources on lesbian and gay people.

1.   Which principles might apply to this situation?

2.   How can you use the principles' ranking in coming to a decision?

3.   As a social worker, what would *you* do in this situation?

Chapter 13
The Social Worker in Court

For many people, going to court is about as appealing as a visit to the dentist. Courts can be scary places filled with behaviors, jargon, and concepts that bewilder the average person. Yet many social workers spend a significant portion of their professional lives in court. The worker may be helping a client deal with a recalcitrant landlord who refuses to return a security deposit, acting as an advocate for a youngster facing potential incarceration, testifying in a case of child abuse, or serving as an expert witness. In all the different roles we may play in the court system, we have an obligation to be professionally knowledgeable and competent.

Sometimes the court system is used to establish new rights for client groups, enforce existing laws, and require that organizations and governments abide by their own rules. The court system is often the last resort when other branches of government refuse to do what is constitutionally right and just. Client system rights to social and economic justice may rest solely on the ability of the courts to act fairly and impartially.

Finally, courts settle all manner of disputes between individuals and between individuals and other societal systems, and they decide the merits of claims brought by everyone from the single individual to the executive branch of the government.

This chapter will:
- Define important terms used in courts
- Outline differences between social work practice and courtroom protocol
- Provide general guidance about testifying in court
- Consider various phases of the adjudication process
- Identify strategies employed during cross-examination

Legal Terminology

Just as you learn new terminology and concepts for the practice of social work, so also will you need a vocabulary appropriate for the courtroom. Like other professionals, lawyers and judges have concepts and principles expressed in specific words. This vocabulary ensures a common understanding of complex issues, but it can be off-putting for the rest of us. Greater familiarity with legal terminology makes you more comfortable and less anxious about the courtroom processes.

Violations

A *violation* is the breaking of a rule or law. You are probably familiar with *criminal violations,* which are punishable by fines, imprisonment, or probation. Criminal violations are further classified by degree of seriousness. Minor infractions—*misdemeanors*—are punishable by less than a year in jail. Serious criminal violations—*felonies*—carry penalties of a year or more in prison. Murder and first degree sexual assault are felonies. Shoplifting and battery of another person are generally classified as misdemeanors.

Civil offenses are penalized by forfeiture of money or property. For instance, a hunter who kills a deer out of season will probably lose his gun and be fined. A physician or attorney convicted of malpractice—failure to provide appropriate services—can be fined and may also lose his or her license to practice. A company which makes a defective widget that later harms someone may be required to make restitution to the injured party.

Ordinance violations involve the breaking of civil or non-criminal laws created by a city or town. For example, most cities have ordinances governing how many unrelated tenants can live in an apartment or specifying a landlord's responsibility to provide hot and cold running water to each apartment. Violation of an ordinance can result in a fine but does not involve incarceration.

Julian Wainwright is part of a social action group protesting at a nuclear power plant. He and other group members who chained themselves to the front gate of the plant were arrested for violating the law and face penalties including fines and up to six months in jail for trespassing. In addition, the city is charging them with loitering, which carries a possible fine of $100.

1. How would you classify the violations facing Julian and his group in terms of the categories discussed above?

2. How serious are the charges against them?

3. If the power plant operator sues Julian and his group for lost income and the costs of providing extra plant security, what kind of violation would this entail?

Jurisdiction

Jurisdiction is the authority to act in a given situation. For example, a court in one state does not have jurisdiction to punish someone for a violation that occurred in another state. The issue of jurisdiction frequently arises when you are dealing with juveniles. Most states give jurisdiction over juvenile cases to a juvenile court. This means that a young person who commits a crime will not be tried in adult court. There are exceptions to this rule: Several states allow juveniles to be "waived" into adult court if they have committed particularly serious crimes.

Since laws sometimes vary greatly from one community or state to another, jurisdiction is an important concept. Determination of the proper jurisdiction is often left to the discretion of the prosecuting attorney.

Exercise 13.2: Who Has Jurisdiction?

Marian, a 15-year-old, is stopped in Georgia for driving her mother's car without permission. Marian and her mother live a few miles away near Tallahassee, Florida. The local Georgia newspaper, in a misguided effort to stamp out youthful crime, has suggested that teenagers like Marian should be flogged. The paper's editors call upon the local prosecutor to charge Marian with auto theft, treat her as an adult, and give her the maximum punishment.

As a social worker in the prosecutor's office you are asked to write a brief letter to the editor informing the paper and its readers about such cases. What would you say in the letter to deal with the jurisdictional issue?

Allegation

When one individual charges that another has committed a violation, this is called an *allegation*. (This should not be confused with the reptiles that frequent local swimming pools in Florida.) Courts refer to someone against whom an allegation has been made as an "alleged offender" because under our system of justice a person is innocent until proven guilty. Get in the habit of calling accused persons "alleged" offenders.

Court Process

What goes on in a court can be broken down into two phases, *adjudication* and *disposition*. During the first phase, adjudication, facts are presented, and the charge is determined by a judge or a jury. Adjudication ends when the judge or jury arrives at a verdict. If the accused is found guilty, disposition begins. In this phase a decision is reached about what punishment or consequences are appropriate. Sometimes the law gives clear guidance: An adjudication of murder may require the death penalty or life imprisonment. In other situations, a judge or jury has considerable latitude. Several days or weeks may pass between adjudication and disposition. The judge may order a pre-sentence investigation prior to the dispositional hearing in order to get additional input and information.

Exercise 13.3: Explaining the Relationship

As a juvenile probation officer, you often give talks to the public about the juvenile court. At the local Rotary Club you are asked to talk about what happens in the courts to "those delinquents." Explain in a few words what you see as the relationship between an allegation of delinquency and the adjudication and disposition process in court.

Due Process

Due process is guaranteed by the Sixth Amendment in the Bill of Rights. It ensures that all proper procedures, rules, and opportunities permitted by law are guaranteed to all individuals before a legal judgment can deprive them of life, liberty, or property. Due process rights were extended to juveniles in 1967 under a Supreme Court decision known as *Gault*. Juvenile court had previously been governed by the principle that adults acted in the "best interest of the child." The extension of due process rights to juveniles was designed to protect them from arbitrary decision-making by courts and judges.

Exercise 13.4: What Is Due?

You are working with Malcolm and Jamal Washington, two brothers who are part of a boys club. Last night, on the way home from the club, they were stopped by the police, their car was searched, and despite their protests they were detained for two hours at the police station. Their requests to speak to an attorney were ignored. They were later released without any charges being filed. The boys ask you if this seems fair and inquire whether their rights were violated. What would you tell them and why?

Stipulation

A *stipulation* is simply a statement that both sides in a court case agree on the accuracy of certain facts or information, thus eliminating unnecessary discussion of evidence that is not in dispute. For example, a stipulation might be used in a murder case involving domestic abuse. The defendant admits to committing the crime, but the defense argues that it was a justifiable response to physical abuse by the deceased. By stipulating to the killing itself, the defense removes the need for argument over opportunity, weapon, and motive.

Burden of Proof

The burden of proof is the obligation of the prosecution (in a criminal case) or the plaintiff (in a civil case) to prove their assertions. Neither a criminal nor a civil defendant is required to prove anything, so both can concentrate on refuting evidence offered by the prosecution or plaintiff.

An editorial in your local newspaper asserts that too many "criminals" are avoiding punishment because courts find them not guilty when "everyone" knows they're guilty as sin. As a social worker working for the judge, you are asked to respond with a letter to the editor. Explain how you would defend the burden of proof principle.

Standards of Proof

In criminal and delinquency cases the prosecution must prove its case beyond a reasonable doubt. The level of certainty is referred to as the *standard of proof*. If it could be quantified, reasonable doubt might constitute about 90 percent certainty. Child abuse and neglect cases generally require a standard of proof referred to as "clear and convincing evidence," roughly a 70 percent degree of certainty. In most civil cases, the burden of proof requirement is "a preponderance of the evidence." This is simply the majority of the evidence, about a 51 percent certainty. The greater the potential punishment for the defendant, the higher the standard of proof.

Exercise 13.6: Why Do It This Way?

1.   What is your opinion of these differing standards of proof?

2.   *Should* there be a different standard for different types of cases or situations? Explain

3.   What if the courts adopted a single standard for all cases?

Evidence

Evidence is proof of the accuracy of an allegation, but not all evidence is equal in nature or importance. *Real evidence* consists of things, such as weapons, blood, and fingerprints. *Documentary evidence* is material identified and authenticated by proper authorities. An emergency room doctor, for example, might testify that the X-rays used in a trial are the same ones he took the night a person was admitted to the hospital. *Testimonial evidence* is actual testimony given in court under oath and is subject to legal regulation and to careful examination by opposing counsels. Mary, for example, cannot testify to what Sam said to her because that would be hearsay. Sam is not available to verify what he actually said, and Mary could have misheard or misunderstood him.

In addition, only statements made under oath are allowed in court. Mary can testify to what she told Sam because she is now under oath, but Sam's statements (as related by Mary) were *not* made under oath. Also, the judge and jury can't see Sam or hear his inflection, so they cannot judge his demeanor based on what Mary reports. Think about it. If Sam said, "I'm going to kill Bob," that could be a serious threat. But what if Sam was laughing at the time? What if he was reacting to one of Bob's practical jokes? What if Sam was just blowing off steam. The statement itself is meaningless without this additional information. If the attorneys cannot bring Sam into court (via subpoena) to testify under oath, his words will be inadmissible.

Evidence presented in court must be competent, relevant, and material. Testimony from a person who was drunk or delusional is not competent. Neither is medical testimony from a baseball player or blood-spatter testimony from a chef. *Competent evidence* comes from qualified people. *Relevant evidence* is information with a direct bearing on the case. The ingredients of Aunt Hattie's apple pie are not relevant unless the pie contained arsenic and Uncle Fred was poisoned. *Material evidence* is more than relevant—it proves or refutes an essential fact.

Therefore, if it's established that Uncle Fred was poisoned *with arsenic,* evidence of Aunt Hattie's whereabouts during the preparation of the poisoned pie would be material—that is, it would show that she was out of the house while the pie was baking or waiting to be baked (thus refuting the allegation that no one else could have administered the poison) or that she was in the kitchen all day long (thus proving that it would have been almost impossible for anyone else to have tampered with the pie). On the other hand, testimony that Boris has a crush on Natasha is probably not material to her trial for poisoning Rocky.

Exercise 13.7: Evidence, Evidence, Evidence

Match each example to the appropriate type of evidence.

1. Documentary _____   5. Relevant _____

2. Testimonial _____   6. Material _____

3. Real _____   7. Competent _____

4. Hearsay _____

A. Statements made to a witness by a person who is not present in the courtroom
B. Evidence considered consequential to the outcome of the trial
C. Evidence provided by a qualified witness
D. Testimony by a crime victim about his injuries
E. A gun used in a robbery
F. Testimony with a direct bearing on a case
G. Medical records authenticated by a hospital records clerk

Witnesses

Courts typically recognizes two types of witnesses: *Lay witnesses* can testify to things they experienced. They may be asked for opinions based on their experience, but those opinions can be challenged by opposing counsel since the witness has no particular expertise. Expert witnesses, on the other hand, are accepted as such based upon academic credentials, experience, and specialized training. Expert witnesses are given greater latitude in expressing their opinions about a case, but expert status is given on a case-by-case basis. Thus, one judge might consider you an expert while another views you as a lay witness. As a social worker you should be prepared to defend your qualifications.

Guardian ad Litem

Children and others judged not competent by a court may have a guardian *ad litem* appointed. This person is often, though not necessarily, an attorney and is charged with guarding the person's best interests. In many cases, the viewpoint of the guardian *ad litem* is different from that of either side in the dispute. For example, when two parents argue in court for custody of a child, a guardian *ad litem* may agree with one or the other, or may firmly believe that the only healthy caretaker for the child at this point is the maternal grandmother.

Confidentiality and Privileged Communication

Confidentiality and privileged communication have important implications for social workers and their clients. *Confidentiality* dictates that information shared by the worker and client is kept from others unless the client gives permission to share what has been said. It is a primary tenet of social work practice, but it is also a relative concept since absolute confidentiality is often impossible. For example, all agencies keep records, have supervisors, and are subject to control by legal authorities, so information must be available to agency supervisors, executives, secretaries, and others. Files and records may have to be turned over to the court to settle a related dispute.

Privileged communication has legal protections, usually in the form of state laws, and it is not subject to disclosure in court. Many states routinely grant this protection to the testimony and records of physicians, lawyers, psychologists, spouses, and sometimes social workers. Interestingly, the patient or client—*not* the doctor or lawyer—has the right to invoke privileged communication. Laws governing these matters are meant to protect clients, not professionals.

Subpoenas

A subpoena is "a writ commanding a person designated in it to appear in court under penalty for failure" (Mish, 1995, p. 1173). Many social workers in the course of their professional careers will be subpoenaed to appear in court to testify regarding a client. Often, the subpoena requires that the professional bring any and all paperwork, files, reports, and informal notes as well. The NASW Code of Ethics notes, however, that the professional maintains client confidences "except for compelling professional reasons." Thus, a social worker must carefully guard a client's confidences and privacy to the greatest extent possible.

Exercise 13.8: Confidentiality and Privilege

What are the primary differences and similarities between confidentiality and privileged communication?

Differences Between Courtroom Protocol and Social Work Practice

There are multiple differences between the structured world of the courtroom and the environment of the generalist social worker, but social workers are trained to work in a variety of arenas, ranging from the one-to-one interview to the legislative chamber. Most social workers, therefore, can successfully make the transition to this new environment. Recognizing and anticipating the differences will help them do so.

The atmosphere of most social work activities is informal. Staff refer to each other by first names, as do many clients. Dress is casual. Language and words used by social workers reflect opinions, are hedged by such phrases as "it seems," and emphasize flexibility. After all, the goal of social work intervention is to achieve client-identified goals, and to serve the client system. Mutual problem solving is the professionally approved means of handling disputes, disagreements, and difficulties. Professional social work values accord certain rights to clients (e.g., confidentiality and self-determination). This is the world of the social worker.

The courtroom is markedly different. The atmosphere is very formal, and participants refer to each other accordingly: Your Honor, Counselor, Ladies and Gentlemen of the Jury. Language is similarly formal, precise, and definitive, and dress in court is "business attire." There is an adversarial relationship between the opposing sides. The parties to a disagreement present their arguments, and the judge or jury makes the final decision. The goal of the court system is to determine the truthfulness of an allegation, and its values reflect this: the right to legal counsel, to refuse self-incrimination, and to face one's accuser, for example.

Many social workers feel uncomfortable in the courtroom. It's an unfamiliar place, and sometimes opposing attorneys go out of their way to make social workers look incompetent. To prepare for your courtroom experience, adopt the conservative appearance that is characteristic of the rest of the participants (attorneys, witnesses, etc.)—more or less what you would wear to a funeral. If you can, visit the courtroom when court is not in session or observe a trial as a visitor. Talk with others who have testified in court and are knowledgeable about the protocol. Don't go in cold.

Exercise 13.9: Social Work/Courtroom Differences

Make a chart on which you briefly identify the primary differences between social work practice and courtroom protocol. Include degree of formality, dress, language, methods of settling disputes, values/rights, and collegial relationships, etc.

Preparation for Testimony

Some general rules will help you prepare for a court appearance.

- Offer documentation that enhances, rather than detracts from, your testimony. Case notes and records should be detailed and clear. Opinions and impressions that are undocumented or too broadly stated undermine the worker's credibility. Dates; descriptions of contacts between worker, client, and others; and impartial presentation of information all contribute to the social worker's air of professionalism. Descriptions of a client or situation should be as free as possible of any value-laden terms. Avoid references to "weird behavior" or "uncooperativeness." Instead, describe precisely what you observed in words that don't inflame or prejudice your listeners. Offer your impressions, but be sure they are clearly labeled as such.

- Review all appropriate documentation—prior court decisions in similar cases, agency records and policies, and appropriate state laws—before you appear in court. For example, if you are testifying about your work with a local anti-gang program, review your agency's policies and procedures for providing this service. The ability to cite the applicable section of a policy manual or state law greatly enhances your credibility. Your awareness of relevant court decisions or precedents is likely to win you greater recognition by the court.

- If an attorney is seeking to have you accepted as an expert witness, prepare for this additional responsibility. Expect to be asked about your education, professional experience, and past work with similar cases.

- One side or the other has requested your presence in court, so review with this attorney the nature of the questions you will be asked. If specific information will be sought, review your notes and the case file. Pay special attention to the *petition* to be presented to the court. A petition is essentially a complaint that specifies the reasons for a case being brought to court and usually identifies a remedy sought by the petitioner (Saltzman & Furman, 1999). The petition is a legal document generally prepared by the district or state's attorney. Since the petition represents a detailing of the basis for the action sought by the petitioner, it is critical that the social worker know what the petition alleges and that it be factually correct. You may suggest strategies that would be appropriate given your own experience, but remember that this is the attorney's world—so let the lawyer lead. He or she may also offer some guidance about questions the judge might raise. You will be better prepared if you can think about such questions beforehand. If necessary (though it should not be), press the attorney to meet with you prior to the trial.

- Help prepare anyone else who will be asked to testify. Perhaps you will need to orient your clients to the formalities of the court, the differences in language and terminology, and the importance of nonverbal communication. You may have colleagues who argue that you and your clients *should not* have to observe all these niceties, that judges and juries *should not* be influenced by factors like attire and whether nonverbal communication matches verbal testimony. Nonetheless, there is empirical evidence that these factors *do* affect a person's credibility. Failure to inform clients about these issues does them a disservice.

On Friday of next week your friend and colleague, Jane, is to appear in court as a witness in a child abuse case. It will be her first court case. What advice would you give her about how to prepare for this "experience"?

Phases in the Adjudication Process

The primary phases in the adjudication process are direct examination of witnesses and cross-examination. (These may be followed by redirect and recross-examination.) Direct examination aims to present an accurate and truthful recitation of the facts. Questions asked in this phase are generally straightforward, and you are permitted to use notes to help you recall information. This is advisable, especially if anxiety is high or your memory poor. Look over the case record before testifying, but don't attempt to memorize data. Stumbling over details reduces your credibility and makes your testimony look rehearsed.

In all phases, including direct examination, you must respond verbally. Nods and gestures cannot be recorded by the court reporter who is making a transcript of the trial. Be prepared to explain professional terms with which attorneys, judges, or jurors may be unfamiliar. Limit your comments to direct responses to the questions. The judge and attorneys may rebuke you for going into long explanations and making tangential remarks. Wait for each question to be asked, and pause, if necessary, to think briefly about the question. If you don't understand the question, ask the attorney to rephrase it. If you still don't understand, say so. Don't be intimidated into giving estimates or opinions with which you are uncomfortable. Feel free to say, "I don't know."

You don't have the option of refusing to answer a question, but if you remember to pause after each question, you give the opposing attorney time to object. If there are no objections, address your answer to the judge or jury. If the opposing counsel or the judge begins to speak, stop immediately. Wait for direction from the judge or the questioning attorney. Usually the judge will rule on any objections lodged by opposing counsel and then direct you to continue or tell the lawyer to move on to another question.

Cross-examination of witnesses is part of the adversary system. The goal of cross-examination is to reduce the credibility of the witnesses or the believability of their information. Expect probing and challenging questions worded in ways that can confuse witnesses or put them on the defensive: "Isn't it true that you really don't know much about this family?" Be prepared for very limited questions that do not let you amplify what you said or that seek yes or no answers to complex questions.

1.   What do you understand to be the primary purposes of direct examination of witnesses and cross-examination?

2.   Why is cross-examination likely to be more stressful for the witness?

Strategies Used in Cross-Examination

     Four strategies are used in cross-examination to undermine the credibility of a witness:

- The first is an attack on testimony. Using this approach, an attorney points out discrepancies in the witness's statements, such as differences between direct and cross-examination testimony, or between testimony and records. Attorneys may attack your impartiality by suggesting you are motivated by animosity, prejudice, or other factors. They may also challenge your competence or experience. For example, a young worker might be challenged about her lack of personal child-raising experience.

- The second strategy is an attack on witnesses' credentials, and its goal is to challenge the professional education and experience of the worker. The questions may aim at undermining your academic degree, your continuing education courses, or other training.

- The third strategy, attacking the person, is employed when other methods have failed. Personal challenges can be directed at your opinions or at other aspects of your life that appear relevant: "You don't really *like* Mrs. Ortega, do you?" would be an attempt to discredit your observations about her.

- The fourth strategy, attacking the profession, attempts to undermine the credibility and expertise of your whole profession: "Isn't it true that just about anyone can be a social worker?" Don't let this upset you. Remain calm, and remember the joke that professional courtesy keeps sharks from eating attorneys.

Other methods of discrediting a witness include forcing yes/no answers to complex questions, bombarding the witness with questions in order to create confusion, and using an overly friendly or condescending attitude. The best response in these situations is to answer politely, pleasantly, and firmly. Don't become angry or upset. And don't think it's over until the fat lady sings. As a witness you can be brought back to the stand by either side. Redirect or recross-examination is always possible—usually when critical information is at stake and the trial's outcome may hinge on the presentation of certain testimony. Recognize that your testimony must be important or you would not be back on the stand.

Working in the court system can be exhilarating, frightening, and fun. The key to making it a reasonably enjoyable experience is to learn what to expect, prepare yourself accordingly, and remember that your knowledge and skills in this area will improve with time.

Exercise 13.12: Cross-Examination Strategies

Julio Stalking Wolf, a social worker with the Astewaubanon County Community Action Agency (ACCAA), is testifying in a civil court case. His agency received a grant that another agency had applied for, but did not receive. The other agency sued both the ACCAA and the foundation that provided the grant. The opposing attorney has asked a series of questions suggesting that Julio is "just a social worker" with a BSW degree who lacks the experience to manage this grant. She says that Julio's agency got the grant only because his wife works at the foundation. Shaken by his experience, Julio talks with you about what happened in court.

How would you explain what the opposing counsel was trying to do and why she used these strategies?

Chapter 14
Developing and Managing Agency Resources

Every human services agency requires a variety of resources—such as money, people, technology, and the support of taxpayers or contributors—to operate, survive, and prosper. Without resources even the most effective agency will go out of existence. You aren't likely to begin your career by managing an agency, but as an agency social worker you must understand the importance of resources and how you can help the agency and ultimately your clients. This chapter will present several ways to develop or enhance critical agency resources, including working with the media to create and maintain a positive public image of the agency, the use of computer technology, and fundraising in support of agency projects and programs.

Specifically, this chapter will:

- Consider ways to build and maintain your agency's image and reputation through working with the media
- Review the use of computer technology to manage agency resources
- Discuss fundraising and grant writing

Working with the Media

We are all media consumers in that we gather information from newspapers, radio, television, and other sources of news. The primary mission of these media is to provide information to the public, not to act as a public relations firm for your agency. It is important that you understand this in order to recognize the several ways in which the media can assist your agency.

- First, the media can enhance public awareness of your agency, thus bringing you new clients, referrals from other agencies, and donors, as well as creating a generally favorable impression of your agency.
- Media coverage can be essential in fundraising activities, because the media can highlight your specific needs for goods, services, or money. If you are trying to raise funds for a new building or for playground equipment for your domestic abuse shelter, the media can help get the word out.
- Positive media can reduce the impact of negative events. If people have a favorable impression of your agency from past media coverage, they are less likely to view a single negative event as all that important. Suppose a residential treatment center for adolescents with emotional problems has an excellent reputation in the community, bolstered in large part by positive media coverage of the institution. When a runaway from the center steals a car and subsequently injures a pursuing police officer, there is substantial potential for public relations damage. However, since the media decide to downplay the event and the public has an otherwise positive impression of the agency, this tragic situation has only minor negative consequences for the agency.
- Finally, the media can publicize problems and influence decision-makers by focusing attention on areas where public servants are shirking their duty or failing to deal with problems. They can highlight instances of social and economic injustice perpetuated by individuals, organizations, or society.

Read your local newspaper for three days, and look for examples of media coverage of human services organizations/issues. Explain how the articles reflect positively or negatively on the organization/issues.

Guidelines for Working with the Media

Obviously, you will be most effective if you have a continuing relationship with media representatives. Calling a reporter cold without a prior relationship is less effective than contacting someone with whom you have regularly worked. You can develop this ongoing relationship by remembering that the media are interested in news. If an event isn't newsworthy, it's not likely to be reported in print or over the air. Providing story ideas to your media contacts is a good way to build relationships. Tell them about the opening of a new facility or the launching of a particularly unique treatment program.

Build contacts with multiple forms of media and a variety of representatives. Perhaps your newspaper is not interested in a given story, but a television station might be. A call-in radio show could invite you or a colleague to talk about your program on the air. Each media outlet has its own limitations and strengths, and a 30-second television news item may lead to more extensive coverage in other media.

Facilitate contacts with members of the media by letting them know how to reach you. Give them home and office numbers and the names of others who can be of assistance. Remember, reporters must have something to report and usually that something comes from other people. Learn the various schedules under which the media operate. An important piece of news that reaches a given media outlet after its deadline is useless.

Avoid playing favorites with the media. If the newspaper finds out about something the television station has already covered, its reporters may wonder why you favored the TV. Unless you are giving an exclusive interview (a permissible exception), treat all of the media with the same degree of respect and consideration.

Recognize that the media make mistakes. Asking a newspaper or radio station to publish or air a correction requires great tact and should be used only in the case of major errors. For instance, it's far less important that they misspelled (or mispronounced) your last name than it would be if they garbled the name of your agency. Whenever you can, praise reporters who covered a story, and let them know you appreciated their help.

Realize that your story may never see the light of day. Editors make the final decision on what gets in the paper or on the air. A good man-bites-dog story may preempt your article. Reporters don't like to see this happen any more than you do so just let it go.

Bear in mind that media representatives tend to print or publish what they choose, so if you say something off-the-record, you may see it in print anyway. Reporters operate under a different set of obligations and with a different mission than social workers. Accept this as a cost of doing business.

Never forget your place in the agency. Unless you have been told specifically to speak for your agency, be careful. Talk with your supervisor before agreeing to appear on the 6:00 p.m. news to discuss your agency's manner of dealing with a particular issue. Failure to heed this warning can leave you with serious tooth marks on the rearmost portion of your anatomy.

Exercise 14.2: Interview a Reporter

Set up an appointment to talk with a news reporter for a local radio station, television station, or newspaper. Focus on the following topics:

1. How are decisions made about what stories to cover?

2. What can a worker in an agency do to help a reporter cover a story?

3. What schedule and deadlines does the reporter work under?

4. What are the primary sources of information used by the reporter in covering a story?

Contacting the Media

There are generally three ways to get in contact with the media.

1. The media may contact you if they're pursuing a story and think you might be of assistance.
2. You can contact the media yourself if you have a newsworthy item. In this case, it helps to have some familiarity with local reporters for the various media, but if you haven't established such relationships, you'll have to start from scratch. If you are right in your appraisal of the information's importance, reporters will readily agree to talk with you.
3. You can issue a news release—a written communication designed to solicit media interest in a story connected with your agency or organization. A sample news release is shown below.

Highlight 14.1: An Example of a News Release

Fremont Street Neighborhood Association
1234 Fremont Street
South Swampland, Missouri 65803
417 863-1000

For Immediate Release:
  Neighborhood Association Pushes City for Action
  South Swampland, MO — August 1, 1997
The Fremont Street Neighborhood Association has filed suit against the City of South Swampland for failing to protect adequately children walking to school along East Doyle Avenue. Association president Diane Chambers said that two children were hurt in drive-by shootings during the past four weeks while the city does nothing about the problem. The Neighborhood Association Board of Directors voted yesterday to sue in Circuit Court, charging the Mayor and Police Chief with discrimination against the predominantly African-American neighborhood along Fremont Street. The association

---

is calling for increased police patrols and arrests of the gang members who frequent the area brandishing weapons and selling drugs to children. They also demand the city close the south end of Fremont Street to prevent drivers from racing down the street. "The city's failure to take action to alleviate the problem left us with no choice" said Chambers. "We are also considering filing a discrimination complaint with the state office of civil rights" she said. Chambers said a rally is scheduled for 10:00 A.M. Monday to draw attention to the problem. Following the rally, former Fremont Street resident and professional ballplayer Sam Malone will hold a news conference along with Association officers.

For further information contact Diane Chambers 863-1000 or 883-5060.

News releases should always be typed and double spaced, with margins of at least one and one-half inches all around. It is recommended that they not exceed one page in length.

Exercise 14.3: Writing a News Release

One of your new tasks is assisting the agency director in working with the media. She asks you to prepare a hypothetical news release to test your media savvy. This news release will announce the opening of a new homeless shelter providing educational services for both adults (job readiness skills) and children (elementary and high school subjects). The director tells you to use your imagination in writing the release. Use the example in highlight 14.1 as an example, and pay attention to the requirements for typing, spacing, margins, and length.

Media Interviews

Being interviewed by the media can be fun. You're in the spotlight for a while and it feels good—but don't forget the purpose of the interview. You have something newsworthy to say and reporters want to capture it in a fashion that meets their organization's needs. Prepare for the interview by recalling the different needs of print and air media. Interviews with a print reporter can last as long as an hour, but covering the same topic with a television reporter may take no more than 10 minutes—and only about 30 seconds will be aired. Prepare yourself for this by thinking about how best to convey the important information you have to share. For television interviews, consider "sound bites," short succinct points that the media are likely to use on the air.

Recognize that reporters are paid to probe and ask tough questions. Don't get defensive and don't be afraid to say you don't have an answer. Offer to get further information if appropriate. Be cooperative, credible, and helpful, and you'll be developing contacts you can talk to in the future.

A local television reporter has decided to interview you further about the news release you prepared above. Remember that the broadcast media tend to prefer comments that are short and to the point. Write two sound bites that take no more than 15 seconds to say and that convey key ideas about the program described in your news release.

1.

2.

Letters to the Editor

Print media normally have a letters-to-the-editor section in which individuals can express opinions or inform the public, as the paper itself does in its editorials. Use this method whenever necessary but always pay attention to the limitations and guidelines established by the publication, including spacing, length of letter, anonymity rules, and possible editing. Short letters are more likely to be published without editing. Expect long letters to be edited.

Don't libel anyone by making defamatory statements. Neither you nor the paper wants to be sued. If you're expressing an opinion, state it as such.

Generally, letters to the editor should be related to something that has appeared in the paper. You may be able to get the editors to write an editorial supporting your plan or program. You'll have to approach the editor or editorial board directly about this, but it's worth the effort because the newspaper's opinion on a topic can carry some weight with the public.

Prepare a letter to be sent to the editorial page of your local newspaper. Express your opinion on a topic that was covered in the paper during the last week. Turn in your letter and the original article or news item to which your letter relates.

Agency Technology

A variety of technological inventions are used in the average social agency. These range from fax machines to voice mail, dictation equipment, and computers. Each is a tool designed to assist us in doing our job. Of all of them however, the computer has perhaps had the greatest impact on everyday operations. In the following section we will discuss computer hardware and software, and their use in the typical agency.

Computer Hardware

Most of us know something about computers. Although our VCR at home may still blink "12:00," we probably understand something about computers because of experiences in high school and/or college. The personal computer found in most agencies has three to four main electronic components.

The central processing unit (CPU) is the internal storage and processing/control system for the computer—the "box" containing the memory chips used to store data. Two primary operating systems—Microsoft Corporation Windows machines, and the less common Apple computers—are found in most personal computers today. Because they have far more business users, we will focus most of our attention in this section on window-based machines.

A number of characteristics affect the performance of the computer's CPU, including the main operating chip and the speed at which it operates. Most computers for sale contain a CPU using what is known as a Pentium chip. The speed of the operating system is usually measured in megahertz with newer machines running at 600 megahertz or more.

Another factor affecting performance is the random access—or short-term—memory (RAM) of the unit. It is common today to see computers with 64, 128, or more megabytes of RAM, and even those newer machines will be out of date very soon.

Each computer has one or more data-storage devices including a hard drive. The hard drive allows permanent storage of data, and its capacity is measured in gigabytes. A byte equals a character, a megabyte a million characters, and a gigabyte a billion characters. For comparison purposes, one megabyte equals about 775 pages of double-spaced text. The hard drive is a small disk similar to a compact disk. Typical machines also have a floppy drive that can be used to store data on disks. The most recent floppy disks are about 3 inches square and hold about 1.44 megabytes of data. Like the hard disk, the floppy disk retains its memory after the machine is turned off.

Additional storage systems include Zip drives, tape back-up systems, CD-Rewriteable ROM drives, and similar devices holding very large amounts of data. The information storage needs of your agency will usually determine what devices are available on your computer.

To display data, each computer uses a monitor, a small television-like screen. These screens, like TV sets, come in different sizes, usually 14-17 inches. Color monitors are common, but monochrome monitors are still in use.

Used in conjunction with the keyboard is another device, the *mouse*. The mouse, a pointing device used in place of keystrokes to send commands to the computer, displays on the screen as a cursor or pointer allowing you to move it to a specific location and take some additional action. For example, if you wish to check the spelling of a word you simply move the pointer to the word in question, click on the mouse button, and then click on the spelling button at the top of the computer screen.

Each computer also has a keyboard from which to operate the CPU. The keyboard typically resembles a typewriter although more recent designs vary the layout somewhat. In addition to the standard typewriter keys, keyboards have special function keys—usually at the top of the keyboard—that operate certain software programs. A separate number pad similar to a calculator is located on the right-hand side of the keyboard.

Getting data out of the computer is simple if the machine is hooked to a printer. Printers allow the user to print whatever is on the computer screen and in its memory. Printers come in various types from dot matrix machines to laser and ink-jet units. Each type of printer offers a variety of options and speeds.

Many machines today are equipped with modems, devices used to exchange data with other computers. "Surfing the Internet" from your computer is not possible without a modem or other connection device. The speed of a modem determines how fast data can be transferred from one computer to another.

Exercise 14.6: Understand the Hardware

If you have a computer at home, describe its hardware in detail, including the characteristics of the CPU, monitor, keyboard, modem, and other devices. If you do not have your own equipment, go to the computer laboratory of your college or university. Interview the lab monitor/director to learn about the equipment in the lab, and use the lab information to complete this exercise.

Computer Software

Without software, the computer makes a great boat anchor or doorstop. It is the software that allows us to do word processing, create databases, keep financial records, and surf the Internet.

Software can serve one or multiple purposes. Integrated software packages, for example, might include word processing, spreadsheets for financial records, and a database for keeping track of names, addresses, and the like. Databases are particularly useful for maintaining large accumulations of information for instance, all clients seen by an agency, their addresses, demographic information, records of worker-client contacts, and more. Look at the sample database below.

Last Name	First Name	Birthday	Spouse	Number of Children
Batchelor	Stephanie	06/12/1950	Bryan	1
Blucher	Sahid	11/07/1949		
Clark	Raymond	08/09/1965		2
Delta	Alexis	09/08/1956	Max	3
Forrest	Richard	10/08/1943	Margaret	
Hobart	Corey	02/06/1970	Lee	
Layton	Leland	12/05/1962		1
Mansard	Rachel	03/10/1965	Leon	4
Martino	Kair	04/06/1939		
Rutondo	Lupe	04/01/1945		
Smith	Fred	05/01/1967		
Trump	Laurie	02/22/1969	Mort	
Wolk	Frank	06/08/1956	Kate	5
Zorro	Ivana	01/07/1960	Niklaus	2

Spreadsheets are used primarily for accounting purposes. Each spreadsheet is a sort of electronic ledger which allows us to keep track of expenditures by category. For example, an agency director might want to know how much was paid for electricity in the agency as a prelude to considering more energy-efficient lighting. A small spreadsheet is displayed below.

Date	Item	Cost	Category
1-3-98	Postage	14.56	O1
1-5-98	Desk	456.00	E3
1-5-98	Chair	134.00	E3
1-7-98	Paper	95.66	S2
Total		**700.22**	

Spreadsheets can have many more columns and rows depending on what financial information you are keeping track of. Spreadsheets allow you to build formulas and automatically recalculate totals. The categories are simply shorthand ways of identifying expenditures by type.

Agencies use many types of software. For example, there are software packages that allow clients to input their social histories or to take certain psychological tests. Other software is used by workers to maintain case notes. Computer software programs can even identify likely agencies to which a client might be referred or discover whether a client qualifies for a particular public assistance program.

Agencies use computers as part of their management information system (MIS) which gathers, organizes, and evaluates data such as demographic characteristics of clients served, primary problems for which clients sought help, and the average number of service hours provided by workers. The MIS can also be used to maintain records on agency personnel and identify gaps in the training or experience of current personnel. Frequently, computers in an agency are networked so that information can be shared by various departments. Thus, a secretary typing a letter, the bookkeeper preparing a bill, and the worker entering case notes may all simultaneously have access to a client's record. Networked computers allow electronic mail (e-mail) to be sent within the agency.

Of course, computers can be used in macro practice outside agencies. Software can track donations for a political candidate or a new domestic abuse shelter. Computers can maintain a database of all neighborhood residents involved in the neighborhood watch program. More sophisticated software can identity pockets of poverty in a community by compiling data on home addresses of children receiving free school lunches. Criminal victimization information can be computerized to pinpoint neighborhoods with high crime rates.

Desktop publishing software can produce brochures and flyers about a program, advertise a new service or a public meeting, or produce other communications. This software rivals in quality anything produced by professional print shops, so anyone with a computer can create a variety of impressive documents.

Increasingly, social workers are using the Internet for research, accessing national and state databases, communicating through e-mail, locating groups and organizations with interests of benefit to clients. Census Bureau data, for example, can be accessed at www.census.gov providing a wealth of information. Similarly, the national office of NASW can be reached at www.naswdc.org. The web page of most major organizations contains information you might find useful as well as a means to contact them. Interested in advocacy for children? So is the Children's Defense Fund and they can be reached at www.childrensdefense.org. Do you want to reach the Association of Community Organizations for Reform Now? They're at www.acorn.org/community. Considering developing a support group for lesbian mothers? The Lesbian Mothers Support Society has its own web site at www.lesbian.org/lesbian-moms/. Would information on the homeless be useful? If so, you might access the Directory of State and National Homeless/Housing Organizations at nch.ari.net/direct.html.

As you can see, the Internet provides many resources for macro practice as well as for other levels of practice. At the same time, it can also be a source of incredibly useless, incorrect, and biased data and information. It is important to maintain a critical perspective when accessing information on web sites. Since anyone or any organization (including those opposed to the basic purposes of social work) can establish a web site, careful analysis of information found on the web is essential.

Of course, computers cause a variety of headaches—as anyone knows who's life has been snarled in a computerized error. Computer problems are difficult to correct because the machines do exactly what you tell them to do. If you make a mistake entering data, the machine doesn't know that. Learning how to effectively use a computer is not difficult, but it is time consuming. Classes are available at every level from post-technical school to university. Most common programs have workbooks and other aids available for purchase at any bookstore. Learning to use a computer can enhance your skill as a social worker. It can also teach you humility.

Interview the administrative assistant or other official who oversees computer use in a local human services agency. If you are currently in field placement, use your own agency. If not, make a telephone appointment to talk about computer use in another agency of your choosing. Describe what kinds of software programs are employed and for what purposes. Be specific in asking about brands and other details.

Fundraising

Both public and private (for-profit and not-for-profit) agencies are deeply involved in fundraising. The need for funds to maintain existing programs, develop new initiatives, and serve different clienteles, places a continuing burden on social agencies. Yet few social workers begin their careers with the goal of becoming fund-raisers. We may not perceive it as a social work function, may lack confidence in our ability to raise money, or may lack the training or experience for this task. In addition to fees paid by clients, there are at least four major sources of funding used in human services:

- The first is public or tax dollars. These funds go to public agencies and, indirectly, to private agencies which have contracts with the public agency. The contracts usually stipulate that the private agency will provide a service the public agency can't or prefers not to offer.
- These contracts represent a second major source of funding for many agencies.
- Grants are a third source. Unlike contracts—which are essentially agreements between two agencies—grants may be considered "free" money, usually to be used for one-time projects. This money supply ends once the project is completed or the program established.
- The fourth source of money is donations and gifts, which often come with fewer restrictions than grants and contracts. Donations and gifts may be received from foundations, individual or corporate donors, benefits, and dues from organizational members. Donations from individuals can be gathered in various ways. Some agencies hold raffles using donated prizes or gifts. Others sponsor events such as concerts, carnivals, or dinners to raise money. Some solicit donors directly for gifts or invite them to benefits. Benefits are events held for the specific purpose of raising money for a particular cause. Musicians and performers, for

287

example, have held benefits to help farmers, children, and others. A sporting event may be held with proceeds going to a given charity. Benefits can include a giant garage sale, an auction, or a pancake dinner, among other possibilities. Benefits work best when the event is attractive enough to draw people and the cost-benefit ratio is high. Some benefits become annual affairs and provide a substantial amount of money for an agency or organization. One family service agency conducts a celebrity auction each year, auctioning items signed or donated by famous athletes, movie stars, and other public figures.

Preparing for a benefit takes careful planning. Poor attendance, cost overruns, or bad weather can end up *costing* the agency money. Benefit organizers must advertise the event, sell tickets, arrange actual activities (dance, auction, golf tournament), and estimate costs and revenues. Anyone who contributed money or time to the benefit must be acknowledged.

The amount of money to be raised from a benefit is generally limited. It is usually not possible to raise the hundreds of thousands of dollars needed to operate an agency year round. Regardless of how much is raised, however, the funds must be accounted for. A local service organization contracted with a professional fundraising firm to operate its carnival benefit. When it was all over, the vast majority of the $80,000-90,000 raised ended up in the pocket of the fundraising firm, which charged for its consultative services and expenses.

Direct solicitation of money is another option. Private individuals can be asked to give money for agency operating funds or to pay for a special project. The amount you ask for depends a great deal on the resources of the donor. If you can identify larger donors, you can amass the same amount of money and approach fewer people. For example, you could ask 200 people to give $10 each, or ask four people to give $500 each.

Potential donors can be gleaned from newspapers, membership lists of professional or business organizations, newsletters of colleges and universities, from other supporters and organizations. Once you identify a potential donor, make an appointment, prepare your pitch, and show up on time. Explain why this donor should want to support your organization or project. Connect the donor's interests with those of your project. Be certain to accept and collect any donation immediately. Promises to give at a later date are often forgotten.

Individuals are not the only source of donations. Corporations routinely donate money, services, and goods to charities. For example, a fast food restaurant may donate a portion of a given day's revenue to a daycare center. Other corporations might donate vehicles, office furniture, computers, and/or cash. Another source of potential gift giving is community groups, organizations, and associations, including social, fraternal, and professional groups—Rotary, Kiwanis, Junior League, etc. A list of these groups is usually available at the public library or from the local Chamber of Commerce. Offer to speak about your agency at one of the group's meetings. Prepare a written request for assistance to give to the group's board of directors or finance committee. Explain the importance of the project to be supported and ask for their help. If money is not needed, ask for their help on a specific project such as constructing a playground for an inner city neighborhood. Donations of labor can be very helpful and give people a sense of involvement in the agency's work.

You can also raise funds by establishing an organization to which members pay dues. The Society of Balding Middle Aged Men may be just the ticket. Once such an organization is created, it can devote itself to bettering the life in your community. Dues paid by members can be spent on such improvements as removal of mirrors from public washrooms (The mirrors just remind us about Mother Nature's ravages.) Americans are "joiners." Most of us belong to multiple groups or organizations, so establishing an organization is not a farfetched idea, but the decision to start a group usually arises from a clearly identified goal. Thus, the Southlake Refuse Group was formed to oppose creation of a landfill in the neighborhood. Money raised from member dues was used to oppose a landfill aimed at Southlake. Sometimes it is easier to ask people to join a group whose purpose they agree with than it is to ask them to donate money. Belonging to a group is a way of feeling connected and the dues raised are less restricted than other kinds of donations. Dues can be spent on anything the organization's leadership and members think is appropriate. The group is usually not accountable to others. Realistically, the amount of money that can be raised through membership groups is limited unless you have a national organization with hundreds of thousands or millions of members.

Money can also be raised through mailings and telephone solicitations, but this is difficult because you are often calling or contacting people with no predisposition to contribute to your cause. It's easier if such solicitations are directed at people with some connection to your group. Obviously, it's much easier for a college to raise funds with phone calls or letters to alumni than with calls to people unaffiliated with the school. Both written and verbal solicitations must be professionally done, well rehearsed, and free of errors in grammar and usage. Nothing loses a donor faster than a poorly prepared pitch or an error-filled letter or brochure.

Exercise 14.8: Where Does the Money Come From?

Using the same agency you used above—or a different one if you prefer—interview the director, deputy director, or other supervisor about the various fundraising approaches the agency employs. (This interview can be conducted in person or over the phone.) Explain that this is a class assignment. Among the questions you will need to ask are:

1.   Does the agency receive tax dollars either directly or indirectly?

2.   Does the agency have any contracts for services with other agencies?

3.   Is the agency currently receiving any grant monies and for what purposes?

4.   Has the agency held or participated in any benefits designed to raise funds?

5.   Has the agency received any donations of money, goods, or services from individuals, groups, or businesses?

6.   Does the agency charge fees for providing services to clients?

Grants and Contracts

We have already mentioned grants and contacts as important sources of funding for human services programs. Grants and contracts are somewhat similar in that both are transfers of assets from one body to another, and both usually require the submission of a written proposal outlining what is to be done with the money. A reviewing agency can approve the grant or contract as written, require modifications in the proposal, and/or supply only a portion of the funds requested. In addition, the granting/contracting agency can simply say no to the request for financial assistance.

Finding Grants

There are several primary sources of grants and/or contracts.
1.   Every level of government from local to national provides grants and contracts.
2.   Many foundations and private organizations are established especially for such purposes. The foundation's money often comes directly or indirectly from a business or other commercial interest.
3.   Some grant money comes directly from companies.
        Each of these sources offers both advantages and disadvantages. Government grants and contracts are more restrictive because this is taxpayers' money. Foundations and businesses may

be more willing to fund untested but promising ideas. Lists of non-governmental grant sources can be found in such library documents as *The Foundation Directory* and the *Annual Register of Grant Support*. Both publications contain substantial information for anyone seeking information about types of programs funded, typical size of grants, and deadlines for submitting proposals. Other periodicals such as the *Foundation News* and the *Foundation Center Information Quarterly* offer additional help. Internet resources include the Foundation Center and the Grantsmanship Center.

Carefully review the interests of a particular foundation to be sure you're not wasting your time by writing them. Writing to a foundation that primarily supports research on the octopus is unlikely to be productive unless you're testing new ways to hug children.

Foundation grants vary in size depending upon the assets of the particular foundation. Some fund new programs, and others only established ones. Some will pay for capital items such as computers, furniture, or a building, but most do not wish to spend money on such items. A given foundation may provide grants on a national basis while another organization may fund only projects in a given state or region. If grant writing becomes a major portion of your job, consider subscribing to such services as the Taft Information System or the Foundation Research Service. Government grants are often identified in the *Federal Register* and the *Catalog of Domestic Assistance*. For state-level grants, check *The State Contract Register*. These sources describe a very large array of possible grantors and announce Requests for Proposals (RFP). The RFP lists the programs a given governmental unit supports, describes the dollar amount, and specifies the appropriate deadline for submission of an application.

Grants from businesses or corporations are usually, but not always, given through a specific charitable division, typically to not-for-profit agencies. Their proposal review process is not much different from that of other potential sources. As might be expected, many businesses provide grants in areas directly related to their own industry or area of commerce. There is always some risk in accepting funding from an organization with a particular agenda, because the money may come with subtle or not-so-subtle pressure to reflect favorably on the granting agency.

Exercise 14.9: Look It Up

Consult one or more of the directories/resources mentioned above. These will probably be found in your college or university library. Locate one granting agency with which you share an interest, maybe an agency that funds human services programs or one that supports some highly specialized cause.

1.   Provide the agency's name and address and identify the kinds of programs/ideas it supports.

2.   What information, if any, is available about grant application deadlines?

3.   List any other information you might need to prepare a grant request to this agency.

Thinking about a Grant?

If you have a particular idea you'd like to explore, send a letter of intent to the agency or organization from which you seek assistance. Most funding organizations will at least respond to your letter, and some may even ask to talk with you further about your ideas. Obviously, the larger the foundation, the greater the likelihood that it can provide some assistance and early feedback. As part of the review process for a grant application, some private foundations and corporations will expect to make a site visit to your agency. This may seem odd, but it beats the heck out of writing a hundred-page proposal when ten pages and a site visit will suffice.

Applying for a Grant

There are generally three steps in the grant application process. In the pre-application phase, you identify potential grantors. Use one or more of the reference documents mentioned earlier, and at the same time keep your eyes and ears open for possible funding sources. Discard those possibilities that offer remote or nonexistent chances of funding your project or whose restrictions are not acceptable. You will have made preliminary contact with the likely grantors, discussed deadlines, and reviewed the funding body's expectations and interests, thereby obtaining an appreciation for the kind of proposal the body seeks, its length, and any other significant information.

In the application phase, you prepare a draft of your proposal containing a statement of intent, an explanation of why the project is worthy of funding, a presentation of the problem it addresses, and specifics about who will do what, when, and why. The potential recipient of the grant will probably be your agency, since grants are less often given to individuals. This means that you will need to fully discuss the proposal with your supervisor and probably with someone higher in the organization. A grant application (or at least the agreement to accept a grant) probably requires permission from the agency's board of directors. The proposal will describe who will administer the grant and outline that person's experience in such endeavors. It will indicate the facilities and staff required to carry out the project. Any contributions and assistance to be provided by your own agency will be listed. Grantors rarely like to fund projects unless the receiving agency provides a significant contribution to the overall effort. This contribution may be in the form of cash, services (such as typing and computer data entry), supervision of workers, and equipment. A grant proposal may also require evidence that no one will be hurt by participating in the project. Human subjects must be protected from harm, records from the project may need to be kept for a number of years to protect the identity of participants, and the proposal should indicate how these steps will be accomplished.

The greater the attention you give to this step, the less likely you are to stumble later on. Details worked out in advance will not slow the project down once money is available.

Writing the Proposal

Writing the actual proposal (in the application phase) means attending to several factors. Your proposal should reflect "a good idea" that the funding agency can support. The problem addressed by the proposal must be important enough to justify spending scarce resources. The soundness of the idea is perhaps the most important consideration. Of course, the proposal must be well written with no grammar or other English usage problems. The track record—or at least a clear indication of professional competence—of those who will carry out the project must be evident. Include all sections of the proposal, including evaluation. Identify measurable objectives. Describe the actual services to be provided. The budget must be clearly indicated and accompanied by an appropriate narrative describing any unusual expenses in detail. Consider whether the objectives of your proposal justify the amount of money you have requested. The length of your proposal can vary depending upon the granting agency's expectations. Some want long detailed proposals while others prefer that you keep to just a few pages. Deadlines must be observed. Granting agencies are not impressed when your proposal arrives a week late.

Kinds of Proposals

There are several typical kinds of grant proposals.

- Program proposals suggest a particular service to a specific group, such as the unemployed. A new job training program for public assistance clients would be an example.

- Research proposals seek funding to study a given problem (such as a study of the educational problems of homeless children) or to test a new intervention.

- Training proposals are requests for funds to train or educate a given population—perhaps to train all agency staff to better serve Hispanic clients.

- Planning proposals request funds for planning new services or programs. (Planning proposals may be followed by a program proposal after the planning phase is completed.)

- A proposal for technical assistance seeks specialized help to assist an agency that needs skills or information not ordinarily available. An agency might seek a technical assistance grant to hire a specialist who could design an intensive in-home child abuse prevention program. Such specialized assistance is sought because the agency has no regular staff with that capability.

- A contract for service—although not exactly a grant proposal—is a written agreement between two or more organizations specifying that one will provide a given service and that the other will pay for that service.

Contents of a Grant Proposal

The several standard components of a grant proposal are identified below:

1. A cover page or a letter should accompany each proposal. Often the granting agency will provide a cover sheet for you to fill in with the appropriate data. If none is provided, your cover sheet should briefly state the title of the proposal and the names, addresses, and phone numbers of both the prospective granting agency and your agency. The subject of the proposal should also be listed, along with the starting and ending dates of the project and the amount of money requested.
2. A table of contents helps readers locate information easily.

3. An abstract or summary of the proposal should state in 200-300 words the objectives, methods, results, and value of your proposal. The abstract is very important. In fact, some granting agencies make their decisions based largely on the quality of this document.

4. The narrative section of the grant describes the problem and your proposed solution. Goals and objectives should be included here, along with the methods to be employed and an evaluation component. A grantor wants to know that you fully understand the problem and expects to see statistics, demographic data, and other references indicating your knowledge of the territory. Your goals and objectives should be clear, reasonable, measurable, and worthwhile. Objectives may include outcome-oriented items such as a decrease in cases of reported child abuse or process objectives that indicate the steps you will take to achieve your desired outcome. The methods section of the narrative will detail how you and your agency intend to accomplish the objectives. Will you begin a new program, expand an existing one, or undertake a time-limited project? Will new staff be needed, job descriptions created or revised, or existing staff trained in new procedures? Carefully consider the evaluation portion of the narrative. Are your goals measurable? Who will conduct the evaluation—an internal person or an external evaluator? Will you assess outcomes, a process, or both? Lacking the expertise and time to conduct a thorough evaluation, some grant writers indicate that this portion of the project will be conducted by an outside group. Finally, the narrative should describe your plans after the grant runs out. Will some other body continue funding if the proposal proves successful? Willingness of the receiving agency to pick up the costs for the program after the grant ends increases the likelihood of funding.

5. A bibliography section should contain the references cited in the proposal.

6. The budget gives explicit detail, usually in a line-by-line format. That is, each item to be purchased is categorized into such areas as personnel, equipment, supplies and expenses, travel, and evaluation. Many granting agencies have their own forms for listing this information and you should use these. If none is provided, develop your own. The budget should describe what expenses the grant recipient is covering and what funds are being requested from the grantor. You may have to apportion these items to show, for example, that your agency is contributing 10 percent of a supervisor's time and salary. At the same time, 100 percent of a worker's salary will be requested from the grantor. You may even have to apportion such things as space: Maybe 10 percent of the rental costs and utility expenses for that supervisor's office are listed as agency contributions. Often the granting agency requires a contribution from your agency (this contribution is called cost sharing or matching funds) to ensure that your agency is truly committed to the proposal. Cost sharing can allow your agency to contribute hard match (money) or soft match (in-kind contributions). An agency that donates a portion of a supervisor's time to a project is making an in-kind contribution. Budgets should be realistic and understandable. Confusing items or amounts may lead the grantor to conclude that you are not sufficiently honest or competent to be trusted with their money. Remember to include indirect costs—such items as clerical support, operation and maintenance of a building, computer time, and other administrative expenditures. This represents an estimate of the actual time and effort the receiving agency will expend on the grant. Many receiving agencies build indirect costs into a proposal so that a proposal for a $100,000 project may increase to $130,000 when the agency adds its indirect costs. That additional $30,000 will be added to the amount requested from the grantor. The actual percentage of indirect costs charged by the grant recipient or allowed by the grantor can vary widely.

7. The final portion of the grant application is agency or institutional endorsements, the signatures of appropriate agency executives or others who are accepting responsibility

for the grant. Letters of support from other agencies can also accompany the proposal and be included in this section.

Post-Application Phase

Once received, grant applications are reviewed by an individual or a committee empowered to fund the proposal as is, reduce the amount of money given to your agency, or reject the project outright. Once the money runs out, your agency will have to decide whether to continue funding the project at full or reduced amounts, expand the program, or end it. Ideally, the program will have demonstrated its effectiveness and become an ongoing part of the agency.

Staff credentials may need to be included in a separate section if they are not detailed in the narrative. The same is true of information about how the agency will deal with such things as rules governing protection of human subjects, civil rights laws, and similar concerns.

Exercise 14.10: Check It Out

Get your hands on a grant application prepared by an agency, organization, or other group. This could be your placement agency if you are currently in the field, another agency with which you are familiar, or your college or university grants office. It doesn't matter whether the grant application was successful or not, because your purpose is simply to compare the actual grant to the guidelines described in this book. For purposes of the assignment, determine the following:

1. What kind of proposal was this—program, research, training, planning, technical assistance, or contract for service? Explain the reasons for your choice.

2. Which if any of the following sections were included in the proposal: cover page, table of contents, abstract or summary, narrative, budget, budget narrative, bibliography, agency or institutional endorsements?

3.   What indirect costs were included in the proposal?

4.   How much money was the receiving organization proposing to spend as its portion of the grant (their match)?

5.   Was the match in-kind or cash?

6.   Are credentials of the staff described in the application? If so, in what ways?

7.   What mention, if any, does the proposal make about protections for human subjects (if such protections would apply)?

8.   To what extent are the objectives contained in the proposal clear and measurable?

Stress is "the overall process" by which external pressures impact individuals emotionally and physically, producing some internal tension (Jex, 1998, p. 2). Most of us recognize certain situations—for example, losing your job or the catastrophic death of a significant other—can be expected to cause unusual stress. Even positive events can be stressful. They, too, can force you to deal with new circumstances and expend energy pursuing unfamiliar or different activities. For example, receiving a promotion, a desirable event for most people, still causes stress. Other stressors include environmental situations such as financial cutbacks at work, personal characteristics such as compulsive perfectionism, and cultural factors such as gender role expectations.

Social workers often consider their profession and the macro work environment to be highly stressful. Certainly, dealing with the complicated needs of multiple clients, confronting the huge amounts of paperwork and documentation required for accountability, and operating within bureaucratic systems can produce significant stress. One of the greatest dangers in social work practice is burnout (Simpson & Simpson, 1992). Burnout is "a nontechnical term to describe workers who feel apathy or anger as a result of on-the-job stress and frustration" (Barker, 1999, p. 57). Burnout can occur when you have too much work and too little control over getting it all done. Obviously, social work usually addresses problems. Constant confrontation with problems is stressful. To avoid burnout and enhance your usefulness, good stress and time management skills are essential.

Specifically, this chapter will:

- Explore stress reactions and stress-related problems
- Propose techniques for changing your perceptions about and subsequently managing stress
- Examine time management approaches as a primary means of managing stress

The General Adaptation Syndrome

Selye (1956), one of the foremost authorities on stress, found that the body reacts to all stressors in the same way, regardless of whether the source of stress is positive or negative. A stressor can be any stimulus that causes stress. Selye (1956) labeled the body's three-stage reaction to stress the General Adaptation Syndrome (GAS):

(1) *The Alarm Phase:* The body recognizes the stressor and responds by preparing for fight or flight. Hormones are produced that release adrenaline. This causes increased breathing and heart rates, higher blood pressure, and a range of other physical symptoms. Thus stimulated, the body is prepared for a burst of energy, better vision and hearing, and increased muscular strength, all of which increase the capacity to fight or to flee.

(2) *The Resistance Phase:* Bodily processes seek to return to homeostasis and to repair any damage caused by the stressors.

(3) *The Exhaustion Phase:* If the body remains in a state of high stress for an extended period of time, it becomes exhausted. At this point, a person is apt to develop a stress-related illness or other negative symptoms including ulcers or heart attacks.

Perceptions of Stress

Stress becomes a problem only when the stressors become so great that they overwhelm the adaptive system. This can result from excessive stress for a short time or from the cumulative effects of stress over an extended period. Both the type of problems you encounter and your perception of how well you can cope with them will affect the stress-related problems you experience. For example, if you feel you simply cannot cope with a particular problem—no matter how serious or how minor it actually is—this perception can increase your anxiety. The anxiety, in turn, increases your stress, and a snowball effect results. The consequence of stress, therefore, can be physiological, psychological, or behavioral.

Exercise 15.1: Assessing Your Stress Level

Stress can be caused both by personal and work factors. Check the factors listed below, placing an X beside those that cause you stress. Indicate whether you consider the stress minor or major. On the blank lines at the end of each list, add any stressors that are not listed. Ignore factors that do not apply to you. Identifying your stress factors will help you complete subsequent exercises in this chapter.

I. Personal Life Factors[1]

	Minor	Major
Illness or injury (either yours or someone's close to you)............	____	____
Divorce or marital separation......................................	____	____
Getting married...	____	____
Marital reconciliation...	____	____
Pregnancy...	____	____
New member joins family..	____	____
Shift in financial status...	____	____
Change in the type or number of arguments with significant other.........................	____	____
Family member leaves family group................................	____	____
Difficulty with in-laws..	____	____
Great personal accomplishment....................................	____	____
Beginning, quitting, or changing schools...........................	____	____
Alteration of living environment...................................	____	____
Major changes in personal behavior or routine.....................	____	____
Change in religious practices or activities.........................	____	____
Change in social life or recreational activities.....................	____	____
Debt..	____	____
Shift in sleeping pattern or practice...............................	____	____
Shift in eating patterns..	____	____
Shift in interactions with other family members....................	____	____
Vacation..	____	____
Observing a major holiday...	____	____
Minor legal infractions (such as getting a speeding ticket)........	____	____
_____...............	____	____
_____...............	____	____
_____...............	____	____

[1]These items are derived from The Holmes & Rahe Life Changes Scale cited in the *Journal of Psychosomatic Research, Vol. 11*, 1967, pp. 213-18, figure 1-1.

II. Work Factors[2]	Minor	Major
Recent job loss	____	____
Changing jobs..	____	____
Interpersonal difficulties with coworkers..........................	____	____
Interpersonal difficulties with supervisor or administration........	____	____
Alteration of work schedule or conditions.............................	____	____
Major change in workload...	____	____
Lack of understanding of work role and responsibilities.............	____	____
Unclear career path..	____	____
Generally hostile work environment......................................	____	____
_____..........................	____	____
_____..........................	____	____
_____..........................	____	____

Results of Stress

Often the first recommendation for coping with stress is to recognize its existence and magnitude. *Physiological* results of stress include headaches, stomach upset (such as ulcers or colitis), skin rashes or hives, and high blood pressure. While most of us have some of these symptoms from time to time, you should recognize that chronic, long-lasting symptoms are warning signs that your stress level is out of control.

Psychological difficulties from chronic stress include anxiety and depression. Anxiety is "painful or apprehensive uneasiness of mind usually over an impending or anticipated ill" (Mish, 1991, p. 93). Depression is an emotional state of sadness and despair often characterized by "inactivity, difficulty in thinking and concentration, a significant increase or decrease in appetite and time spent sleeping, feelings of dejection and hopelessness, and sometimes suicidal tendencies" (Mish, 1995, p. 311).

Behavioral correlates of stress include any behaviors resulting directly from excess stress. For example, verbally or physically lashing out at someone close to you, or else withdrawing and isolating yourself.

Figure 15.1. illustrates an example of stress in a macro context—reacting to pressures at work. First, a stressor occurs—in this case, the problem is too much paperwork. Second, an individual's perception of the problem shapes the reactions to stress. Figure 15.1 illustrates how people may experience physical symptoms such as stomachaches, headaches, or hives; psychological symptoms such as anxiety or depression; or behavioral symptoms such as uncontrollable emotional outbursts. Depending on the individual, the environmental context, the problem, and the person's perception of the problem, each individual will react differently to stressors.

---

[2]These items are derived from The Holmes & Rahe Life Changes Scale cited in the *Journal of Psychosomatic Research, Vol. 11*, 1967, pp. 213-18, figure 1-1 and from those discussed in *The Stress Check* by G. L. Cooper (Englewood Cliffs, NJ: Prentice-Hall, 1981), pp. 175-91.

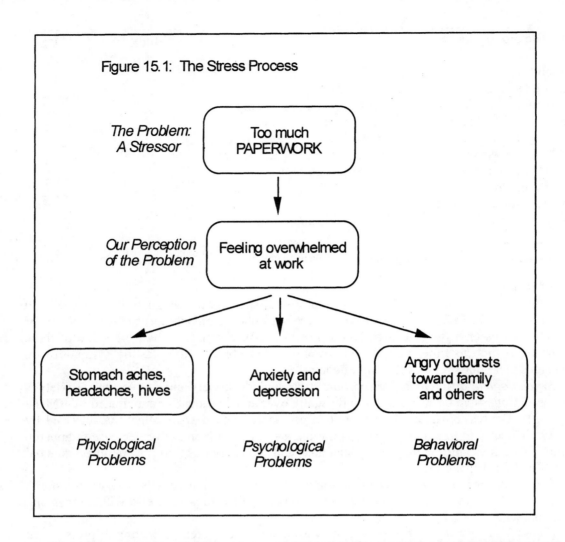

Figure 15.1: The Stress Process

The Problem:
A Stressor — Too much PAPERWORK

Our Perception
of the Problem — Feeling overwhelmed at work

Stomach aches, headaches, hives — *Physiological Problems*

Anxiety and depression — *Psychological Problems*

Angry outbursts toward family and others — *Behavioral Problems*

Describe below how and when you tend to react to stress.

1.   Physiological Problems:

2.   Psychological Problems:

3.   Behavioral Problems:

Managing Your Stress

Managing stress often means reducing it or finding ways to keep it under control. Three primary approaches to stress management—whether in your macro setting at work or in your personal life—include changing the stressful event, changing the way you think about the stressful event, and adopting specific strategies and techniques to help control your stress level.

Change the Stressful Event

At least seven areas of problems in a work context can cause you undue stress which you need to control. These include:

1.   *Inadequate Setting* (Jex, 1998; Sheafor et al., 1997): Is your immediate work environment conducive to getting your work done? Do you have sufficient privacy? Is it quiet enough to concentrate? Do you have enough time to take care of necessary paperwork without interruption? Does your office look pleasant and feel comfortable?

2.   *Urgent Deadlines* (Sheafor et al., 1997): Do you feel unable to catch up on your paperwork no matter what you do? How can you assume greater control of deadlines and paperwork? Is there any way to decrease the urgency of deadlines? To decrease the amount of paperwork you must do? Can you record less? Are you incorporating too much detail? Are there ways for you to become more efficient in your completion of paperwork? Can you find more lead time for accomplishing tasks and goals? Can you manage your time better? Can your supervisor help you better organize your priorities?

3.   *Too Much Work and Too Little Time* (Brody & Nair, 1998; Jex, 1998; Sheafor et al., 1997): Do you clearly understand your job role? Are your expectations for your own performance appropriate? Are you spending your time on the most significant tasks? Or are you wasting time on overly repetitive or low-priority tasks? Note that having too little to do can also produce stress (Brody & Nair, 1998). Staff may be bored or feel they have no purpose. Inequitable workloads can cause resentment among staff that can also result in stress.

4.   *Distractions and Interruptions* (Sheafor et al., 1997): Are people constantly popping into your office? Does the phone ring incessantly? Do you feel you never have an opportunity to *think?* How can you get better control of your time? Can you shut your door during certain times of the day? Can you put up a "Please do not disturb" sign? Can you set aside some predetermined amount of time to finish your paperwork? Can an administrative assistant or secretary hold your calls and take messages so that you're not constantly distracted?

5.   *Problematic Interpersonal Relationships* (Jex, 1998; Sheafor et al., 1997): Are there other personnel in the office whose poorly developed interpersonal skills continuously annoy you? Can you approach these people and try to work out your differences? Can you ask your supervisor to act as a mediator? If you don't think resolution is realistically possible, can you minimize your involvement or interaction with the individual without interfering with your own ability to do your job? Can you change your perspective on those you find annoying?

6. *Role Ambiguity* (Jex, 1998; Brody & Nair, 1998): When job descriptions, worker expectations, or administrative policies are unclear, it's difficult to know the right thing to do. This can cause anxiety and stress.

    Agencies having an extremely laid back atmosphere may contribute to such ambiguity (Brody & Nair, 1998). Likewise, contradictory expectations for worker performance can add to role ambiguity and create stress (Jex, 1998; Brody & Nair, 1998).

7. *Poor Match between Staff and Jobs* (Brody & Nair, 1998): Stress can result when workers are given responsibilities for which they aren't qualified. It can be amazingly frustrating when a practitioner doesn't have a clue about what to do. Stress can also occur when required work is way below a person's ability level when boredom and tedium take over.

Exercise 15.3: Changing Stressful Events in Your Life

1. In the list below, check the events you feel are stressful in your life.

Inadequate Setting	_____ yes	_____ no
Urgent Deadlines	_____ yes	_____ no
Too much Work and Too Little Time	_____ yes	_____ no
Controlling Distractions	_____ yes	_____ no
Problematic Interpersonal Relationships	_____ yes	_____ no
Role Ambiguity	_____ yes	_____ no
Poor Match between Staff and Jobs	_____ yes	_____ no

2. Describe in detail the reasons each event you checked above causes you stress.

3.   Think carefully about events and aspects of these events over which you might work to gain control. Explain in detail what you could do to change these stressful events.

Change How You Think About the Stressful Event

      If you can't change the stressful event or situation itself as discussed above, a second approach to stress management is changing how you think about the stressful event. Consider the following suggestions:

1.   Accept that some stress cannot be avoided. Do you have to worry about every stressor? Or can you accept the fact that some stressors are going to exist regardless and put them out of your mind as much as possible?
2.   Realize that the primary changeable element in your life is you. Appreciate the fact that you can control your thinking and your behavior.
3.   Separate insoluble problems from others. If you can't solve the problem, can you put it out of your mind and stop worrying about it?

4. Examine your expectations. Put plainly, dump the unrealistic ones. Both positive thinking (reframing a negative event to look more positive) and talking to others about your expectations can be helpful. Try to become realistic.

5. Avoid *should/should not* thinking. This limits your options. Are you wasting time worrying about what you should be doing while you're not doing it? Either do it or don't, but don't waste time worrying about it.

6. Analyze your needs. What do you *really* need? How much does the stressful event really affect you? To what extent should you let it bother you? Are you wasting time and energy thinking about it?

7. Emphasize your strengths—physical, emotional, and spiritual. Could your time be better spent placing greater emphasis on positive aspects or your life instead of dwelling on the stress-producing negatives?

Exercise 15.4: Change Your Thinking about a Stressful Event

Select a stressful event or condition that you feel you cannot change. Describe the event or condition below.

Describe how you might change your thinking about this event or condition. (For example, is your instructor's grading scale exceptionally hard in your estimation? Can you change your thinking about this issue by, say, lowering your expectations from getting an A to getting a B?)

Adopt Stress Management Strategies

The third way to manage stress is by adopting specific strategies and techniques to subdue your stress level. There are at least four types of stress management strategies: relaxation techniques, physical exercise, reinforcing activities, and social support.

Relaxation techniques include deep breathing relaxation, imagery relaxation, progressive muscle relaxation, and meditation. Making yourself comfortable and at ease, avoiding noisy distractions, and closing your eyes are helpful for each of these approaches. Regular practice of any relaxation technique will help you become less tense and less susceptible to stress.

Deep breathing relaxation helps you stop thinking about day-to-day concerns and focuses concentration on your breathing processes. For five to ten minutes, slowly and gradually inhale deeply and then exhale. Meanwhile, tell yourself something like, "I am relaxing, breathing more smoothly. This is soothing, and I'm feeling calmer, renewed, and refreshed."

Imagery relaxation switches your thinking from your daily concerns to a ten-to-fifteen-minute focus on your ideal relaxation place. You imagine lying on an ocean beach, soaking in a frothing hot tub, or viewing a majestic mountain landscape. Whatever scene you choose, focus on everything about the image that you find calming, soothing, relaxing. Sense your whole body becoming refreshed, revived, and rejuvenated.

Progressive muscle relaxation is based on the principle that people cannot remain anxious if their muscles are relaxed (Jacobson, 1938). You can learn the technique by tightening and relaxing muscles, set by set. As you relax each set of muscles, concentrate on feeling relaxed and being aware that your muscles are becoming less tense. Watson and Tharp (1973) provide a brief description:

> Make a fist with your dominant hand (usually right). Make a fist and tense the muscles of your (right) hand and forearm; tense it until it trembles. Feel the muscles pull across your fingers and the lower part of your forearm . . . . Hold this position for five to seven seconds, then . . . relax . . . . Just let your hand go. Pay attention to the muscles of your (right) hand and forearm as they relax. Note how those muscles feel as relaxation flows through (twenty or thirty seconds) (pp. 182-83).

The procedure of tensing and then relaxing is continued three or four times until the hand and forearm are relaxed. Next, other muscle groups are tensed and relaxed in the same manner, one group at a time. These groups might include: left hand and forearm; right biceps; left biceps; forehead muscles; upper lip and cheek muscles; jaw muscles; chin and throat muscles; chest muscles; abdominal muscles; back muscles between shoulder blades; right and left thigh muscles; right and left calf muscles; and toes and arches of the feet. With practice, you can develop the capacity to relax simply by visualizing your respective sets of muscles.

A variety of *meditative approaches* are used to decrease stress and tension. (Deep breathing relaxation and imagery relaxation are both forms of meditation.) Benson (1975) has identified four basic components of meditative approaches that induce the relaxation response: (1) being in a quiet environment free from external distractions; (2) being in a comfortable position; (3) having an object to dwell on, such as a word, sound, change, phrase, or image (since any neutral word or phrase will work, Benson suggests repeating silently to yourself the word *one);* and (4) having a passive attitude that allows you to stop thinking about day-to-day concerns. This last component, Benson asserts, is the key element in inducing the relaxation response.

Check any of the following relaxation responses you are willing to try.

_____ Deep breathing relaxation
_____ Imagery relaxation
_____ Progressive muscle relaxation
_____ Meditation

Describe when and where you will begin (or explain why they won't work for you).

Physical Exercise

Since the alarm phase of the General Adaptation Syndrome (GAS) automatically prepares us for large muscle activity, it makes sense to exercise. Through exercising, we use up fuel in the blood, reduce blood pressure and heart rate, and reverse the other physiological changes set off during GAS's alarm stage. Exercising helps keep us physically fit so we have more physical strength to handle crises. Exercising also reduces stress and relieves tension, partly by switching our thinking from our daily concerns to the exercise we are involved in. A key to making yourself exercise daily is selecting a program you enjoy. A wide variety of exercises are available including walking, jogging, isometric exercises,[3] jumping rope, swimming, lifting weights, and so on.

---

[3]Isometric exercises involve those in which "opposing muscles are so contracted that there is little shortening but great increase in tone of muscle fibers involved" (Mish, 1995, p. 621).

306

Describe what kinds of exercise in which you are willing to participate (or explain why this approach won't work for you).

When will you begin?

Where will you exercise and under what circumstances?

Reinforcing Activities and Social Support

Reinforcing activities and social support are personal pleasures that relieve stress, change our pace of living, are enjoyable, and make us feel good. What is a pleasurable experience for one person may not be for another. Common positive experiences are: listening to music, going shopping; being hugged, taking a bath, going to a movie, having a glass of wine, taking part in family and religious get-togethers, taking a vacation, going to a party, singing, participating in a sports activity, and so on.

Exercise 15.7: Reinforcing Activities

Identify and describe behaviors you enjoy and could use in a stress management plan.

Under what circumstances and when do you plan to use your identified pleasurable goodies (for example, as a work break or a reward)?

Managing Your Time

Disorganized people often feel as if they were living on the brink of imminent catastrophe. The key is that they feel out of control, swept this way and that by torrents of time demands. Time management techniques can help by giving people a sense of control over their lives.

As a social worker, you will have to juggle many responsibilities. Your macro environment is saturated with demands and potential stressors. The ability to manage both time and workload successfully is an essential skill for an efficient, effective generalist social worker. Learning specific ways to use your time more effectively and efficiently will help you manage your workload better. This section will present a variety of helpful ways to manage your professional (and personal) time.

Exercise 15.8: What Are Your Time "Troublers" and Controllers[4]

There are a number of elements that cause you and just about everyone else to waste time. Review the "time troublers," likely reasons, and possible options listed below. Then answer the subsequent questions.

Time Troublers	Likely Reasons	Possible Options
What a mess!	Confusion, disorder	Throw out, re-organize, file
Hurry, hurry!	Doing too much too fast, too little attention to detail	Undertake less, allow more time, just say no
I just can't decide.	Terror at making mistakes, cowering at responsibility, can't prioritize and set goals	Use decision-making, problem-solving, and goal-setting skills

---

[4]Most of this material is adapted from R. A. Mackenzie, *The Time Trap: Managing Your Way Out,* 1972. New York: AMACON.

Oops! forgot to plan.	Just didn't think, things happened too fast	Take time to think things through ahead of time, allow time for thought
There's just too much to do!	Unable to say no, too much pressure to perform, can't prioritize	Prioritize goals, just say no, evaluate what is possible to accomplish
I'll do it later.	Being overwhelmed, don't feel like it, it's too hard	Prioritize tasks, plan how to accomplish the most significant
There's that phone again!	Can't resist answering, too nonassertive to not answer or speak briefly, can't control yourself	Talk briefly, stick to the main points, offer to return call later
Unwanted guests	Just can't say no, talking is fun, allows you to avoid work	Limit easy access and availability, be assertive

Now answer the following questions:

1. What is your #1 time troubler? _____

   What are the likely reasons for this troubler?

   What are your potential options for controlling this troubler?

2. What is your #2 time troubler? _____

What are the likely reasons for this troubler?

What are your potential options for controlling this troubler?

3. What is your #3 time troubler? _____

What are the likely reasons for this troubler?

What are your potential options for controlling this troubler?

How Poor Time Management Causes Stress
If you are not managing your time efficiently, you are probably not as effective as you could be. At least the following five reasons explain *why* insufficient or totally nonexistent time management results in stress (Curtis & Detert, 1981, pp. 190-91).
1. "Preoccupation" is being lost in thought over something other than what you are supposed to be doing.
2. Poor Task "Pacing" means not allowing yourself adequate time to complete a set of necessary activities, goals, or tasks.
3. "Stimulus Overload" occurs when you have so much to do that you could not possibly complete all of the tasks in the amount of time allowed.
4. "Stimulus Underload" occurs when you don't have enough interesting things to do—things that hold your attention or concentration—so you don't get anything done.
5. "Anxiety" was defined earlier as "painful or apprehensive uneasiness of mind usually over an impending or anticipated ill" (Mish, 1995, p. 93).

Which if any of the following problems characterize how you manage your work time. Check all that apply.

_____	Preoccupation	_____	Poor task pacing
_____	Stimulus overload	_____	Stimulus underload
_____	Anxiety		

Give specific examples of how the time management problems you checked above interfere with your ability to complete necessary tasks. What were you trying to accomplish? How did you react? What were the results?

Issues Involved in Time Management

At least three issues are involved in time management. In all three cases, learning new approaches to handling time and changing old behavior patterns requires expending some amount of effort. You'll need to plan, control your own behavior, and deal with procrastination.

Planning Your Time

Planning your time involves four primary steps.

- First, you must figure out how you currently spend your time. You can't make changes until you know what you need to change.
- Second, establish goals for yourself. How would you ideally like to spend your time? What would you really like to get done?
- Third, prioritize your goals. What goals are the most important? What do you need to accomplish first, second, etc.?
- Fourth, consider each prioritized goal and specify what action steps you must complete in order to attain that goal.

Step 1: Figure Out Where Your Time Goes. The first step in time management is to figure out where all of your time goes. Are you spending too much time on some activities and not enough on others? Are you avoiding unappealing tasks you know you should be doing? Do you dawdle? Do you spend more time than you think you should watching *The X-Files* or *The Young and the Restless*?

Monitoring and writing down how you spend your time in hour, half-hour, or 15-minute segments allows you to "keep a record of what you do and how long each task takes" (Filley, 1978, p. 126). It can help you more accurately identify how you really spend your time.

Exercise 15.10: Where Does Your Time Go?

The time-tracking format illustrated below shows you how to begin tracking 30-minute time blocks. Select what you consider a "typical" workday. You may simply block or "x" out whatever period or periods of time you spend sleeping. Completing this exercise should help you pinpoint those periods when you waste time. Subsequently, this information can focus on those time periods over which you want to gain greater control.

We assume here that you are a student. Therefore, your time-tracking will be substantially different than it would be if you were working in a full-time professional social work position in the macro environment. Many of the methods used to gain control over your time during this period of your life are nevertheless identical to the techniques you can use to control your agency work time.

Time-Tracking Format

Day: _____

Time Segment	**How Time Was Spent**
12:00 a.m.:	
12:30 a.m.:	
1:00 a.m.:	
1:30 a.m.:	
2:00 a.m.:	
2:30 a.m.:	
3:00 a.m.:	
3:30 a.m.:	
4:00 a.m.:	
4:30 a.m.:	
5:00 a.m.:	

5:30 a.m.:

6:00 a.m.:

6:30 a.m.:

7:00 a.m.:

7:30 a.m.:

8:00 a.m.:

8:30 a.m.:

9:00 a.m.:

9:30 a.m.:

10:00 a.m.:

10:30 a.m.:

11:00 a.m.:

11:30 a.m.:

12:00 p.m.:

12:30 p.m.:

1:00 p.m.:

1:30 p.m.:

2:00 p.m.:

2:30 p.m.:

3:00 p.m.:

3:30 p.m.:

4:00 p.m.:

4:30 p.m.:

5:00 p.m.:

5:30 p.m.:

6:00 p.m.

6:30 p.m.:

7:00 p.m.:

7:30 p.m.:

8:00 p.m.:

8:30 p.m.:

9:00 p.m.:

9:30 p.m.:

10:00 p.m.:

10:30 p.m.:

11:00 p.m.:

11:30 p.m.:

Summarizing How You Spend Your Time

Circle A below illustrates how one individual spent a day.[5] Proportionate pieces of the 24-hour pie display how much time was spent doing what.

[5]This figure is adapted from an exercise in the *Student Manual of Classroom Exercises* and *Study Guide for Understanding Human Behavior and the Social Environment,* 2nd ed., by K. Kirst-Ashman & C. Zastrow, 1990, Chicago: Nelson-Hall, pp. 133-35.

CIRCLE A: AN EXAMPLE OF UNMANAGED TIME SPENT IN A TYPICAL WEEKDAY

Studying

Spending time with significant other

Exercising

Church

Partying

Being Lazy

Watching TV

Working

Sleeping

After dividing your day as the person above did, determine how you would *prefer* to spend your time. Circle B below depicts how the individual whose actual time tracking is illustrated in Circle A would prefer to spend her time. It displays a visual plan for more effective time management.

CIRCLE B: AN EXAMPLE OF AN IDEALLY TIME-MANAGED DAY

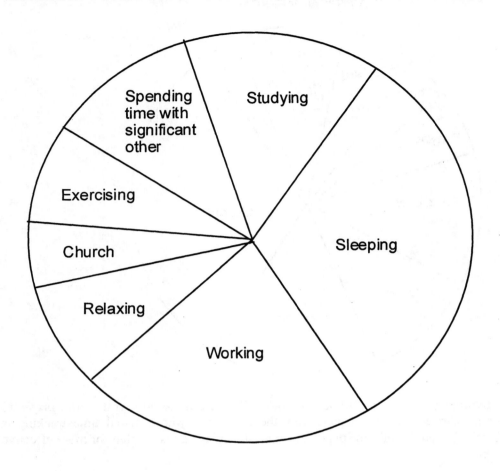

Take the information you gained earlier from completing Exercise 15.10 on time-tracking a typical day. Proportionately, divide Circle C below to depict how you spent your time. The result might resemble the example of unmanaged time depicted in Circle A.

Circle C: How You Spent Your Typical Day

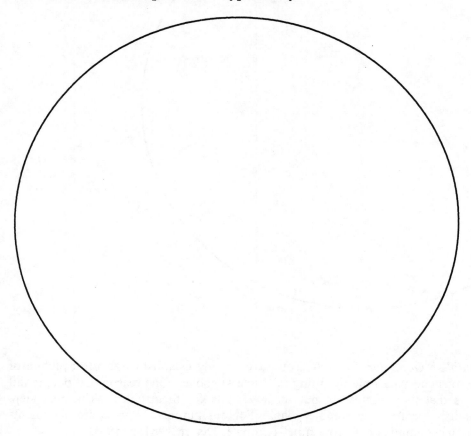

Scrutinize Circle C and determine (1) where you are wasting your time, and (2) how you ideally want to spend it. Now divide Circle D below to reflect how you would *like* to use your time. This may resemble the example of an ideally time-managed day depicted earlier in Circle B. It should provide you with a beginning plan for daily time management.

Circle D: How Would You Spend Your Ideal Day?

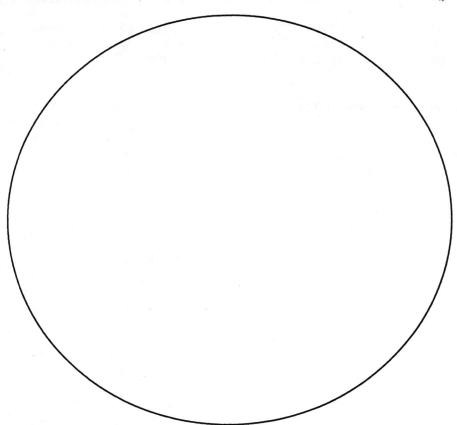

Step 2: Establish Goals for Yourself. You have already established an ideal picture of how you would like to spend your time by filling in Circle D above. One reason that people fail to use time wisely is that they simply do not set any goals for themselves. The next step, therefore, is to establish specific, measurable goals. For our purposes, "goals are statements about what you want to accomplish with your time" (Curtis & Detert, 1981, p. 193).

Note that your goals as a student will be different from your goals as a full-time professional social worker. However, once again, you can use these same procedures to manage your work time and workload in the future.

Exercise 15.12: Establish Your Time Goals

Below list ten goals that you would like to accomplish in a given day. Remember that goals don't have to be set up on a daily basis. They can extend over weeks, months, or years, depending on the unit of time over which you wish to gain control. In reality, the number of goals you set for yourself is arbitrary. Likewise, the goals you set during any particular day may vary radically. The intent of this exercise is to teach you a procedure for goal-planning that you can use for any day you choose.

Ten goals for _____ include:
                 (date)

1. _____

2. _____

3. _____

4. _____

5. _____

6. _____

7. _____

8. _____

9. _____

10. _____

Step 3: Prioritize Your Goals. Part of gaining control over time is deciding which goals are most important. Making this decision helps you avoid becoming immobilized by an overwhelming cluster of goals all at one time. Therefore, after you identify your goals, prioritize them according to their importance.

One common method of prioritizing goals is the ABC method (Curtis & Detert, 1981; Lakein, 1973). Assign a value of A, B, or C to each goal you cite. A goals are top priorities that you absolutely want to get done no matter what. C goals, on the other hand, are relatively unimportant, things you would *like* to accomplish, but probably never will. Don't waste precious time worrying about things that you cannot or will not do. C goals often get relegated to the circular file.

B goals lie somewhere between A and C goals. You should get them done pretty soon, but you probably don't have time to do them today. Frequently, today's B goal becomes tomorrow's A goal as a deadline approaches (or as your anxiety increases when you don't accomplish something you were supposed to). If you can't decide whether a goal should be A or B, automatically assign it a B (Curtis & Detert, 1981). If you're not certain that it's critical enough to be an A goal, then it probably isn't.

Category A, B, and C goals are then further prioritized by assigning them numbers: Goal A1 is the one you *absolutely* must get done today. Goal A2 is second in importance, A3 third, etc. When you finish prioritizing your A goals, go on to do the same thing with your B and C goals. This process will produce a clearly prioritized plan for your day. First, pursue goal A1, then A2, and so on down the line.

Note that you can prioritize goals in at least three major life areas including "self, work, and family" (Curtis & Detert, 1981, p. 199). You can do this either separately or in one prioritized list. Figure 15.2—which focuses on work goals—illustrates a prioritized goal list for a professional social worker employed in a health-care center for the elderly.

Figure 15.2: Prioritizing an Unprioritized Plan for a Professional Workday

The numbered items to the left below comprise a nursing home social worker's unprioritized goal list for one workday. The arbitrarily prioritized ABC and numerical standings are depicted to the right of each goal.

Day: <u>Monday</u>
1. Finish last week's progress notes............................ C1
2. Call Sybil about Ms. Sicperson............................... A1
3. Meet with supervisor... B1
4. Get resources for Mr. Ed.. B2
5. Take Ms. Harrington to her daughter-in-law's......... A2
6. Complete resource file... C2
7. Attend two-hour inservice.. B3
8. Run social support group... A3

Exercise 15.13: Prioritizing Your A, B, and C Goals

Take the time goals you listed in Exercise 15.12 and rank each of them as an A, B, or C goal. Next, prioritize each category by numbering its goals.

Looking at your new prioritized system, identify and discuss which goals you think you will actually achieve and which you will not.

Will you be able to complete all of your A goals in one day? If so, explain how you intend to do so. If not, explain why not. Discuss when you *will* accomplish them.

If you have listed any B goals, discuss what you think you will do about them. Explain when, if ever, you think you will complete them. Discuss the consequences of completing them or not completing them.

If you have listed any C goals, discuss what you think you will do about them. Explain when, if ever, you will complete them. Discuss the consequences of completing them or not completing them.

Step 4: Specify Tasks for Each Goal. After prioritizing your goals, it is helpful to list the specific tasks involved in accomplishing each goal (Curtis & Detert, 1981; Filley, 1978). For example, a hospital social worker might identify the goal of arranging Ms. Jones' transfer from the hospital to a nursing home. She arbitrarily labels this goal A1. Specific tasks to accomplish this particular goal include notifying Ms. Jones' son and daughter, locating an appropriate nursing home, arranging transportation, working out financial arrangements, and notifying the nursing staff that arrangements are complete.

Obviously, these tasks need to be accomplished in a particular order. For example, you arrange transportation only after you know the nursing home in which the client will be placed. Thus, it is probably wise to assign numerical priority to each goal as a guide to your progress from one task to the next.

Leave sufficient time to complete each step. Think ahead and try to estimate how much time each step will take.

Look at the A goals you listed earlier in Exercise 15.12. Now list the respective steps you must follow in order to achieve each. Six task steps are arbitrarily listed for each goal of four A goals below. In reality, you may have more or fewer goals or tasks. Complete this exercise for each A goal you cited above.

Goal A1

Task 1:

Task 2:

Task 3:

Task 4:

Task 5:

Task 6:

Goal A2

Task 1:

Task 2:

Task 3:

Task 4:

Task 5:

Task 6:

Goal A3

Task 1:

Task 2:

Task 3:

Task 4:

Task 5:

Task 6:

Goal A4

Task 1:

Task 2:

Task 3:

Task 4:

Task 5:

Task 6:

Get Control of Your Own Behavior

In addition to planning your time, effective time management requires getting control of your own behavior. The following recommendations can help you acquire this control.

1. *Look at Yourself.* Develop a time management perspective. Instead of falling prey to the various stresses discussed earlier, look yourself right in the eye and commit to time management.

2. *Understand Your Job.* Effectively fulfilling your job responsibilities means fulfilling them at all levels—micro, mezzo, and macro. Discuss with your supervisor what your job description and specific responsibilities really involve (Sheafor et al., 1997).

3. *Bunch Similar Activities Together.* Try to block portions of time for completing similar types of tasks (Filley, 1978).

4. *Use a Calendar.* Select a daily, weekly, or monthly format that works best for you, and plan your time on a longer term basis.

5. *Handle Each Sheet of Paper Only Once.* Don't waste time shuffling paper. Deal with the issue right away.

6. *Delegate* (Filley, 1978; Sheafor et al., 1997). Determine which tasks, if any, others can, will, or should do, and arrange for them to do so.

7. *Don't Do Other People's Work* (Sheafor et al., 1997). Especially if you tend to have high expectations for the quality of your work, be vigilant that you do not end up doing other people's work because you do it better than they do. View each individual as responsible for her or his own tasks, accomplishments, and failings.

8. *Bring Order to Your Desk.* Organize items on your desk so you can find them easily. (Sheafor et al., 1997). It is also useful to make certain that information you use frequently is readily available (Sheafor et al., 1997).

9. *Develop a System.* Devise some system for keeping track of your deadlines (Sheafor et al., 1997). For example, you could note deadlines on your regular monthly calendar or use a more sophisticated computer program. Try various methods. Whatever works for you is the best system.

10. *Leave Time for Contemplation.* Even with a busy schedule, allow yourself some "down" time each workday (Filley, 1978). You need time to organize your thoughts and evaluate the progress you have made toward your designated goals.

11. *Designate Leisure Time for Yourself.* To avoid burnout, regularly incorporate some leisure time into your schedule.

12. *Manage Meetings Effectively.* Plan ahead and consider following these suggestions:
    - *Start meetings on time*
    - *State the ending time at the start*
    - *Pre-schedule regular meetings*
    - *Distribute printed matter well before the meeting*
    - *Hold meetings in meeting rooms—not in your office*
    - *Don't hold meetings and eat simultaneously*

13. *Manage Your Correspondence.* Filley (1978) makes a number of suggestions to facilitate the efficient handling of paperwork: Write brief replies by e-mail or by hand as quickly as possible to messages and correspondence you receive. Remember that it's time efficient to handle paper or address an e-mail message only once.

    Always keep a copy of what you send. Many office correspondence forms have several layers allowing the sender to keep a copy of her reply. However, if this is not the case, make a copy even if it somewhat delays your response. Otherwise, especially if you have a deluge of paper and e-mail, you may not remember what you said, or worse yet, whether you responded to the correspondence at all.

    If possible, use established formats to structure your correspondence instead of "reinventing the wheel" and writing a totally new response each time. You might keep examples of exceptionally well-written letters you receive or have sent to give you ideas about how to phrase things effectively.

    Open second and third class mail including the "junk mail" we get both at home and at the office once a week.

14. *Use the Phone Efficiently.* Consider using conference calls instead of holding meetings. Outline what you want to accomplish during your phone calls before dialing.

15. *Review Your Weekly Progress.* At each week's end, review the extent to which you actually achieved your time management goals and make changes to increase effectiveness.

Which four of the fifteen suggestions for changing your behavior mentioned above would be useful for you? Explain the reasons why each would be useful and how you plan to implement the change.

Procrastination

In addition to planning and getting control of your own behavior, the third major time management factor is fighting your own tendencies to procrastinate. To procrastinate simply means "to put off intentionally [and, sometimes, habitually] the doing of something that should be done" (Mish, 1995, p. 929). Most of us—perhaps all of us at some time—put off what we're supposed to do. However, when procrastination significantly or continually interferes with your ability to accomplish goals, you are no longer in control of your time. To gain such control, you can implement a number of techniques for fighting procrastination.

The reasons that people procrastinate include

1. Seeking flawlessness or perfection—"I don't have time to do this perfectly, so I'll put it off till I do"—which will probably be never.

2. "Fear of failure" (Curtis & Detert, 1981, p. 205)—"Even if I get this done, I know it won't be good enough. I might as well put it off"; or "I'm just too overwhelmed to do a good job."

3. Feeling overwhelmed—If you perceive a task as awesomely difficult, and perhaps even scary, it may be easier for you to avoid it altogether than to do it and get it over with.

4. Non-assertive acceptance of too many responsibilities—"I have so much to do that I don't know where to begin."

5. Idling away time with useless "busy-ness" in order to look busy—"Maybe I'll just clear off my desk and make a few phone calls before I get started."

Procrastination has uniformly negative results. Shirking responsibility irritates clients, coworkers, and supervisors. Unappealing tasks don't disappear—they just become more unappealing. The longer you put something off, the more aversive it becomes (Lakein, 1973).

The following are suggested techniques for battling procrastination:

1. *The "Swiss Cheese" Approach (Lakein, 1973, p. 71).* You can often drastically reduce procrastination when you break a large, threatening, or overwhelming task into a number of smaller, more manageable tasks that you can do gradually over time. For example, if you're faced with a ten-page term paper, you might break up the task into doing research, recording notes, putting together an outline, typing a rough draft, editing the draft, and typing the final copy.

2. *Do the Worst Job First.* Often, anticipating a tough job keeps you from getting it done. Doing the job immediately means that other, less unappealing tasks will look better and easier in comparison. Also, by doing tough jobs first you ensure sufficient time to see the job through to completion. Saving the hard jobs until the end of the day often means they will not get done.

3. *Complete Whatever You Start.* Always try to complete whatever you have started (Filley, 1978). Coming back to an old project or task means having to get oriented to it again, thereby wasting precious time in rethinking what you have already done.

4. *Do It Right Now.* How many times have you heard friends say that they're *going to* quit smoking, lose 20 pounds, stop drinking, or study harder—sometime in the future? When people say they're *going to* do something, they obviously have not done it yet. Framing plans within the *going to* perspective is a good way to procrastinate.

Exercise 15.16: Self-Analysis of Procrastination

Answer the following questions:

1. What tasks do you procrastinate over?

2.   What are your reasons for procrastinating over them? Why do you find them aversive?

3.   What tactics can you employ to control your procrastinating behavior?

4.   When and how will you begin implementing these tactics?

Chapter 16
Resumés, Interviewing, and Getting the Job

This last chapter in our macro workbook addresses material relevant to getting a job, because we anticipate that you are approaching graduation. We assume that macro skills are built on a foundation of micro and mezzo skills, respectively. Therefore, we also assume that you are nearing completion of your practice skill acquisition—at least in a formal educational setting.

This chapter will:
- Assist you in assessing your own capabilities and interests in preparation for seeking professional employment
- Explain how to identify and investigate professional employment possibilities
- Propose principles for developing your resumé
- Request your responses to specific questions concerning the *best* resumé for you
- Discuss the contents of cover letters
- Propose suggestions for job interview preparation
- Prepare you for answering a wide range of questions commonly asked in job interviews
- Propose ways to follow-up on job applications and interviews

Getting a Job

Like much of social work practice, successful job-hunting is a combination of hard work and good luck. This chapter will address six steps to enhance your credibility as a candidate for employment (National Association of Social Workers, undated). These include: assessing your own capabilities and interests; investigating actual job possibilities; constructing a resumé and cover letters; preparing for interviews; and following up on contacts.

Assessing Your Own Capabilities and Interests

The first exercises will focus on assessing your "competencies," "accomplishments," "job preferences," "employment goals," and "personal attributes" (NASW Program Advancement Fund, undated, pp. 2-11). This is the initial step in both constructing a resumé and preparing to put your best foot forward in job interviews.

Exercise 16.1: Assessing Your Competencies

Competencies are skills and abilities. Below are areas that may reflect *your* professional knowledge, skills, and values—but this list is only a beginning. After considering your capabilities, explain your strengths in each area that applies to you. This can help you articulate for yourself (and later for potential employers) the reasons why you will be a capable professional.

1. Assessment of individual, family, group, community, and organizational problems and functioning:

2. Writing skills:

3.   Understanding people:

4.   Problem-solving:

5.   Decision making:

6.   Planning:

7.   Organizing:

8.   Recording:

9.   Critical thinking:

10.   Acceptance of responsibility:

11.   Dependability:

12.   Self-motivation:

13.   Coordination:

14.   Case management:

15.   Conducting of meetings:

16.   Advocacy:

17.   Creativity:

18.   Initiation of ideas:

19.   Team work skills:

Exercise 16.2: Identifying Your Accomplishments

Think about what you have achieved educationally and professionally that makes you most proud. Try to identify five such accomplishments below. To become comfortable with the types of words you'll use later in a resumé, try to use clear, vivid, vibrant verbs (Bloch, 1991) such as those in box 16.1.

Have you taken courses that are especially relevant to social work practice? Did you write an exceptionally good paper on a topic relevant to practice? Did you supervise a volunteer? Have you formulated case plans? Did you initiate and implement a new policy in some organization of which you were a member? Did you lead a support group? Have you presented in class on a topic relevant to practice? The possibilities are endless.

Accomplishment #1:

Accomplishment #2:

Accomplishment #3:

Accomplishment #4:

Accomplishment #5:

Box 16.1: Vibrant Verbs to Capture Your Achievements

Assess	Formulate	Facilitate	Manage
Develop	Appraise	Supervise	Counsel
Organize	Achieve	Employ	Construct
Propose	Implement	Direct	Demonstrate
Assemble	Create	Improve	Initiate
Negotiate	Research	Analyze	Lead
Write	Design	Establish	Present
Teach	Administer	Revise	Coordinate
Plan	Evaluate	Solve	Examine

Exercise 16.3: What Are Your Job Preferences?

Think about the perfect job for you. This will help you seriously consider your own goals and career objectives. The better you know yourself, the more capable you will be of both presenting yourself to others (such as potential employers) and making decisions about what job to pursue and accept. First check all of the following preferences that apply to you. Second, prioritize the options in each of the four categories, with #1 being most important to you, #2 second in importance, and so on.

1. What types of professional activities are you most interested in pursuing?

___ Counseling	___ Supervising volunteers
___ Brokering resources	___ Writing grants
___ Running groups	___ Case management
___ Management	___ Supervising staff
___ Community organizing	___ Lobbying
___ Program evaluation	___ Research
___ Public relations	___ Fundraising
___ Running meetings	___ Training staff
___ Budgeting	___ Policy development
___ Administrative	___ Advocacy
activities in general	
___ (What else?) _____	
___ _____	

2. If you had your druthers, with what client population would you prefer to work?

___ Children	___ Teenagers
___ Young adults	___ Middle-aged adults
___ Elderly people	___ Married couples
___ Women	___ Men
___ Intact families	___ Single parents
___ Minority groups (If so, specify which) _____	
___ Other client populations (If so, specify which) _____	

3. What problems and issues are you interested in addressing?

___ Community development	___ Crime in communities
___ Alcohol and other drugs	___ Teen pregnancy
___ Child maltreatment	___ School problems—truancy
___ Battered women	___ Financial resource acquisition
___ Probation and parole	___ Prison populations/conditions
___ Mental illness	___ Couples conflict
___ Family problems	___ Unemployment
___ Vocational rehabilitation	___ Suicide prevention
___ Developmental disability	___ Physical challenges
___ Health	___ HIV/AIDS
___ Eating disorders	___ Homelessness
___ What else? _____	
___ _____	

4. In what type of agency setting would you prefer to work?

<u>General type:</u>

___ Private	___ Public
___ Large agency	___ Smaller agency

<u>Specific Type:</u>

___ County social services	___ Institution
___ Group home	___ Primary social work setting
___ Primary medical setting	___ Primary educational setting
___ Hospital	___ School
___ Community organization	___ Prison
___ Family planning agency	___ Mental health center or counseling agency
___ Hospice	___ Shelter (for example, for homeless people or survivors of domestic violence)
___ Serving clients with a wide range of problems	
___ Receiving close, directive supervision	___ Serving clients with specialized problems
	___ Receiving supervision primarily on a consultative basis

Exercise 16.4: What Are Your Employment Goals?

This exercise concerns the context of your employment. First, on the list below check the aspects of work that are important to you. Second, prioritize them, #1 being the most important.

____ Salary
____ Sick leave
____ Hours of work
____ Social work supervision
____ Geographic location
____ Potential for advancement
____ Substantial discretion in decision-making
____ Low stress levels
____ Realistic recording requirements
____ Being rewarded for achievement
____ Little travel
____ Potential for new skill development
____ Competent colleagues
____ Good office
____ Is there anything else that would be motivating to you? If so, specify.

____ _____

____ Vacation time
____ Health care benefits
____ Not being "on call"
____ In-service training opportunities
____ Clear job description
____ Opportunity to function independently
____ Challenging environment
____ Good relationships with colleagues
____ Working as part of a team
____ Potential for travel
____ Respect from other staff
____ Clear rules and regulations
____ Responsive administration
____ Time flexibility

Exercise 16.5: What Are Your Positive Personal Attributes?

Identify your three most significant personal attributes and explain why. You may refer back to exercise 5.1 to help generate ideas.

Investigating Actual Job Possibilities
The following are possible sources for learning about job openings.

1.   *State Merit System Lists.* Some state merit systems issue periodic listings of social work openings. You can probably find the address and telephone number of the division that advertises such jobs in your state capital's phone directory. Look under the listing for

governmental agencies. Making a phone call to this agency will quickly tell you whether such a listing is available in your state.

2. *NASW Publications.* Positions for MSW graduates are often included in the *NASW News,* published by the National Association of Social Workers. This newspaper, published almost monthly, lists positions by state. Occasionally, BSW positions are mentioned, but only rarely.

3. *Networking.* Networking in the job-finding context means establishing and nurturing linkages with other social work professionals. An obvious linkage is with colleagues at your field placement agency. Other contacts may include faculty, professionals from other agencies you've met during meetings or in-services, colleagues from prior jobs, family, and friends. Membership in state and local NASW branches can also help you form relationships with other social workers. One way to carry networking even further is to expand your primary contacts to secondary contacts. You can ask your primary contacts to refer you to other professionals they know, even though you don't know them personally.

4. *College or University Resources.* Many, perhaps most, colleges and universities have some type of career placement service. Your social work department at school may also post job announcements. If you are hoping to move to another state following graduation, you might ask the head of your college social work program for the names of colleagues in that state.

5. *Using New Technology.* More and more information is becoming available via computer technology and the Internet. To investigate what is available on your campus, contact either your career counseling and placement services, or your computer center for on-line information.

6. *Using Newspapers.* Most public and private social work position openings appear in local newspapers especially in Sunday editions. Thus, you would be wise to target this source first. Since many smaller communities either lack a newspaper or have papers with more limited audiences, administrators often advertise in the newspapers of nearby larger cities. Most university and college libraries have a collection of newspapers from various areas within the state or region.

Exercise 16.6: Searching the Newspaper's Employment Section

This exercise will acquaint you with the classified ads listing social work positions and help you zero in on the kinds of positions that may interest you. Select a Sunday newspaper from a large city nearby. Look carefully for job announcements under a range of categories: "social worker," "counselor," "group worker," "caseworker," "probation and parole officer," "youth worker," "medical social worker," "alcohol and other drug counselor," "case manager," "protective services worker," "youth counselor," "juvenile court intake worker," "job coach," "community support worker," "co-facilitator," "residential counselor," "surveillance officer," "public health advisor," or "director." Since classified ads in many larger newspapers are divided into subsections (such as professional, general, and sales), it is important to search each section carefully. For example, one social work position might be advertised under the "Professional" heading and another under "Health Care."

Clip three job announcements that interest you. Tape them in the space below and answer the subsequent questions.

Job Announcement #1:

What aspects of this job announcement did you find attractive?

What aspects of this job announcement did you find unattractive?

What additional information would you like to have that was not provided in the ad?

Job Announcement #2:

What aspects of this job announcement did you find attractive?

What aspects of this job announcement did you find unattractive?

What additional information would you like to have that was not provided in the ad?

Job Announcement #3:

What aspects of this job announcement did you find attractive?

What aspects of this job announcement did you find unattractive?

What additional information would you like to have that was not provided in the ad?

Preparing Your Resumé

The following exercises will take you through some procedures for preparing or updating your resumé. A first-time resumé is usually difficult because you must make hard decisions about what to include and what to omit, what to emphasize and what to ignore. A resumé should be free of spelling and grammatical errors because it is usually your only introduction to a potential employer.

What is the "perfect" format for a resumé? No one really knows. Each individual has an opinion about what should be in a resumé, how long it should be, what color paper or print is best, and what contents must be included. Therefore, my advice is to ignore anyone who tells you exactly how your resumé *has to be*. The number one rule of resumé-writing is to make independent decisions about what to include and how. Every tiny piece of information you include in your resumé—indeed, every period and comma—should be there for a clearly defined reason.

You must also keep in mind what you think the employer is looking for. What do *you* think is important in an employee? Dependability? Neatness? Good writing skills?

Exercise 16.7: What Content Should You Include in Your Resumé?

Answer the following questions about typical kinds of content included in resumés (Bloch, 1991). You should have a reason for every item you include.

1.   Identifying Information

    a.   What identifying information do you want to include, and how will you place it on the page?

b.   How will you print your name (for example: font; font size; bold, italics, or plain; placement on the page?)

c.   Do you have both a temporary and a permanent address and telephone number? If so, how will you include them?

d.   Do you want to label the document "resumé" or "vita"? Explain your choice.

2.   Education

a.   What information about your education will you include? (This usually appears early in a resumé, before work experience. The first thing an employer will want to know is whether you are qualified for the job so that she doesn't waste her time if you're not. In most cases, the date of graduation or expected graduation is the most significant item.)

b.   Will you mention that the social work program is accredited by the Council on Social Work Education? Why or why not?

c.   Is there a reason to include your cumulative or social work grade point? (I recommend including it only if it is *very* high.) Why or why not?

d.   Have you received any honors or scholarships related to educational achievement that should be noted? If so, what are they?

3.   Certificates or Licenses

a.   What content, if any, will you include? (All states now have some kind of licensing or certification for social workers, although not always at the baccalaureate level).

b.   Identify any other special training or credentials that merit mentioning (for example, Alcohol and Other Drug Counseling certification, CPR training, a black belt in tae kwon do).

4.   Work History, Related Experience, and Volunteer Experience

a.   Identify and explain how you will divide and label these three content areas. (They are addressed together here because there are a number of ways to include this information, depending on your individual strengths and what you want to emphasize.)

b.   Should social-work-related experience be put first? Explain why or why not.

c.   Identify and explain how you will label your social-work-related experience (for example, "social work experience," "social-work-related experience," "job experience," "paid work experience").

d.   How and where will you cite your field experience? (Be careful not to imply that you were paid if you were not.)

e.   Cite any significant volunteer experience that should be identified separately for emphasis.

f.   Identify what work experience—other than social-work-related—you will include and explain why. Specify what work experiences you will leave out and discuss why. (Even minimum-wage employment can demonstrate that you are a hard worker.)

g.   Describe any jobs you held that carried substantial responsibility. (For instance, handling budgets, supervising or training workers or volunteers, or planning activities all reflect skills related to those used in social work.)

h. How will you handle any time gaps in your resumé? (For example, did you stay home to care for your pre-school children? How can you present these gaps to your best advantage?)

i. Identify any jobs that you quit or from which you were fired. Discuss whether you want to include or omit them. (There is no rule that you must include everything you have ever done. Additionally, you need never say why you left a particular job. However, employers will likely inquire about any obvious gaps in your employment history, so prepare your answers before interviewing.)

j. For each experience you choose to include in your resumé, give the specific dates, job title, correct name and address (probably city and state will suffice) of the agency or business, primary job responsibilities, and special skills required.

k.   What vibrant active verbs can you use to describe the responsibilities you handled on specific jobs? Cite them and then indicate how they might be relevant to a social work position.

5.   Special Work-Related Activities or Accomplishments

a.   Is there anything in particular that you want to emphasize about your skills? What makes you special? (For example, do you have a Spanish or journalism minor, a specialization in gerontology or recreation, a working knowledge of behavior modification techniques, or computer skills?)

b.   Cite instances where you have been involved in campus or other organizations (perhaps, you used your writing skills to publish a newsletter or rewrite sections of an agency policy manual, held a leadership position, ran meetings, or won awards).

6.   Publications and Presentations

a.   What if anything have you published, and where? (Don't be put off by this. You might have put together a community resource directory as an independent study, written an article for the school paper or department newsletter, or worked on an improved agency policy manual as part of your field placement requirements. Any such activity counts.)

b. Have you given presentations? If so, what, where, and when? (This can include presentations given in class, at any agency workshop, at professional conferences, or at church.)

7. Other Possible Content

a. Do you want to include a clearly stated *job objective* (Parker, 1989)? Evaluate the pros and cons of this tactic. (If you state a specific objective [for example, "Position working with children having a developmental disability in a group home setting"], you may limit your opportunities. A potential employer in an agency not exactly fitting this objective may automatically eliminate you. If you state a very general objective [for example, "Gain a professional social work position"], what does that tell a prospective employer? Isn't this fact assumed? In this case an employer may feel your interest is not specific enough to fit into her particular agency.)

b. Do you want to include *"Qualifications Summary"* or *"Highlights of Qualifications,"* usually at the resumé's very beginning, immediately following your name and address (Fry, 1992; Parker, 1989)? (This approach is probably best if you have a substantial amount of experience to highlight.) Explain why or why not.

c. Do you want to include a section on *personal interests* or *hobbies?*
Explain why or why not.

d. Do you want to include a *personal information* section (for example, date of birth, marital status, or health: excellent? Why or why not? (By including subjective, non-work related content, you risk touching a potential employer's biases.)

e. Is there any other information that might enhance your chances of being interviewed and hired? If so, explain what it is and why it should be included. (There are almost endless categories of information you can include in a resumé. For brevity's sake, you can combine categories that have little or nothing to do with each other. For example, you might follow the information about your education with a topical heading entitled "Significant Educational Activities" and then list any honors, scholarships, or committees on which you were selected to serve during your education.)

8. References

a. Will you include your references or simply a statement such as, "References furnished upon request"? State your reasons (for example, brevity or employer convenience).

b. Determine how many references you would ideally want to have and explain why. (A typical number is three, although some people include more to prove that they're not "hard up" for references.)

c.   Who will provide your best references—that is, who will be positive, thorough, and able to write about social work or related skills and qualities, and represent a variety of experiences? List full names, titles, full addresses including zip codes, and telephone numbers including area codes. (Ask for permission to use these individuals as references.)[1]

Exercise 16.8: What Should Your Resume Look Like?

Answer the following questions concerning how you want to format your resumé.

1.   Discuss how long you want your resumé to be. (There is no "right" answer to this question. Most resumés written by people new to the field are one or two pages. Many sources stress that resumés should be no longer than that (Fry, 1992). However, excellent three- or four-page resumés have been written by students who had substantial experience prior to returning to school for their social work degrees. You need to determine what will make you look your very best. Resumés longer than one page should be very well organized, clear, and easy to read.)

---

[1]Do not feel obligated to list all prior supervisors as references. Supervisors come and go. They even die. No employer expects to contact each and every one. Cite only your best. What if you would really like a reference about a particular experience, but you did not get along well with that supervisor? No problem—simply ask another staff member or colleague to write the reference for you. Once again, it is impossible for you or potential employers to track down all of your prior supervisors. Other staff who know you and your performance will suffice.

2. How will you format your resumé in terms of spacing? How will you establish your margins on the sides, top, and bottom? How will you organize your resumé so that it doesn't look "squished" but doesn't waste precious space?

3. How will you organize your experiences in terms of sequence? (Most are arranged in reverse chronological order with the most recent experience cited first.) How and where will you cite dates on your resumé?

4. What format and spacing will you use to arrange content in a consistent manner (e.g., job positions, locations, and responsibilities)? Can you use bold type, underlining, and italics to organize information so that it is easy to read?

5. Discuss what color and quality of paper will you use and explain why.

Exercise 16.9: Doing Your Resumé

You have now gone through many of the steps involved in writing a resumé. Now put them all together and write your resumé. Below are some examples of resumé formats. Please note that real resumés will have wider margins than those indicated.

(Sample Resumé A:)　　**LYNN GWEENY**

Permanent Address:　　　　　Temporary Address:
1950 Rock Knoll　　　　　　515 Skid Road, Apt. #235
Elvisville, Wisconsin 55894　　Happyville, Wisconsin 23584

Telephone: (747) 247-7526　　Telephone: (313) 786-6357

EDUCATION:

May 1999　　　　　　　Bachelor of Social Work (Accredited Program)
　　　　　　　　　　　Improveyourself University, Happyville, Wisconsin

HONORS:

Spring 1999　　Dean's List

SOCIAL WORK AND RELATED EXPERIENCE:

January 1999　　Social Work Intern　　　　Justincase County Mental Health Center
to present　　　　　　　　　　　　　　　Porta Bella, Wisconsin

　　　　　　　Responsibilities: Counsel individuals and groups; assess
　　　　　　　resource needs; serve as liaison between community
　　　　　　　residents and resources; record case histories and
　　　　　　　progress notes.

June 1998 to　　Co-Coordinator　　　　University Women's Center
December 1998　(Volunteer)　　　　　Improveyourself University
　　　　　　　　　　　　　　　　　　Happyville, Wisconsin

　　　　　　　Responsibilities: Plan programming; run support groups;
　　　　　　　assist students in information retrieval; plan and administer
　　　　　　　budget.

EMPLOYMENT:

May 1998 to　　　　　　　　　Waitress—HeeHaw Truck Stop
September 1998　　　　　　　　Countrywestern, Wisconsin

May, 1997 to　　　　　　　　　Computer Assistant—Stellar Aeronautics
September 1997　　　　　　　　Havemercy, Wisconsin

　　　　　　　Responsibilities: Enter data using Word, Wordperfect
　　　　　　　and Access; assist in document preparation; file; type.

REFERENCES FURNISHED UPON REQUEST

(Sample Resumé B:)   **LYNN GWEENY**

1950 Rock Knoll
Elvisville, WI 55894
Telephone: (747)247-7526

OBJECTIVE: Social work position counseling children and families.

QUALIFICATIONS: Bachelor of Social Work, Improveyourself University, Happyville, WI, 5/99.

EXPERIENCE: Social Work Intern, Justincase County Mental Health Center, Porta Bella, WI, 1/99 to present.
- Counseled individuals and groups;
- Assessed resource needs;
- Acted as liaison between community residents and resources;
- Recorded case histories and progress notes.

Waitress, HeeHaw Truck Stop, Countrywestern, WI, 5/98 to 9/98.
- Served food and communicated with customers.

Computer Assistant, Stellar Aeronautics, Havemercy, WI, 5/97 to 9/97.
- Entered data using Word, Wordperfect, and Access
- Assisted in document preparation;
- Typed and filed.

VOLUNTEER
EXPERIENCE: Co-Coordinator, University Women's Center, Improveyourself University, Happyville, WI, 6/98 to 12/98.
- Planned programming;
- Ran support groups;
- Assisted students in information retrieval;
- Planned and administered budget.

REFERENCES:

Frank Bizarre, Ph.D.	Sheila Weber, MSW
Associate Professor	Supervisor
Social Work Program	Justincase County Mental
Improveyourself University	Health Center
Happyville, WI 54908	Porta Bella, WI 52765
(747) 298-4333	(747) 256-9860

Myrtle Bureaucrat
Computer Analyst
Stellar Aeronautics
Havemercy, WI 57362
(747) 243-7987

(Sample Resumé C:)
RESUMÉ

Name: **Notfarg Lluh**   Telephone: Home: (714) 388-0506
                                                        Office: (714) 638-2545
Address: 2732 N. Inferiora   Car: (714) 168-9002
         Autumnfield, NE 70856

Formal Education:

    Bachelor of Science, Social Work
    University of Nebraska, June, 1982

    Master of Social Work
    Florida State University, May, 1985

Professional Experience:

    December 1991   Social Work Supervisor I, Cowotinam County
        to present   Department of Social Service, Cowotinam,
                         Nebraska.

                         Responsible for supervision and direction of Foster
                         Care Unit, Delinquency Rehabilitation Unit, Group
                         Home Project, and Day Care licensing.

    May 1988 to   Social Worker IV, (Foster Home Coordinator),
    December 1991   Cowotinam County Department of Social Service,
                         Cowotinam County, Nebraska.

                         Responsible for home finding, study and licensing.

    June 1986 to   Captain, Medical Service Corps, U. S. Army
    June 1987   (Assigned as Chief of the Social Work Section)
                         Mental Hygiene Consultation Service.

                         Responsible for providing clinic's outpatient and
                         outreach services.

    July 1985 to   Group Home Director, MGM Group Homes, Inc.,
    June 1986   Lazybeach, Florida.

                         Responsible for staff supervision and scheduling,
                         treatment planning, case management, budgeting,
                         and serving as community liaison.

| June 1982 to August 1983 | Social Worker I, Children's and Adolescent Units, Southwestern State Hospital, Buffalo Chip, Nebraska. |

Responsible for providing direct social work service, both individual and group for two units.

Grants:

| 1991 | Independently wrote and presented successful state grant proposal to establish and fund a group home for delinquent boys. |

Seminars Attended (Recent):

| 1994 | Human Services Management Institute; Needs Assessment; Supervision Seminar; NASW National Conference |

| 1993 | The Dynamics of Childhood Sexuality; Adolescent Diagnostic and Treatment Issues; Total Quality Service; NASW National Conference |

| 1992 | Family Therapy in the 1990s; Quality through Accountability; Alcoholism and Adolescence |

| 1991 | Gangs in America; NASW National Conference |

| 1990 | Just Say No to Drugs; NASW National Conference |

Miscellaneous Community Service:

Member, Cowotinam City Council (elected), 1992-1994

Member, Cowotinam Landmarks Commission, 1990 to present

Member, Board of Directors, Comehome Refuge House, 1990 to 1994

Memberships in Professional Organizations:

National Association of Social Workers
Academy of Certified Social Workers
Delinquency Prevention Council of America

References:

Mary Poppins, MSW
Director
Cowotinam County
  Department of Social Service
Cowotinam, Nebraska 43789
(714) 638-8990

Gene Yuss, MSW
Unit Supervisor
Foster Home Placement
Cowotinam County
  Department of Social Service
Cowotinam, Nebraska 42789
(714) 638-4982

Kari Meeback, MSW
Social Work Supervisor I
Cowotinam County
  Department of Social Service
Cowotinam, Nebraska 43789
(714) 638-1135

Minnie Series, Ph.D.
Executive Director
MGM Group Homes, Inc.
Lazybeach, Florida 34879
(908) 353-5713

Harry Kari
Social Worker
Cowotinam County
Department of Social Service
Cowotinam, Nebraska 43789
(714) 638-2321

The Application Cover Letter

Always send a cover letter with your application. The cover letter tailors you and your experience to fit the particular job for which you're applying in addition to emphasizing your greatest strengths.

NASW (Program Advancement Fund, undated) makes the following suggestions for writing good cover letters.

- First, write only one page. A cover letter's purpose is to get your potential employer's attention.
- Second, each cover letter should be individualized for a particular job at a specific agency. One of a cover letter's purposes is to individualize and personalize your more generic resumé.
- Third, try to establish "a picture frame" effect so that type is centered with wide margins (p. 22). The letter should look good.
- Fourth, use straightforward, understandable language in fairly simple, direct sentences. Make certain that your writing is grammatically correct.
- Fifth, let your letter reflect your individual personality, at the same time being sensitive and tactful.
- Sixth, make sure you sign the letter above your printed name.
- Seventh, if at all possible address the letter to a specific individual within the organization and make certain to use the correct title.
- Eighth, get feedback from other people about your cover letter.
- Ninth, never send a cover letter out without keeping a copy.

Contents

NASW (Program Advancement Fund, undated) recommends using four paragraphs in your cover letter. The first should explain why you are sending the letter in the first place (e.g., responding to a specific newspaper's classified ad on a particular date). The second paragraph should explain why you're perfect—or almost perfect—for the job. The third paragraph should refer to the fact that a resumé is enclosed. (For the sake of brevity, you may choose to combine the second and third paragraphs.) The last paragraph should re-emphasize your interest in the position and thank the reader for her or his time, consideration, or attention. Make certain the cover letter contains no errors.

Formatting the Letter

Your letter of application and resumé are the first contacts an agency administrator will have with you. Make them pay off. Cover letters should always be typed, preferably on the same quality and color of paper used for the resumé.

Using block style for your letter is often easiest. Position the date at least one inch down from the top of the paper (more if the letter is short). After the date, leave at least five spaces before the name, title, name of agency, and agency address. All sentences can begin at the left margin with no indenting required. Single space and leave a blank line between paragraphs. You should always include your full address in the letter, your telephone number, and possibly your e-mail address. You can use any of a number of complimentary closings including "Sincerely," "Very sincerely," "Yours truly," or "Very truly yours." Below are two examples of cover letters. Please note that real cover letters will have wider margins than those illustrated.

(COVER LETTER #1:)

May 28, 1999

Russ T. Hinge
Social Services Director
Kneebend County Social Services
Kneebend, NY 98576

Dear Mr. Hinge:

I am responding to the advertisement for Case Manager published in the Kneebend News on May 24, 1999.

As my enclosed resumé reflects, I am well qualified for the position. I received my social work degree from an accredited program and have applied for state licensure which should be forthcoming. My field practicum at a child welfare agency has provided me with experience in case management. My work experience includes serving as care counselor for adult group home clients who have a cognitive disability. My volunteer experiences include visiting elderly adults living in health care settings. These experiences have provided me with a well-rounded exposure to a variety of social service settings that, I feel, will readily prepare me for the case management position.

Thank you very much for your attention. I hope to hear from you soon.

Sincerely,

(Signature)

Ernest Endeavor
4995 Truthful Avenue
Wholesome, Massachusetts 48069

Telephone: (401) 859-4833
E-mail: ernestend@ma.net

(COVER LETTER #2:)

84 Hot Street, Apartment #1
Boiling, New Mexico 48300
January 13, 2000

The Penguin Press
Box 8888
Frigid, Alaska 68349

To Whom It May Concern:

This letter is in response to the advertisement published in your January edition for the position of Social Work Counselor.

My primary interest and career goal is to work with people who have developmental disabilities. I am hardworking and committed to enhancing people's well-being. I am open to constructive criticism and consistently strive to improve my skills. My intent is to become the best social worker I can be.

My resumé is enclosed. It reflects my accomplishments which include: a field internship at a sheltered workshop; volunteer experience with the Special Olympics; and a concentration of coursework related to developmental disability.

Thank you for your consideration. I look forward to hearing from you.

Very truly yours,

(Signature)

Burr Bank

Enclosure

Select one of the following three classified ads from a Sunday paper and respond to the subsequent questions.

Classified Ad #1:

SOCIAL WORKER. Okyfenoky County seeks individual to fill a full-time social work position in its Developmental Disabilities program. Must have a degree in social work. Duties include case management/coordination of children and adults with developmental disabilities. Assessment, service plan development, and follow-up services are performed. Implementation and monitoring of a variety of complex state, federal and local funding sources requires a high level of skill in program organization and documentation.

Send resumé to Okyfenoky County Personnel Department, 4321 Getajob Av., Heavenshome, AL 68394.

Classified Ad #2:

SOCIAL WORKER/CASE MANAGER. Full time position in an exciting community based program for older adults. Knowledge of funding sources preferred. Car required. Competitive salary and benefit package. Send resumé to: Community Happycare, 388 Blizzard Dr., Snowbound, MN 27485.

Classified Ad #3:

SOCIAL SERVICE OUTREACH WORKER. City Health Habitat has full time outreach worker position for lead poisoning project. Conduct home visits, parent education, conduct finger stick blood draws. Send resumé to: City Health Habitat, 10234 Tinaturner Pl., Cowtown, WI 53678.

1.   Selecting one of the three ads above, describe how you would format your cover letter in response to this ad. Would you use bold, indented, or some other style? Explain your choice.

2.   How would you address your letter?

3.   Write your first paragraph below?

4.   Write your second and third paragraphs (or one condensed paragraph if you prefer) below.

5.   What complimentary closing would you choose?

The Job Interview

Preparing for a job interview involves several steps.

- First, find out as much as you can about the agency so you can respond to and ask questions as appropriately and effectively as possible.
- Second, prepare specific questions so you can take an active part in the interview process and find out significant information about the job. This may concern anything from the agency's benefits, its programs and clientele, to its dress code.
- Third, prepare answers for potential questions the interviewer is likely to ask you.

Exercise 16.11: Preparing Yourself for the Job Interview

Refer back to the classified ad you chose in exercise 16.10, and answer the following questions.

1.   How can you find out more about an agency such as this? Whom can you call? To what written information and other sources can you refer?

2.   Identify three questions you might ask during your interview for the designated position.

1.

2.

3.

Once again refer to the classified ad you chose in exercise 16.10. Answer each of the following questions as if you were being interviewed for that position.

1. We would like to get to know you a little better; could you tell us about yourself?

2. What made you choose social work as a major? Who influenced you the most in choosing social work and in continuing in the major?

3. What interests you about this agency and position?

4. What are your major strengths? What are your major weaknesses?

5. With what type of clients would you like to work?

6. Are there any clients with whom you might have difficulty working?

7. What makes you the best candidate for this position?

8.   What is your definition of a family system?

9.   What kind of information would you collect on a new case?

10.   What can you bring to this agency?

11.   What are your long-term goals?

12.   How well do you work under pressure?

13.   How do you deal with criticism?

14.   What experiences have you had that might help you in our agency?

15.   With what type of supervisor do you work best?

16. What do you do to unwind?

17. What motivates you the most?

18. What do you tend to have the most difficulty with on the job?

19. What salary range are you looking for?

20. What type of work environment makes you most at ease?

21. Are you planning to stay in social work?

22. (To BSWs) Are you planning to go to graduate school? If so, when?

23. Have you ever done a job ineffectively?

24.   Are you willing to work overtime?

25.   Do you mind being on-call with a beeper?

26.   How long do you think you would remain with this agency?

27.   What type of decisions are most difficult for you?

28.   What do you expect to be doing five years from now?

29.   What do you know about our agency?

30.   What personal characteristics do you think are important in social work?

31.   Do you feel you did as well in college as you could have? Why or why not?

32.   Have you ever had trouble getting along with people, such as other students or faculty?

33.   How would you define the word cooperation?

34.   What type of work interests you the most?

35.   What have you done that demonstrates initiative?

36.   Describe your time management skills.

37.   How do you prioritize your workload?

38.   What frustrates you the most?

39.   In what ways has a prior supervisor of yours assisted—or failed to assist—in your skill
        development?

40.   How do you react to being evaluated?

41.   Why should you be hired for this position instead of other candidates?

42.   What do you think you could do positively for this agency?

43.   What has been your worst difficulty with a prior supervisor? Explain.

44.   Explain why you quit or were let go from a prior job.

Exercise 16.13: How Do You Answer Illegal Questions?

Illegal questions include those involving marital status, pregnancy, religion, skin color and its relationship to race, religion or religious participation, credit history, ancestry, personal characteristics such as weight, organizational memberships, children, and the person or persons with whom you live (Berk, 1990). However, such questions are asked all the time, perhaps out of ignorance or perhaps because interviewers feel the questions are harmless. You might respond with a blunt refusal to reply, a partial answer, or a full answer that emphasizes that your work performance has nothing to do with such personal characteristics or choices.

How would you respond to the following questions?

1.   Are you married?

Explain how you think the interviewer might react to your response.

2.   Do you have children or are you (or your partner) planning on getting pregnant or adopting soon?

Explain how you think the interviewer might react to your response.

3.   I have a Native American grandfather. What's your ethnic status?

Explain how you think the interviewer might react to your response.

4.   Whom do you live with, or do you live alone?

Explain how you think the interviewer might react to your response.

5.   Where do you go to church, or don't you attend?

Explain how you think the interviewer might react to your response.

Follow-up after an Interview

It's wise to write a brief thank-you letter following your interview. This will make you stand out as an exceptionally conscientious job candidate.

Interviewees commonly ask whether to call the interviewer or agency within a week or two after the interview if they haven't heard from the agency. You might wait a few days or a week. Then it is appropriate to call and inquire about the search status. If the agency indicates that no decision has yet been made, it is up to you whether you feel comfortable calling again after another week or two. Contacting the agency too frequently can be obnoxious or make you appear overly anxious.

Exercise 16.14: What Is Your Follow-up Plan?

1.　　Describe below what you might say in the main body of a follow-up thank-you letter.

2.   Suppose you have participated in a job interview. The interviewer said you would be notified about the results within two weeks. Two weeks have passed, and you've heard nothing. What is your plan for contacting the agency at this point? Explain your reasons for this plan.

3.   Consider the situation described above. You decide to call the agency and are told that the decision has not yet been made—but it will be made soon. How long will you wait before contacting the agency again if they do not contact you? Explain your reasons for this plan.

References

Alberti, R. E., & Emmons, M. L. (1976). *Assert yourself—It's your perfect right: A guide to assertive behavior.* San Luis Obispo, CA: Impact.

Alinski, S. (1971). *Rules for Radicals.* New York: Vintage Books.

Austin, M. J., Kopp, J., & Smith, P. L. (1986). *Delivering human services: A self-instructional approach* (2nd ed.). New York: Longman.

Barker, R. L. (1987). *The social work dictionary.* Silver Spring, MD: National Association of Social Workers.

Barker, R. L. (1995). *The social work dictionary* (3rd ed.) Washington, DC: National Association of Social Workers.

Barker, R.L. (1999). *The social work dictionary* (4th ed.) Washington, DC: NASW Press.

Bedwell, R. T., Jr. (1993). Total quality management: Making the decision. *Nonprofit World* 2 (3), 29-31.

Benjamin, A. (1974). *The helping interview.* Boston: Houghton Mifflin.

Benjamin, M. P. (1994). Research frontiers in building a culturally competent organization. *Focal Point* 8 (2), 17-19.

Benson, H. (1975). *The Relaxation Response.* New York: Avon.

Berk, D. (1990). *Preparing for your interview.* Oakville, Ontario: Crisp.

Bloch, D. P. (1991). *How to write a winning resumé.* Lincolnwood, IL: VGM Career Horizons.

Brager, G., & Holloway, S. (1983). A process model for changing organizations from within. In R. M. Kramer & H. Specht (Eds.), *Readings in community organization practice* (3rd ed., pp. 198-208). Englewood Cliffs, NJ: Prentice Hall.

Brody, R., & Nair, M. D. (1998). *Macro practice: A generalist approach* (4th ed.). Wheaton, IL: Gregory.

Canadian Association of Social Workers. (1994). *Social work code of ethics.* Ottawa, Ontario: Author.

Chess, W. A., & Norlin, J. M. (1988). *Human behavior & the social environment: A social systems model.* Boston: Allyn&Bacon.

Compton, B. R., & Galaway, B. (1999). *Social work processes* (6th ed.). Pacific Grove, CA: Brooks/Cole.

Cross, T.; Bazron, B.; Dennis, K.; & Isaacs, M. (1989). *Towards a culturally competent system of care: A monograph on effective service for minority children who are severely emotionally disturbed* (Vol. 1). Washington, DC: CASSP Technical Assistance Center, Georgetown University Child Development Center.

Curtis, J. D., & Detert, R. A. (1981). *How to relax: A holistic approach to stress management.* Palo Alto, CA: Mayfield.

Daft, R. L. (1983). *Organization theory and design.* St. Paul, MN: West.

Daft, R. L. (1992). *Organization theory and design.* St. Paul, MN: West.

Daft, R. L. (1998). *Organization theory and design* (6th ed.). Cincinnati, OH: South-Western College Publishing.

Dworkin, J., & Kaufer, D. (1995). Social services and bereavement in the lesbian and gay community. *Journal of Gay & Lesbian Services, 9* (3/4), 41-60.

Emery, S. E., & Trist, E. L. (1961). The causal texture of organizational environments. *Human Relations, 18* (1), 21-32.

Etzioni, A. (1964). *Modern organizations.* Englewood Cliffs, NJ: Prentice-Hall.

Farmer, E. E., Monohan, L. H., & Hekeler, R. W. (1984). *Stress management for human services.* Beverly Hills, CA: Sage.

Fatout, M. & Rose, S. (1995). *Task groups in the social services.* Thousand Oaks, CA: Sage.

Federal Electric Corporation. (1963). *A programmed introduction to PERT.* New York: Wiley.

Filley, A. C. (1978). *The complete manager: What works when.* Champaign, IL: Research Press.

Fry, R. (1972). *Your first resumé* (3rd ed.). Hawthorne, NJ: Career Press.

Gibbs, L., & Gambrill, E. (1996). *Critical thinking for human service workers: A workbook.* Newbury Park, CA: Pine Forge/Sage.

Gibbs, L.; Gambrill, E.; Blakemore, J.; Begun, A.; Keniston, A.; Peden, B.; & Lefcowitz, J. (1994). A measure of critical thinking about practice. Unpublished paper presented at the fall Conference of the Wisconsin Council on Social Work Education, Stevens Point, WI.

Gibelman, M. (1995). *What social workers do.* Washington, DC: NASW Press.

Ginsberg, L. (1992). *Social work almanac.* Silver Spring, MD: National Association of Social Workers.

Greenberg, H. H. (1980). *Coping with job stress. A guide for all employers and employees.* Englewood Cliffs, NJ: Prentice-Hall.

Gummer, B. (1990). *The politics of social administration: Managing organizational politics in social agencies.* Englewood Cliffs, NJ: Prentice-Hall.

Guttierrez, L. M. (1995). Working with women of color: An enpowerment perspective.

In J. Rothman, J. L. Erlich, & J. E. Tropman (Eds.), *Strategies of Community Intervention* (pp. 204-217). Silver Spring, MD: National Association of Social Workers.

Halley, A. A., Kopp, J., & Austin, M. J. (1992). *Delivering human services: A learning approach to practice* (3rd ed.). New York: Longman.

Halley, A. A., Koop, J., & Austin, M. J. (1998). *Delivering human services: A learning approach to practice* (4th ed.). New York: Longman.

Hartman, A. (1993). The professional is political. *Social Work, 38* (4), 365-66.

Hasenfeld, Y. (1983). *Human services organizations*. Englewood Cliffs, NJ: Prentice-Hall.

Hasenfeld, Y. (1984). Analyzing the human service agency. In F. M. Cox, J. L. Erlich, J. Rothman, & E. Tropman (Eds.), *Tactics and techniques of community practice* (pp. 14-26). Itasca, IL: Peacock.

Hasenfeld, Y. (1987). Program development. In F. M. Cox, J. L. Erlich, J. Rothman, & J. E. Tropman (Eds.), *Strategies of community organization* (4th ed., pp. 450-73). Itasca, IL: Peacock.

Hepworth, D. H., & Larsen, J. (1987). Interviewing. In A. Minihan (Editor-in-chief), *Encyclopedia of social work* (18th ed., Vol. 1, pp. 996-1008). Silver Spring, MD: National Association of Social Workers.

Hepworth, D. H., & Larsen, J. (1990). Direct social work practice (3rd ed.). Belmont, CA: Wadsworth.

Hepworth, D. H., Rooney, R. H., & Larsen, J. A. (1997). *Direct social work practice: Theory and skills* (5th ed.). Pacific Grove, CA: Brooks/Cole.

Hodge, B. J., Anthony, W. P., & Gales, L. M. (1996). *Organization theory: A strategic approach* (5th ed.). Upper Saddle River, NJ: Prentice-Hall.

Hoffman, K. & Sallee, A. (1993). *Social work practice: Bridges to change*. Needham Heights, MA: Allyn & Bacon.

Holland, T. P. (1995). Organizations: Context for social service delivery. In *Encyclopedia of social work* (Vol. 2, pp. 1787-1794). Washington, DC: National Association of Social Workers.

Holland, T. P., & Petchers, M. K. (1987). Organizations: Context for social service delivery. In A. Minahan (Editor-in-chief), *Encyclopedia of social work* (18th ed., Vol. 2, pp. 204-17). Silver Spring, MD: National Association of Social Workers.

Holloway, S. M. (1987). Staff-initiated change. In A. Minihan (Editor-in-Chief), *Encyclopedia of social work* (18th ed., Vol. 2, pp. 729-36). Silver Spring, MD: National Association of Social Workers.

Homan, M. (1995). *Promoting community change*. Pacific Grove, CA: Brooks/Cole.

Hooyman, G. (1973). Team building in the human services. In B. R. Compton & B. Galloway (Eds.), *Social work processes* (pp. 456-78). Homewood, IL: Dorsey.

Hull, G. H., Jr. (2000). The appointment letters. In R. F. Rivas & G. H. Hull, Jr., *Case Studies in Generalist Practice* (pp. 166-70). Pacific Grove, CA: Brooks/Cole.

Ivey, A. E., & Ivey, M. B. (1999). *Intentional interviewing and counseling: Facilitating client development in a multicultural society* (5th ed.). Pacific Grove, CA: Brooks/Cole.

Jacobson, E. (1938). *Progressive relaxation* (2nd ed.). Chicago: University of Chicago Press.

Jay, A. (1984). How to run a meeting. In F. M. Cox, J. L. Erlich, J. Rothman, & J. E. Tropman (Eds.), *Tactics and techniques of community practice*. Itasca, IL: Peacock.

Jex, S. M. (1998). *Stress and job performance: Theory, research, and implications for managerial practice*. Thousand Oaks, CA: Sage.

Johns, G. (1996). *Organizational behavior: Understanding and managing life at work (4th ed.). New York: HarperCollins.*

Johnson, D. W. (1986). *Reaching out: Interpersonal effectiveness and self-actualization* (3rd ed.) Englewood Cliffs, NJ: Prentice-Hall.

Johnson, L. (1998). *Social work practice: A generalist approach*. Boston: Allyn & Bacon.

Johnson, L. C. (1998). *Social work practice: A generalist approach.* (6th ed.) Boston: Allyn & Bacon.

Kanter, R. M. (1989). The new managerial work. *Harvard Business Review, 67* (6), 86- 92.

Kettner, P. M., Daley J. M., & Nichols, A. W. (1985). *Initiating change in organizations and communities: A macro practice model.* Monterey, CA: Brooks/Cole.

Kirst-Ashman, K. K. & Hull, G. H. (1999). *Understanding generalist practice*. Chicago: Nelson-Hall.

Kirst-Ashman, K. K., & Hull, G. H. (1997). *Generalist practice with organizations and communities*. Chicago: Nelson-Hall.

Kadushin, A., & Kadushin, G. (1997). *The social work interview: A guide for human service professionals* (4th ed.) New York: Columbia University Press.

Kazdin, A. E. (1994). *Behavior modification in applied settings*. Pacific Grove, CA: Brooks/Cole.

Kretzmann, J. P., & McKnight, J. L. (1993). *Building communities from the inside out*. Chicago: ACTA Publications.

Lakein, A. (1973). *How to get control of your time and your life*. New York: Signet.

Landon, P. S. (1995). Generalist and advanced generalist practice. In *Encyclopedia of social work* (Vol. 2, pp. 1101-1108). Washington, DC: NASW Press.

Landon, P. (1999). *Generalist social work practice.* Dubuque, IA: Eddie Bowers.

Larson, C. E., & LaFasto, F. M. (1989). *Teamwork.* Newbury Park, CA: Sage.

Lauffer, A. (1982). *Getting a grant in the 1980s* (2nd ed.). Englewood Cliffs, NJ: Prentice-Hall.

Lauffer, A.; Nybell, L.; Overberger, C.; Reed, B.; & Zeff, L. (1977). *Understanding your social agency.* Beverly Hills, CA: Sage.

Lewinsohn, P. M.; Munoz, M. A.; Youngren, M. A.; & Antonette, M. Z. (1978). *Control your depression.* Englewood Cliffs. NJ: Prentice-Hall.

Lindsay, M. (1995). Understanding and enhancing adult learning. Unpublished paper prepared for presentation at the Spring Conference of the Wisconsin Council on Social Work Education, Wisconsin Dells, WI.

Loewenberg, F. M., & Dolgoff, R. (1996). *Ethical decisions for social work practice* (5th ed.). Itasca, IL: Peacock.

Lutheran Social Services of Wisconsin and Upper Michigan (LSS). (1993). *Getting started: TQS at LSS: A workbook on total quality service for employees.* Milwaukee, WI: LSS.

Martinez-Brawley, E. E. (1995). Community. In *Encyclopedia of social work* (Vol. 1, pp. 539-548). Washington, DC: NASW Press.

Mason, J. L. (1994). Developing culturally competent organizations. *Focal Point, 8* (2), 1-8.

Meenaghan, T. M., Washington, R. O., & Ryan, R. M. (1987). *Macro practice in the human services.* New York: Free Press.

Mish, F.C. (ed.). (1995). *Merriam-Webster's collegiate dictionary* (10th ed.). Springfield, MA: Merriam-Webster, Inc.

National Association of Social Workers. (1996). *The National Association of Social Workers Code of Ethics.* Washington, DC: National Association of Social Workers.

Netting, F. E., Ketter, P. M., & McMurtry, S. L. (1998). *Social work macro practice* (2nd ed.). White Plains, NY: Longman.

Okun, B. F. (1976). *Effective helping: Interviewing and counseling techniques.* Belmont, CA: Duxbury.

Parker, Y. (1989). *The damn good resumé guide.* Berkeley, CA: Ten Speed Press.

Patti, R. J. (1983). Limitations and prospects of internal advocacy. In H. Weissman, I. Epstein, & A. Savage (Eds.), *Agency-based social work* (pp. 214-23). Philadelphia: Temple University Press.

Perrow, C. A. (1961). The analysis of goals in complex organizations. *American Sociological Review, 26* (6), 856-66.

Pincus, A., & Minahan, A. (1973). *Social work practice: Model and method.* Itasca, IL: Peacock.

Rapp, C., & Poertner, J. (1992). *Social administration: A client-centered approach.* White Plains, NY: Longman.

Reamer, F. G. (1990). *Ethical dilemmas in social service* (2nd ed.). New York: Columbia University Press.

Reamer, F. G. (1983). Ethical dilemmas in social work practice. *Social Work, 28* (1), 31-35.

Resnick, H. (1980a). Appendix: A workshop on organizational change for supervisors and practitioners. In H. Resnick & R.J. Patti (Eds.), *Change from within: Humanizing social welfare organizations* (pp. 307-23). Philadelphia: Temple University Press.

Resnick, H. (1980b). Effecting internal change in human service organizations. In H. Resnick & R.J. Pattie (Eds.), *Change from within: Humanizing social welfare organizations* (pp. 187-99). Philadelphia: Temple University Press.

Resnick, H. (1980c). Tasks in changing the organization from within. In H. Resnick & R.J. Patti (Eds.), *Change from within. Humanizing social welfare organizations* (pp. 200-16). Philadelphia: Temple University Press.

Resnick, H., & Patti, R.J. (Eds.). (1980). *Change from within: Humanizing social welfare organizations.* Philadelphia: Temple University Press.

Robert, H. M. (1989). *Robert's Rules of Order Revised.* New York: Berkeley Books.

Rubin, H.J., & Rubin, I.S. (1992). *Community organizing and development* (2nd ed.). New York: Macmillan.

Saltzman, A., & Furman, D.M. (1999). *Law in social work practice* (2nd ed.). Chicago: Nelson-Hall.

Sarri, R. (1987). Administration in social welfare. In A. Minahan (Ed.), *Encyclopedia of social work* (18th ed., Vol. 1, pp. 27-40). Silver Spring, MD: National Association of Social Workers.

Schriver, J.M. (1998). *Human behavior and the social environment.* Needham Heights, MA: Allyn & Bacon.

Selye, H. (1956). *The stress of life.* New York: McGraw-Hill.

Sheafor, B. W., Horejsi, C. R., & Horejsi, G. A. (1991). *Techniques and guidelines for social work practice* (2nd ed.). Boston: Allyn & Bacon.

Sheafor, B. W., Horejsi, C. R., & Horejsi, G. A. (1988). *Techniques and guidelines for social work practice* (3rd ed.). Boston: Allyn & Bacon.

Sheafor, B. W., Horejsi, C. R., & Horejsi, G. A. (1997). *Techniques and guidelines for social work practice* (4th ed.). Boston: Allyn & Bacon.

Shulman, L. (1993). *Interactional supervision.* Washington, DC: NASW Press.

Shulman, L. (1991). *International social work practice.* Itasca IL: Peacock.

Simpson, C., & Simpson, D. (1992). *Exploring careers in social work.* New York: Rosen Publishing Group.

Sundel, S. S., & Sundel, M. (1980). *Be assertive: A practical guide for human service workers.* Beverly Hills, CA: Sage.

Warren, R. (1978). *The community in America* (3rd ed.). Chicago: Rand McNally.

Watson, D. L., & Tharp, R. G. (1973). *Self-directed behavior.* Monterey, CA: Brooks/Cole.

Webster's Tenth New Collegiate Dictionary. (1995). Springfield, MA: Merriam-Webster.

Weissman, H., Epstein, I., & Savage, A. (1983). *Agency-based social work.* Philadelphia: Temple University Press.

Whittacker, J. K., & Tracy, E. M. (1989). *Social treatment: An introduction to social work practice.* New York: Aldine.

Yessian, M. R., & Broskowski, A. (1983). Generalists in human service systems: Their problems and prospects. In R. M. Kramer & H. Specht (Eds.), *Readings in community organization practice* (pp. 180-98). Englewood Cliffs, NJ: Prentice-Hall.

Zippay, A. (1994). Should today's community organizer use the tactics handed down from earlier generations? No. In M. J. Austin & J. I. Lowe, *Controversial issues in communities & organizations* (pp. 119-24). Needham Heights, MA: Allyn & Bacon.